Aggression Replacement Training

Aggression Replacement Training

REVISED EDITION

A Comprehensive Intervention for Aggressive Youth

Arnold P. Goldstein
Barry Glick
John C. Gibbs

Research Press
2612 North Mattis Avenue
Champaign Illinois 61822
www.researchpress.com

Figure 4.2: "Nonreader's Hassle Log," unpublished form for clinical use, by J. Gilliam, 1997, Horseshoe Bay, Texas. Reprinted by permission.

Figures 5.1, 5.2, 5.3 and Table 5.1: From *The EQUIP Program: Teaching Youth to Think and Act Responsibly through a Peer-Helping Approach* by J.C. Gibbs, G.B. Potter, and A.P. Goldstein, 1995, Champaign, IL: Research Press. Reprinted by permission.

Table 4.2: From *Anger Control: The Development and Evaluation of an Experimental Treatment* by R.W. Novaco, 1975, Lexington, MA: D.C. Heath. Adapted by permission.

Chapter 8: Portions of *Program Manual*, Positive Alternative Learning Program, 1996, Ferguson-Florissant School District, St. Louis. Reprinted by permission. Portions of *Operating Manual*, Taberg Residential Center, 1994, Taberg, New York. Reprinted by permission.

Jim's, Jerry's, Sam's, and Antonio's Problem Situations: From *The EQUIP Program: Teaching Youth to Think and Act Responsibly through a Peer-Helping Approach* by J.C. Gibbs, G.B. Potter, and A.P. Goldstein, 1995, Champaign, IL: Research Press. Reprinted by permission.

Mark's and Alonzo's Problem Situations: From *An Analysis of Social Behavioral Skill Deficits in Delinquent and Nondelinquent Adolescent Boys* by B.J. Freedman, 1974, unpublished doctoral dissertation, University of Wisconsin, Madison. Adapted by permission.

George's Problem Situation: From *Dilemmas for Applied Use* by A. Colby and B. Speicher, 1973, unpublished manuscript, Harvard University, Cambridge, Massachusetts. Adapted by permission.

Leon's and Reggie's Problem Situations: From *Moral Dilemmas at Scioto Village* by D.W. Meyers, 1982, unpublished manuscript, Ohio Department of Youth Services, Columbus. Adapted by permission.

Juan's Problem Situation: From *Dilemma Session Intervention with Adult Female Offenders: Behavioral and Attitudinal Correlates* by H.H. Ahlborn, 1986, unpublished manuscript, Ohio Department of Rehabilitation and Correction, Columbus. Adapted by permission.

Copies of this book may be ordered from the publisher at the address given on the title page.

Cover design by Linda Brown, Positive I.D. Graphic Design, Inc.
Composition by Tradewinds Imaging
Printed by McNaughton & Gunn, Inc.

ISBN 0–87822–379–7

Library of Congress Catalog Number 98–66599

CONTENTS

Figures and Tables   vii
Acknowledgments   ix
Introduction   1

Chapter One   Aggression: Sources, Scope, and Solutions   3
Chapter Two   An Overview of ART   33
Chapter Three   Skillstreaming:
                 The Behavioral Component of ART   47
Chapter Four   Anger Control Training:
                 The Emotional Component of ART   69
Chapter Five   Moral Reasoning Training:
                 The Values Component of ART   99
Chapter Six   Trainee Motivation and Resistance   119
Chapter Seven   Enhancing Generalization of Performance   155
Chapter Eight   Application Models and
                 Evaluations of Program Effectiveness   179

Afterword: Summary and Future Directions   209

Appendix A   Skillstreaming Skills for Adolescents   211
Appendix B   Skillstreaming Checklists and Grouping Chart   263
Appendix C   Moral Reasoning Problem Situations   295
Appendix D   The Transfer Coach   325

References   331
Name Index   343
Subject Index   347
About the Authors   355

FIGURES & TABLES

FIGURES

3.1   A Sample Skillstreaming Skill   52
3.2   Room Arrangement for Skillstreaming   56
3.3   Homework Report 1   66
3.4   Homework Report 2   68
4.1   Hassle Log   78
4.2   Nonreader's Hassle Log   79
4.3   Sample Drawing of Participant's Anger Cues   87
5.1   Jerry's Problem Situation   108
5.2   Responses to Jerry's Problem Situation   110
5.3   Social Decision Making Meetings:
      Group Leader Review/Self-Evaluation Checklist   112
7.1   School-Home Note   168
7.2   Parent/Staff Skill Rating Form   169

TABLES

1.1   Approaches to School Violence and Vandalism   16
1.2   Reasons for School Suspension   21
1.3   Antecedents of Aggressive Behavior   26
1.4   Prescriptive Interventions by Type of Aggression   28
1.5   Categories of Student Aggression   28
1.6   Environmental Methods for
      Preventing and Reducing Vandalism   31
2.1   Ten-Week ART Curriculum   38
3.1   Skillstreaming Skills for Adolescents   51
3.2   Skillstreaming Training Steps   57
4.1   Overview of a 10-Week Anger Control Training Sequence   81
4.2   Self-Instructional Reminders for Use
      before, during, and after Provocation   90
5.1   Stages of Moral Reasoning   100
5.2   Cognitive Restructuring Strategies for
      Self-Instruction Training   106

6.1   Types of Trainee Resistance   125
6.2   Commonly Used Reinforcers   135
7.1   Transfer- and Maintenance-Enhancing Procedures   159
8.1   Frequency of Rearrest by Condition in the
       Community-Based Evaluation   201
8.2   Rearrest Outcomes for Delinquent Youths
       Plus Significant Others   207

ACKNOWLEDGMENTS

The product of an intervention application and evaluation effort lasting a dozen years reflects the wisdom and labor of many people. *Aggression Replacement Training* circa 1998 is clearly the collective outcome of such multiple efforts and shared thinking. Some of its contributors are fellow psychologists; others are school, agency, and residential center personnel of diverse types. Contributing a very great deal to this book are the hundreds of youths who over these years have served as the intervention's trainees. To all such persons, we offer a warm and grateful thank you for the many insights you have shared regarding this intervention-in-progress.

Karen Steiner, our friend and editor at Research Press, has brought her many talents, her considerable energies, and patience without limit to the task of nurturing and shaping this book. We are most appreciative of her countless contributions to both its structure and substance.

INTRODUCTION

Aggressive behavior, for reasons we will suggest, is typically quite difficult behavior to change. For many youths, its teaching is repetitive, its success is frequent, its rewards are generous, and its punishments are few. Of special importance is the complex character of aggression. It is an overt *behavior* often employed by those weak or lacking in prosocial alternatives. It is often initiated by anger growing from the youth's *cognitive* misperceptions of the interpersonal world. And it typically is given energy and sustenance by the *emotional* arousal such cognitions usually generate. It is simultaneously a behavioral, cognitive, and emotional phenomenon. So, too, must be the interventions designed to address it.

Aggression Replacement Training, or ART, was initiated in 1987 as a comprehensive attempt to concretize such multichannel thinking. Skillstreaming is its behavioral component, Anger Control Training is its emotion-targeted component, and Moral Reasoning Training is its cognitive component. Since 1987, ART's use in school, delinquency, and other settings frequented by aggressive youths has grown substantially. As program use has proliferated, so have short- and long-term evaluations of its effectiveness in a number of diverse sites. Feedback from both these sources—applied settings and research—has led to valuable modifications and improvements in content as well as implementation of ART's constituent procedures. In this book, we share the journey by which this intervention has developed.

The first two chapters orient the reader to the problem of aggression and attempt to place ART in the context of this real and present problem. Specifically, chapter 1 details likely sources of aggression, provides updated information on aggression in schools and society, and discusses the broad range of interventions designed to prevent aggression and curb its effects. Chapter 2 gives an overview of the ART program, illustrating how the ART components are integrated by outlining one commonly used curriculum.

Chapters 3 through 5 are the heart of the ART program. Each of these chapters is devoted to a single program component: Skillstreaming, Anger Control Training, or Moral Reasoning Training. Each chapter in turn describes the background and rationale for the component's use, discusses particular implementation concerns, and presents step-by-step training procedures to ensure effective group sessions in that area.

The next two chapters focus on two areas critical to program success: Chapter 6 examines trainee motivation and resistance, describing common types of trainee resistance and offering effective means for dealing with it. Often interventions with aggressive youths result in short-term gains, but, as discussed in chapter 7, ensuring generalization of performance is a much more difficult matter. This chapter specifies transfer- and maintenance-enhancing procedures to increase the likelihood that ART trainees will continue to use what they learn from the program outside the training setting.

Over the years, ART has been employed in a wide variety of settings and has undergone extensive evaluation. Chapter 8 describes specific program applications and the efforts to assess ART's effectiveness, indicating that, when applied properly, ART does indeed help trainees think and behave less aggressively.

Finally, in our brief afterword we summarize what ART has contributed so far to prevent and reduce aggression in youths, and we point toward future explorations that we hope will make the program of even greater value.

CHAPTER ONE

Aggression: Sources, Scope, and Solutions

SOURCES: LEARNING TO BE AGGRESSIVE

Once aggression was viewed as an instinctive human behavior, a combative energy that must be expressed. For many years, repetitively aggressive people—chronically aggressive adolescents, spouse abusers, child abusers, and others who regularly behaved violently—were told to find a safe way to release this instinctive energy: Blow off steam; beat on the couch or the punching bag or the bobo doll instead. In recent years, however, such cathartic thinking about aggression has changed, as the idea of an inborn and inevitable aggressive instinct has been shown to be a convenient but incorrect myth. Instead, research has demonstrated that aggression is primarily learned behavior, learned by observation, imitation, direct experience, and rehearsal. Bandura (1969, 1973) was an early proponent and demonstrator of the validity of this belief; many since then have followed his lead (e.g., Baron, 1977; Eron & Huesmann, 1984; Montagu, 1978).

Effects of Coercive Parenting

Aggression often begins with interactions described by the Oregon Social Learning Center as "coercive parenting" (Patterson, Reid, Jones, & Conger, 1975). This parental behavior is marked by irritability and inconsistency. Parental warmth and affection are infrequent. At times, the parents' supervision of the child is lax or even nonexistent, at other times harsh and severe. The coercion takes the form of threats, reprimands, and frequent corporal punishment.

The aggressive pattern continues with the child's response to the coercive parenting: Temper tantrums, whining, yelling, and hitting become the child's preferred and often successful techniques for getting what he or she wants. By age 2 or 3, such children are often called "temperamental."

As ages 4 and 5 approach, such youngsters become more social beings. They go outside to play with other children. Having learned in the home that coercion pays, they begin employing aggressive tactics with newfound peers. Johnny pushes Mary off her tricycle so that he can have a ride. He grabs Freddie's soccer ball and runs off to kick it around. He barges ahead of three or four other children waiting their turns on the slide. Mary's mom, Freddie's dad, and the parents of the children in line object, intervene, and tell their children not to play with Johnny because he doesn't play nicely.

Johnny's parents have not served as positive models for him, and now his peers, who in some ways could, are withdrawn for their own protection. Johnny—who might now be labeled "oppositional"—still has social needs, desires playmates, and begins to gravitate toward and play with other coercive, frequently aggressive children. He finds ample opportunity to employ, expand, and refine his aggressive behaviors. He enters school already primed for trouble, and it doesn't take him long to find it. By regularly using the aggressive behaviors he has learned, he becomes to school personnel a "difficult" child, a "problem" child, an "acting-out" child, perhaps receiving the formal label "conduct disordered."

School personnel and Johnny's fellow students now see him as a troublemaker. Since his aggression usually brings attention and approval from his violence-prone friends, he works hard to live up to this negative expectation. If he continues to get his way by being aggressive, the frequency and intensity of aggressive acts will grow. By the preteen or teen years, "conduct disorder" may give way to "juvenile delinquency." Johnny has learned his lessons well.

Classrooms for Learning Aggression

Given that aggression is learned, who is teaching it and where are they teaching it? In most western societies, and perhaps most clearly in the United States, there appear to be three major classrooms for the learning of aggression—the home, the school, and the mass media.

Home

The first major classroom for the teaching and learning of aggression is the home. In the home, 4% of parents physically abuse their children (e.g., burn, fracture bones, shake to the point of concussion), and 90% make at least occasional (and sometimes frequent) use of corporal punishment (e.g., spank, hit, slap; Straus, 1994). What happens when an adult hits a child? The child ceases the behavior(s) that resulted in the punishment. Punishment results in the cessation of an aversive event and, thus negatively reinforced, the adult is now more likely to use corporal punishment in response to the child's next transgression. Not only has the adult learned the correctness of the adage "might makes right," so too has the child.

Bandura (1969, 1973) and others have shown that aggression is learned in one of two ways, directly or vicariously. Direct learning (the adult in our example) follows from reinforced practice (i.e., the behavior is tried and brings the expected, desired result). Vicarious learning (the child in our example) occurs by observing others behaving aggressively and their receiving a reward for doing so.

School

The school is a second major location in which aggression is learned. This assertion is supported by the increasingly aggressive nature of many adolescent peer groups (Csikszentmihalyi & Larson, 1984; Goldstein, Apter, & Harootunian, 1984; Manaster, 1977) and also by means directly analogous to those described previously for parents and their children. As noted in our later discussion of the use of punishment in U.S. schools, the teacher often inadvertently becomes a skilled instructor in "Aggression 101."

Media

Aggression is taught and learned not only in schools and homes. Perhaps its most effective teaching occurs via the mass media—newspapers, books, comic books, radio, movies, video games, and television. The impact of the mass media on human behavior is immense. One of its effects is to increase the level of violence in our society. This assertion is still disputed in some quarters, but our reading of the combined evidence regarding the influence of television leaves little room for doubt or equivocation. The continuous display of violence on television is a substantial contributor to the learning and enactment of aggressive behavior. The negative effects of this barrage of media violence include an *aggression effect* (increased copycat violence and self-directed violence), a *victim effect* (increased fearfulness, mistrust, and self-protectiveness), and a *bystander effect* (increased desensitization and callousness; Comstock & Paik, 1994; Donnerstein, Slaby, & Eron, 1994; Hoberman, 1990).

Aggressive Thoughts and Actions

Youngsters growing up as we have described not only learn to behave aggressively, they are also characteristically preoccupied with aggressive thoughts. Most people, most of the time, choose not to behave aggressively because they think such actions are immoral, antisocial, and just plain wrong. Frequently angry and aggressive people—especially those who commit violent crimes—think and act differently than most of us. First, their thinking is typically *self-centered:* "When I get mad, I don't care who gets hurt"; "If I see something I like, I take it"; "If I want to do something, I don't care if it's legal or not." Their view of the world is "me first."

Along with an egocentric perspective, frequently aggressive people often view others as being hostile toward them even when such is not the case. They misinterpret neutral behavior by others, seeing it instead as aggression directed toward them. This is why so many youths interpret being looked at (a neutral act) as a challenge, threat, or put-down (a hostile act). Similarly, if they are accidentally bumped in a crowded school hallway, they believe it is intentional. Such thinking in frequently aggressive people often takes the form of *minimizing/mislabeling,* in which one's own aggressive behavior and its negative consequences are downplayed or portrayed as something other than what they really are. Statements such as "It's no big deal if you steal—everybody does it" or "You have to get even with somebody who doesn't show respect" exemplify this error.

Minimizing and mislabeling are often combined with two other common thinking distortions to make overt aggression inevitable. One distortion is *assuming the worst* ("If I don't smack him I'll look like a punk"). The other is externalizing or *blaming others* ("It's his fault, he's asking for it, I'll smack him").

Added to these are two other distorted ways of thinking. One is *false consensus:* the rationalization that "other people think and act as I do, so there is nothing unusual about me." *Anchoring,* the final thinking mode common in aggressors, is a resistance to changing one's thinking, even when new evidence to the contrary is presented.

Thoughts do lead to actions. In trying to reduce aggressive behavior in our schools, on our streets, and in society at large, one important step is to work on changing the kinds of thinking likely to lead to such behavior.

Why Is Aggression Difficult to Change?

For a growing number of adolescents, aggressive thoughts and behaviors are "overlearned," consistently successful, and generously supported by the important people in their lives. Parents, teachers, delinquency workers, and others seeking to change such youths continue to find it difficult to succeed. Their first obstacle is the frequency with which the lesson "aggression works" is taught to youngsters in our society during their developing years.

Many young people grow up with parents who settle their own disputes aggressively. They frequently hit their children as a means of discipline. Young people play for long periods with toys in aggressive games with aggressive peers. They spend thousands of hours playing aggressive video games and viewing televised violence. They may attend a school that uses corporal punishment, perhaps join an aggressive gang or another antisocial peer group.

They are surrounded by aggressive experiences that promote rapid and lasting learning—at home, on the street, at school, and in front of the television. These aggressive experiences, arousing and seen in specific "how-to" detail, are often carried out by people the youths admire, appear to be painless, and, most important, very often succeed.

Aggressive lessons learned well and used successfully will persist if the important people in a youth's life support such thinking and behavior. Unfortunately, encouragement of the notion "might makes right" is very common—from family, peers, and others. In a recent survey comparing chronic fighters with nonfighters in one large U.S. city's secondary schools, 80% of the fighters but less than half of the nonfighters said that their families want them to hit if provoked (Goldstein & Conoley, 1997). Many youths will, in fact, be severely punished and humiliated if they *don't* use force when parents or others think they should. Similar demands for aggressive action, and praise for its use, are an equally frequent feature of peer group pressure for many youngsters. Such pressure is increasingly apparent at younger and younger ages, for both gang and nongang adolescents, and for boys and girls alike.

Having learned well how to be aggressive, found aggression to be consistently successful, and received generous encouragement and support from important others to keep being aggressive, chronically aggressive youngsters have a final quality that keeps such behavior going. Stated simply, they don't know what to do instead. The positive, nonviolent, constructive alternatives to aggression that such youngsters might use instead of fists or guns are alternatives that they have seldom seen and tried, and at times even been punished for using. Hitting the adversary is the means chosen because negotiating, walking away, getting help from an uninvolved adult, making light of the disagreement, and other nonviolent solutions are alternatives rarely seen or attempted by the youth and rarely supported by the significant people in his or her life.

In summary, aggression is often difficult to change because it is taught early, often, and well, and because it is supported and encouraged by important others. It seems to be the best and often only alternative for children and adolescents who have never really learned otherwise.

Aggression as Addiction

For some youths, aggression is so difficult to change that one is justified in wondering whether, for them, aggression is an addiction. We have not seen aggression described by others as addiction, and certainly the term *addiction* is overused today. But it is nevertheless curious that aggressive behavior has so much in common with dependence on drugs, alcohol, tobacco, gambling, and other habit-forming substances and activities. Just as is true for each of these "traditional" addictions, for some individuals aggression is:

- A long-term, repetitively used, stable behavior. The chronically aggressive youngster is likely to become a chronically aggressive adult.

- A behavior that provides short-term satisfaction but long-term problems. Beyond mere satisfaction or pleasure, some youths even describe an addiction-like physical "rush" accompanying their violent acts.

- Frequently accompanied by denial. "I didn't do it," "I didn't mean it," or "I didn't start it." Such denial, minimizing, and attribution of responsibility to others is the drug addict's rejoinder, the aggressor's frequent response.

- Described as behavior that is difficult to control, hard to reduce, and at times compulsive. When some time passes without aggression, relapses and a return to aggressive actions are likely.

- Used for a variety of reasons, including to relieve stress, deal with unpleasantness from others, alter a negative mood, or reduce a heightened level of physical arousal.

- Sustained not only by the fact that it "feels good" but also by the encouragement and support of others, many of whom could be described as friend and family "enablers." Such encouragement is also often provided by mass media portrayals and community tradition. Drink beer, bet on the lottery, light up a smoke, don't take lip from anybody—all common themes.

- A preoccupation with others' use of the behavior, be it drug taking, gambling, or aggression. Chronic aggressors, for example, watch more television violence than do others less prone to such behavior.
- A behavior that results in a high level of health risk, injury, and even death.

SCOPE: AGGRESSION IN SCHOOLS AND SOCIETY

Before the second half of the 20th century, school-based aggression apparently occurred infrequently, was low in intensity, and, at least in retrospect, was almost quaint in character. "Misbehavior," "poor comportment," "bad conduct," and the like took the form of getting out of one's seat, refusing to obey a teacher, throwing a spitball, dipping a girl's pigtail in an inkwell, or even (rarely) breaking a window. These events of another era are so mild in comparison to the aggressive acts of today that it is difficult to think of the two types of behaviors as the extremes of a shared continuum. The nature of fights between students has changed from using words and fists to aggravated assault with lethal weapons. The years prior to the 1960s might appropriately be called the "preescalation period" in U.S. school violence. For example, according to a 1956 National Education Association survey, two-thirds of the 4,270 teachers sampled from across the United States reported that fewer than 1% of their students caused disruption or disturbance, and "95% [of the responding teachers] described the boys and girls they taught as either exceptionally well behaved, or reasonably well behaved" (p. 17).

In 1975, a U.S. Senate subcommittee headed by Birch Bayh issued a report on safety in schools. This survey of 750 school districts indicated that in U.S. schools between 1970 and 1973, homicides increased by 18.5%, rapes and attempted rapes increased by 40.1%, robberies increased by 36.7%, assaults on students increased by 85.3%, assaults on teachers increased by 77.4%, burglaries in schools increased by 11.7%, drug and alcohol offenses increased by 37.5%, and the number of weapons confiscated by school personnel (pistols, knives, chukka sticks, and even sawed-off shotguns) increased by 54.4%. The National Association of School Security Directors (1975) reported that in 1974, there were 204,000 assaults and 9,000 rapes in U.S. schools. There were 18,000 assaults on teachers in 1955, 41,000 in 1971, and 63,000 in 1975; by 1979, the number of such attacks had risen to 110,000. Matters had come a very long way from spitballs and pigtails.

The situation has not improved since the 1970s. In the 1988–1989 school year, compared to the preceding year, school crime increased by 5%, and in-school weapons possession rose by 21% in California's public schools (California Department of Education, 1990). In a similar comparison, the New York City public school system reported a 35% increase in assaults on students and school staff, a 16% increase in harassment, a 24% increase in larceny, and an overall increase in crime of 25%. Noteworthy is the fact that the greatest increases in crime rates are occurring at the elementary school level (U.S. Department of Justice, 1993).

The assault level on teachers in U.S. public schools is so high that the vocabulary of aggression has been expanded to include what Block (1977) has called the "battered teacher syndrome"—a combination of stress reactions including anxiety, depression, disturbed sleep, headaches, elevated blood pressure, and eating disorders. The National Center for Education Statistics indicated in 1991 that nearly one out of five U.S. school teachers reported being verbally abused by students; 8% reported being physically threatened; and 2% indicated they had been attacked by students during the previous year. A survey by the Metropolitan Life Insurance Company (1993) indicated that 11% of U.S. teachers reported being assaulted at school—in 95% of the instances, by students.

The seriousness of these attacks notwithstanding, it must be remembered that most student aggression in U.S. schools is directed toward other students. During the first half of 1990, according to the U.S. Department of Justice (1993), approximately 9% of all students ages 12 to 19 were crime victims in the United States; 2% were victims of violent crimes, and 7% were victims of property crimes. In addition, 15% of these 12- to 19-year-olds said that their schools had gangs, and 16% claimed that their schools had had an actual or threatened attack on a teacher. Siegel and Senna (1991, p. 37) add that "although teenagers spend only 25 percent of their time in school, 40 percent of the robberies and 36 percent of the physical attacks involving this age group occur in school."

A report aptly titled *Caught in the Crossfire* (Center to Prevent Handgun Violence, 1990) fully captures the central role of firearms in the more recent surge of school violence. From 1986 to 1990, 71 people (65 students and 6 employees) were killed by guns in U.S. schools. Another 201 were seriously wounded, and 242 were held hostage at gunpoint. Older adolescents were more frequently perpetrators as well as victims. An estimated 270,000 students carry handguns to school one or more times each year.

The American School Health Association (1989) estimates that 7% of boys and 2% of girls carry a knife to school every day.

During the 1991–1992 school year, 14.4% of New York City middle school children reported being threatened by another student at least once each month, and 7.7% of them were in an actual fight (Youth Violence, 1991). A 1990 California survey of fifth through twelfth graders revealed that in the month prior to the survey, a third of them had had personal property stolen, had been grabbed or shoved, or had seen a weapon at school. Two-thirds reported being put down or cursed at by a fellow student (California Department of Education, 1990). A national crime survey (U.S. Department of Justice, 1993) reported nearly 3 million crimes per year on or near school campuses—16,000 per school day.

Consequences of Low-Level Aggression

Parallel to (and in many instances also underlying) the substantial levels of student assault, use of weaponry, theft, intimidation, and other serious violence is lower level aggressive behavior. Both Wilson and Petersilia (1995) and ourselves (Goldstein, Palumbo, Striepling, & Voutsinas, 1995) have focused in depth upon such low-level disorder as significant aggressive behavior in its own right, as well as a frequent precursor to and promoter of higher levels of such behavior. Wilson and Petersilia view such behavior—for example, students coming to school late, wandering the halls, writing graffiti on the walls, and throwing debris in the corridors—as the foundation upon which more serious violence rests:

> [Low-level] disorder invites youngsters to test further and further the limits of acceptable behavior. One connection between the inability of school authorities to maintain order and an increasing rate of violence is that, among students with little faith in the usefulness of the education they are supposed to be getting, challenging rules is part of the fun. When they succeed in littering or writing on walls, they feel encouraged to challenge other, more sacred rules, like the prohibition against assaulting fellow students and even teachers. (p. 149)

In the same spirit, we have written about the tendency in schools and other settings to "downsize deviance"—the tendency, as high levels of violent behavior demand the attention of teachers and administrators, to pay insufficient remedial attention to lower, less intense levels of such actions (Goldstein et al., 1995). We surveyed a national sample of U.S. teachers for their descriptions of violent school incidents and their management of them. In incident after incident, it is clear that the demands of high-level violence cause teachers to turn away from, ignore, or fail to adequately address low-level transgressions.

We believe all of us pay a price for this failure. As stated earlier, aggression is primarily a learned behavior. Youngsters who perpetrate low-level aggression and are rewarded for their efforts by peer approval or other means are youngsters primed both to continue such behaviors and to escalate their intensity. Two such lower level aggressive behaviors deserve special mention. Both occur frequently in schools, are covert, and are more serious in their potential consequences than those holding a "downsizing of deviance" perspective usually recognize. One is bullying, a behavior that can take several forms (e.g., name-calling, physical attack, threats, theft, spreading rumors, racial slurs, and shunning). The other is sexual harassment (e.g., sexual jokes, gestures, or looks; touching, grabbing, or pinching; spreading sexual rumors; brushing up against, flashing, or mooning).

Weapons

The counterpart of this relative inattention toward low-level aggression is the considerable professional and public concern that has been focused on more severe or intense forms of school aggression, particularly possession and use of weapons. The following list is a compilation, based on a variety of formal and informal sources, of the nature of such weaponry (National School Safety Center, 1993):

- Guns
- Knives
- Screwdrivers
- Mace
- Pens/pencils
- Baseball bats
- Rocks
- Bottles
- Brass knuckles
- Large rings
- Two- and three-finger rings
- Scissors
- Stun guns
- Chairs
- Heavy belt buckles
- Heavy false gold chains
- Box cutters
- Pen guns
- Auto batons
- Weighted gloves
- Ammonia-filled spray bottles
- Staplers
- Padlocks

- Metal nail files
- Steelies (ball bearings or steel marbles)
- Nunchakus
- Slap jacks
- Bayonets

It is our impression that box cutters (which often slip through metal detectors) are causing the most actual injury; however, guns are clearly causing the greatest concern. Though the phenomenon of students bringing guns to school is relatively recent, it has become sufficiently widespread that much is known about the particulars of such behavior. For example, 63% of the incidents of gun violence surveyed by the National School Safety Center (1993) took place in high schools, 24% in junior high schools, 12% in elementary schools, and 1% in preschools. The types of incidents reported were intentional shootings (65%), accidents (13%), suicides (8%), hostage-taking incidents (8%), and undetermined (6%).

Guns are widely available and continue to make their way into schools, in spite of the growing use of metal detectors. Although obtaining a gun is an act often based on a perceived need for self-protection, using it is typically a response to the perception of being treated disrespectfully (a perception that can arise from bad looks, bumps in the hall, or minor insults). Though students spend most of their school day in the classroom, guns are most often used during between-class transition times, in school hallways, on stairs, or in similar venues. It is in these unsupervised or inadequately supervised locations that the bad looks, bumps, and perceived insults are most likely to occur.

Vandalism

Numerous surveys and reports during the past 25 years have supported the contention that school vandalism is high and continues to grow in the United States, regularly costing over 600 million dollars each year. Such costs reflect theft as well as damage and destruction of school property. In 1991, for example, one of eight teachers and one of nine students in U.S. schools reported incidents of stealing within any given month (Miller & Prinz, 1991).

Vandalism not only costs money, it typically has social costs as well. As Vestermark and Blauvelt (1978) suggest, the social cost of vandalism is the total of three components: (a) its impact on the school's educational program, (b) its psychological impact on both students and adults, and (c) its degree of disruptiveness to group or intergroup relations. One social cost in particular may be very high—namely, the arousal of fear among students and staff.

In terms of monetary and social costs, two forms of serious aggression toward school property must be mentioned: arson and bombings. Though fortunately both are rare, when they do occur the costs can be immense. Karchmer (1982) estimates that 25 to 50% of all school fires begin by arson. Herbert (1990) describes two types of school-age fire setters—children under 10, whose fires are typically the result of play or experimentation, and adolescents, whose more complicated motivations may include life crises, peer or family concerns, independence and power issues, desire for revenge, or attention seeking.

Bombing is a serious aggressive act, causing great bodily, site, and psychological damage. In the years 1993–1995, there were 42 school bombings, occurring in 20 states. Thirty-three of these took place in high schools, and most involved the use of pipe bombs.

Violent Crime by Juveniles

We have described a pattern of serious and sustained levels of aggression by youths in U.S. schools. Outside the school—on the street, in the home, and in other community settings—a similarly grim picture emerges. According to the U.S. Office of Juvenile Justice and Delinquency Prevention (1994):

- From 1980 through 1994, an estimated 326,170 people were murdered in the United States. Nine percent of these victims, 30,200 people, were youth under age 18. Twenty percent of these victims were killed by a juvenile offender.

- There were more than 2,300 victims killed by juveniles in 1994—more than two and a half times the number in 1984.

- More than 500 youths under age 12 were arrested for rape in 1991; of these, 81 were less than 10 years old.

- In 1994, 2.7 million juveniles were arrested, one-third of them under age 18. Arrests for violent crimes included murder (3,700 arrests), rape (6,000), robbery (55,200), aggravated assault (85,300), other assaults (211,700), and vandalism (152,100).

- Between 1985 and 1994, juvenile arrest rates for all violent crimes increased substantially—murder (150%), robbery (57%), aggravated assault (97%), other assaults (144%), and vandalism (112%).

- Between 1985 and 1994, arrests for violent crimes increased 125% for juvenile females, 67% for juvenile males.

- Between 1985 and 1994, the adult arrest rate for weapons law violations increased 26%, while juvenile arrests grew 103%.

- Between 1994 and 1997, arrests for violent crimes in the United States decreased in number in many jurisdictions, but this decrease occurred primarily at the adult, not juvenile, level.

- By the year 2010, the United States will have 74 million people under age 17. If the 1985–1994 trends continue, juvenile arrests for violent crimes will more than double by that year.

SOLUTIONS: A RANGE OF RESPONSES

Currently, several approaches are in use in our 84,000 schools to moderate, control, or reduce student aggression. Some are student oriented, some are school oriented, and some are system oriented. A few are all three. Table 1.1 lists these intervention strategies. It is an impressive array, demonstrating the creativity and energy currently being applied in a continuous effort by educators, psychologists, and other professionals who seek to solve this escalating social problem.

However, little is known about which of these efforts, used singly or in combination, actually reduce aggressive behavior. Most interventions originate in the wisdom and experience of an applied practitioner— a school administrator, delinquency worker, or teacher. These interventions seem in the eyes of the practitioners or target youths to be of benefit, but this impression is based only on anecdotal and grossly inadequate evidence.

The same inadequate bases for intervention selection and use also apply in the area of juvenile delinquency. Many approaches exist and even flourish, but few have been shown to "deliver the goods" reliably.

Ineffective Intervention Strategies

A few generalized intervention strategies have significantly influenced the development and implementation of many specific approaches for dealing with violence in our schools today and with chronic aggression by children and adolescents in nonschool settings. These strategies are punishment, catharsis, and cohabitation.

Punishment

By far the preferred familial, legal, and educational response to adolescent and child aggression is punishment. Such punishment is more

Table 1.1

APPROACHES TO SCHOOL VIOLENCE AND VANDALISM

Student Oriented
- Diagnostic learning centers
- Regional occupational centers
- Part-time programs
- Academic support services
- Group counseling
- Student advisory committees
- Student governing boards
- Student patrols (interracial)
- Behavior modification: Contingency management
- Behavior modification: Time-out
- Behavior modification: Response cost
- Behavior modification: Contracting
- Financial accountability
- School transfer
- Skillstreaming
- Anger Control Training
- Stress inoculation training
- Problem-solving training
- Moral Reasoning Training
- Aggression Replacement Training
- Values clarification
- Individual counseling
- Self-esteem enhancement
- More achievable reward criteria
- Identification cards
- Peer counseling
- Participation in grievance resolution
- Security advisory councils
- School safety committees
- Codes of rights and responsibilities

Teacher Oriented
- Aggression management training for teachers
- Increased teacher-student nonclass contact
- Teacher-student-administration group discussions
- Low teacher-pupil ratio
- Firm, fair, consistent teacher discipline
- Self-defense training
- Legalization of teacher use of force
- Compensation for aggression-related expenses
- Individualized teaching strategies
- Enhanced teacher knowledge of student ethnic milieu

- Increased teacher-parent interaction
- Robbery, rape, hostage-taking survival training
- Instruction on dangerous settings

Curricular
- Art and music courses
- Law courses
- Police courses
- Apprenticeship programs
- Courses dealing with practical aspects of adult life
- Prescriptively tailored course sequences
- Work-study programs
- Equivalency diplomas
- Schools without walls
- Schools within schools
- Learning centers (magnet schools, educational parks)
- Continuation centers (street academies, evening high schools)
- Minischools
- Self-paced instruction
- Idiographic grading
- Career preparation courses and activities

Administrative
- Use of skilled conflict negotiators
- Clear lines of responsibility and authority among administrators
- School safety committees
- School administration–police coordination
- Legal rights handbooks
- School procedures manuals
- Written codes of rights and responsibilities
- Aggression management training for administrators
- Democratized school governance
- Human relations courses
- Effective intelligence networks
- Principal visibility and availability
- Relaxation of arbitrary rules (regarding smoking, dressing, absences, etc.)

Physical/Environmental
- Extensive lighting program
- Blackout of all lighting
- Reduction of school size
- Reduction of class size
- Closing off isolated areas
- Increasing staff supervision
- Rapid repair of vandalism targets
- Electronic monitoring for weapons detection
- Safety corridors (school to street)

Table 1.1 (continued)

APPROACHES TO SCHOOL VIOLENCE AND VANDALISM

Physical/Environmental (continued)
- Removal of tempting vandalism targets
- Recessed fixtures where possible
- Installation of graffiti boards
- Encouragement of student-drawn murals
- Painting lockers bright colors
- Using ceramic-type, hard-surface paints
- Sponsorship of clean-up, pick-up, fix-up days
- Paving or asphalting graveled parking areas
- Using plexiglass or polycarbon windows
- Installing decorative grillwork over windows
- Marking all school property for identification
- Preventive custodial maintenance
- Intruder detectors (microwave, ultrasonic, infrared, audio, video, mechanical)
- Personal alarm systems
- Altering isolated areas to attract people traffic

Parent Oriented
- Telephone campaigns to encourage PTA attendance
- Antitruancy committees (parent, counselor, student)
- Parent skills training
- Parents as guest speakers
- Parents as apprenticeship resources
- Parents as work-study contacts
- Increased parent legal responsibility for child behavior
- Family education centers
- Parent-student nonviolence contracts

Security Oriented
- Police K-9 patrol units
- Police helicopter surveillance
- Security personnel for patrol
- Security personnel for crowd control
- Security personnel for intelligence gathering
- Security personnel for record keeping
- Security personnel for teaching (e.g., law)
- Security personnel for counseling
- Security personnel for home visits
- Development of school security manuals

Community Oriented
- Helping-hands programs
- Restitution programs
- Adopt-a-school programs

- Vandalism prevention education
- Mass-media publication of cost of vandalism
- Opening school to community use after hours
- Improved school–juvenile court liaison
- Family back-to-school week
- Neighborhood day
- Vandalism watch on or near school grounds via mobile units
- Reporting by CB users of observed vandalism
- Community education programs
- More and better programs for disruptive/disturbed youngsters
- School-community resources coordination

State and Federal Oriented
- Uniform violence and vandalism reporting systems
- State antiviolence advisory committees
- Stronger gun-control legislation
- Enhanced national moral leadership
- Better coordination of relevant federal, state, community agencies
- Stronger antitrespass legislation
- More prosocial child labor laws

---

often punitive (e.g., corporal punishment, reprimands, school suspension) than corrective and empirically based (e.g., time-out, response cost, over-correction).

Corporal punishment is now permitted in schools in 23 states, and that number is unlikely to decrease in our current "get tough" political climate (Hyman, 1997). Ten of these states are located in the Southeast (Russell, 1989). There are approximately three-quarters of a million applications of corporal punishment in schools in the U.S. each year (Hyman, 1997). Minority youth, who constitute 30% of the school population, receive 40% of such punishments (Richardson & Evans, 1992). Emotionally disturbed and learning disabled youngsters are also targeted disproportionately to their numbers (Jones, 1993). In addition to the popular paddle, other instruments employed in administering punishment include hands, fists, straps, hoses, and bats. Students have been forced to perform exercise drills and to eat noxious substances. Most schools that employ corporal punishment have established policies and procedures regulating its use. Included in these regulations are specifications for the size of the paddle, the number and intensity of strokes to be administered, the presence of a witness, and the need for prior parental approval.

Teachers and administrators frequently respond to student misbehaviors with reprimands. Both Thomas, Presland, Grant, and Glynn (1978) and White (1975) have shown that teachers deliver an average of one reprimand every 2 minutes in both elementary and junior high school settings, a rate that substantially exceeds their rate of praise for appropriate behaviors. Evaluations of the effectiveness of reprimands have demonstrated positive short-term results in reducing aggressive student behavior (Jones & Miller, 1974; O'Leary, Kaufman, Kass, & Drabman, 1970). Nonetheless, one is justified in questioning the long-term effectiveness of reprimands, especially in light of the remarkable stability of aggressive behavior. The chronically aggressive adolescent was undoubtedly an aggressive preschooler—and because of such behaviors has received many parental reprimands—yet his or her aggression continues.

The last ineffective intervention strategy to be discussed is school suspension. Ninety-seven percent of children in the U.S. arrive at school safely every day, do their work conscientiously, experience no aggression, and return home without fear or injury. Three percent do not (Goldstein & Conoley, 1997). They are the perpetrators of sometimes serious disruptive and aggressive behaviors. It is understandable that administrators and teachers, acting on behalf of the majority of students, choose out-of-school suspension for the minority of aggressive students. Yet we believe such an administrative action is overused in many schools. Table 1.2 lists transgressions that typically result in suspension.

The climate of the school community may be enhanced by the suspension of disruptive students, but the larger community has no effective means to deal with suspended students, who may wander the streets or sit at home watching (often violent) television. Such experiences create even more potential for misbehavior outside the schools.

Why are corporal punishment, reprimands, and suspension often ineffective or, at best, of value only temporarily? Perhaps this is the case because the results of these intervention strategies have been shown to be shaped by a complex combination of their likelihood, consistency, immediacy, duration, severity, avoidability, level of instigation to aggression, and level of reward, as well as by the characteristics of the person delivering the punishment.

Yet because these strategies often succeed in the short term, the punisher believes they work, which in turn encourages the use of more punitive measures. The one punished perceives from the use of punishment that "might makes right" and becomes that much more likely to pass this message on. In a national survey, incarcerated delinquent youths consistently responded with harsh solutions when asked how

Table 1.2

REASONS FOR SCHOOL SUSPENSION

- Insubordination
- Fighting
- Use of vulgar and abusive language
- Cutting class
- Leaving the school building
- Persistent disobedience
- Loitering
- Trespassing
- Assaulting, striking, threatening, or harassing a student or staff member
- Possessing an illegal drug or drug paraphernalia
- Using or selling an illegal drug
- Possessing or using alcohol
- Reckless endangerment
- Possessing or using weapons or dangerous objects
- Smoking
- Theft
- Arson
- Extortion
- Gambling
- Destruction or defacement of school or personal property
- Sexual harassment
- Vandalism
- Tardiness
- Indecent exposure
- Truancy
- Failing to obey the reasonable request of a staff member
- Leaving the classroom without permission
- Being unprepared for class
- Falsifying information
- Possessing stolen property
- Being in an area where an illegal drug or alcoholic beverage is being used
- Possessing pornographic or obscene material
- Being disrespectful, uncooperative, or disruptive
- Refusing to stay for detention
- Failing to follow suspension rules

they would reduce aggressive behavior (Goldstein, 1990). Such findings lend credence to the belief that familial aggression is transmitted from generation to generation.

In addition to its only temporary effectiveness and the manner in which its use teaches the lesson "might makes right," punishment tells the individual what *not* to do. It fails to teach alternative, prosocial behaviors. As we have noted elsewhere:

> A reprimand or a paddling will not teach new behaviors. If the youngster is deficient in the ability to ask rather than take, request rather than command, and negotiate rather than strike out, all the teacher scolding, scowling, and spanking possible will not teach the youngster desirable alternative behaviors. (Goldstein, 1988, p. 572)

Catharsis

Catharsis is another aggression reduction strategy popular among both laypersons and education and mental health professionals. In this strategy, for example, the physical education teacher urges the volatile youngster to "get rid of the anger" on the punching bag, not a classmate's head. The marital therapist instructs the abusive husband to blow off steam and beat the couch, not his spouse. In a similar manner, experiencing aggression vicariously by watching televised sports is recommended as an outlet for aggressive tendencies.

Catharsis is the draining off, venting, or purging of emotion. Purportedly, catharsis may occur vicariously, as when one observes and empathically identifies with another person. This concept of catharsis first appeared in reports of emotional purging experienced by the audiences of early Greek dramas. Freud's (1950) view and the ethological perspective of Lorenz (1966) suggest a more direct cathartic response. Freud wrote that "there is a continuous welling up of destructive impulses within the individual representing an outgrowth of the death instinct" (p. 160). Lorenz held that in both animal and human "aggressive energy is continuously being generated within the species member and seeks periodic release" (p. 161). In these views, aggression is inevitable, and the best way to release it is by having a socially acceptable, minimally injurious "aggressive" experience, such as debating or playing competitive sports. Proctor and Eckerd (1976) present this viewpoint clearly:

> People's emotions are similar to steam locomotives. If you build a fire in the boiler of a locomotive, keep raising the steam pressure and let it sit on the tracks, sooner or later something will blow. However, if you take it and spin the wheels and toot the whistle, the steam pressure can be kept at a safe level. Spectator sports give John

Q. Citizen a socially acceptable way to lower his steam pressure by allowing him to spin his wheels and toot his whistle. (p. 83)

Is it correct to view aggression as stored, constantly growing energy that needs to be directly or indirectly vented in order to be maintained at a manageable level? To help answer this question, research relevant to this subject is next described.

Static comparisons

One research approach is simply to compare the aggression levels of people who do and do not regularly engage in aggressive activities. If the catharsis notion is correct, those who do engage in aggressive activities, having vented their feelings, should show less aggression. Zillmann, Bryant, and Sapolsky (1979) compared contact-sport athletes (in football and wrestling) with noncontact-sport athletes (in swimming and tennis) and with nonathletes. They found no between-group differences on behavioral measures of aggression. Le Unes and Nation (1981) compared football players and nonathletes in the same way, and Ostrow (1974) compared tennis players and nonathletes. Their results matched Zillmann et al.'s in that there were no between-group differences on aggression. To say it another way, there was no evidence that the expression of aggression reduces its occurrence.

Before-after comparisons

In before-after comparisons, two groups are randomly constituted, and one is given the opportunity to act out aggressively. If the catharsis concept is correct, the after comparisons should find the group permitted to express aggression to be less aggressive than the comparison group. Ostrow (1974) and Ryan (1970) each conducted this type of study and found no support for such an effect. Surprisingly, three other before-after comparison studies of catharsis found the opposite effect! People who behaved aggressively became more aggressive, not less. This was the result in Hornberger's (1959) study, in which research participants were required to hammer nails, in Loew's (1967) study, in which participants were required to say a series of aggressive words, and in Patterson's (1974) comparison of football players and physical education students before and after the football season. Compared with their respective nonaggressive groups, the nail hammerers, aggression verbalizers, and football players all became more aggressive—the direct opposite of a catharsis effect. J.H. Goldstein and Arms (1971) measured aggression levels in randomly selected fans before and after an Army-Navy football game. Contrary to experiencing catharsis, fans of both the winners and losers had higher aggression levels after the game than before the game. As the investigators comment, "Exposure to the aggression of others seemingly acts to weaken one's internal mechanisms controlling the expression of similar behavior" (p. 165). Arms, Russell, and Sandilands (1979) replicated this result and showed, furthermore, that fan aggression increased after football and hockey matches (aggressive sports) but not after a swim meet (a nonaggressive sport).

Archival studies

If catharsis is a real phenomenon, archival studies of short- and long-term records of aggressive sports and other events should result in a decrease of aggression over the course of the event. In five separate archival studies, Russell (1981) showed the opposite of a cathartic effect: Aggression increased as athletic events progressed. A similar anti-cathartic result emerged in Russell's study of aggression between two teams as they met over a season: More, not less, aggression took place. The early proponents of competitive sports as an ideal ground for venting human aggression saw sports in their grand vision as a substitute for war. Unfortunately, this cathartic vision, too, fails to find support in archival studies. Sipes (1973) showed a positive correlation between the number of combatant sports in a society and its involvement in wars, conflicts, and revolutions. Similarly, Keefer, J.H. Goldstein, and Kasiary (1983) found a positive correlation between a country's participation in the Olympics, on the one hand, and the number and length of wars in which it had engaged.

Laboratory studies

Consistent with the research outcomes reported previously, Berkowitz (1964) conducted a series of investigations in which research subjects were or were not shown either brutal, staged sports violence (e.g., the fight scene from the movie *The Champion*) or equally brutal actual fights from hockey, football, and basketball. In all instances, those viewing the aggressive scenes, compared with nonviewing control subjects, significantly increased their own levels of aggression.

Conducted mostly in the 1960s and 1970s, these several methodologically diverse investigations—static comparisons, before-after comparisons, archival studies, field-based studies, laboratory-based studies—

combine with more recent studies of the consequences of catharsis (J.H. Goldstein, 1986; Phillips & Henley, 1984; Wann & Branscombe, 1990) to converge toward a strong conclusion: Catharsis is a myth. Sports violence increases participant and spectator aggression. As Goranson (1970) has aptly suggested:

> I think that this is one of those rare occasions in behavioral research where an unqualified conclusion is warranted. The observation of violence does not reduce aggressiveness. . . . Observed violence serves to facilitate the expression of aggression, rather than reduce aggression by "draining off aggressive energy"! (p. 12)

Cohabitation

Cohabitation is the defeatist, overwhelming, resigned sense that aggression is a part of human nature and will always be with us, and that one has no other choice than to live with it. Many living with aggression do so poorly—the burned-out teacher, the constantly fearful student, the city-dwelling senior citizen who locks her door in fear of becoming victim to violent crime, and the millions of people (perhaps all of us) who have become increasingly desensitized to and more tolerant of high levels of aggression. We definitely do not share this perspective. Much has already been accomplished in schools and communities to control, reduce, and even eliminate aggressive behavior. As the remainder of this discussion suggests, more can be done if we are willing to change our customary thinking about how to reduce aggression.

Effective Intervention Strategies

Complexity

There is a tendency, stemming perhaps from the "can do" attitude characteristic of those of us in the United States, to hope for and expect to find one "big solution" for major social problems. We seek the single breakthrough or intervention program that will wipe out poverty (e.g., the War on Poverty of the 1960s), cancer (e.g., various "miracle cures"), illiteracy (e.g., early education and stimulation interventions), hunger and malnutrition (e.g., food stamps), drug abuse (e.g., "Just Say No" campaigns), and, most certainly, aggression. The "magic bullets" aimed at reducing aggression over the past few decades have included an array of programs. These magic bullets all miss the target. Hoped-for breakthroughs—whether for the elimination of poverty, cancer, illiteracy, hunger, drug abuse, or aggression—become more elusive as the complexity of the problems increases.

Simply put, we suggest that complex problems will yield only to complex solutions. Every act of aggression has multiple causes. When Johnny throws a book at his teacher, it is unproductive to reduce the causes of such a behavior to Johnny's "aggressive personality," "economic disadvantage," "peer group encouragement," "testosterone level," or any other single cause. Johnny's aggressive act, as well as all other acts of aggression, stem from a variety of societal and individual causes. Table 1.3 lists some of the specific causes and examples of aggression.

As this table shows, the complex causes of aggression indicate the need for correspondingly complex solutions. The call for complex solutions for reducing major social problems has been heard before from the community psychologist (Heller, Price, Reinharz, Riger, Wandersman, & D'Aunno, 1984), the ecological psychologist (Moos, 1974), the environmental designer (Krasner, 1980), and the systems analyst (Plas, 1986). This view certainly applies in the context of school violence (Goldstein, Harootunian, & Conoley, 1994). Our view is that to have even a modest chance of enduring success, interventions designed to reduce aggression must be aimed not only at the aggressor, but also at teachers, administrators, and the larger community context of which the youth is a part. Furthermore, optimally complex intervention strategies designed

Table 1.3

ANTECEDENTS OF AGGRESSIVE BEHAVIOR

Causes	*Examples*
Physiological predisposition	Male gender, high arousal, temperament
Cultural context	Societal traditions and mores that encourage or restrain aggression
Interpersonal environment	Parental/peer criminology, video/film aggressive models
Physical environment	Temperature, noise, crowding, traffic, pollution
Person qualities	Self-control, repertoire of alternative prosocial values and behaviors
Disinhibitors	Alcohol, drugs, successful aggressive models
Presence of means	Guns, knives, other weapons
Presence of potential victim	Spouse, child, elderly person

to reduce school violence should do so through the use of various inter-vention modes or channels. The first requirement, then, for the planning of an effective aggression reduction intervention is multilevel, multi-channel complexity.

Prescriptiveness

Having first developed an appropriately complex aggression interven-tion procedure, the next step is to implement it. We believe aggression reduction will be more likely if interventions are applied in a differen-tial, individualized, or prescriptive manner. Prescriptive programming considers all interacting components of an intervention, including the individual differences of the youths involved, the types of change agents to be used, and the types of interventions that will yield optimal outcomes. This view runs counter to the "one-true-light" assumption underlying most intervention efforts, which holds that specific treatments are sufficiently powerful to override individual differences and are equally effective for all individuals in heterogeneous groups.

Research in all fields of psychotherapy and education has shown the one-true-light assumption to be erroneous (Goldstein, 1978; Goldstein & Stein, 1976). Palmer's (1973) research disproves the efficacy of this assumption as it relates to aggressive and delinquent adolescents. Instead, a "many-true-lights" perspective has been proposed. In elementary and secondary education contexts, examples of prescriptive program-ming include Keller's (1966) personalized instruction; Cronbach and Snow's (1977) aptitude-treatment interactions; Hunt's (1971) matching of student conceptual level and teacher instructional style; and Klausmeier, Rossmiller, and Sailey's (1977) individually guided education model.

In the context of school violence, two additional promising prescriptions may be offered. Both await empirical scrutiny. The first intervention is from the seminal work of Dodge (1990). As Table 1.4 illustrates, Dodge has proposed two major subcategories of aggression: proactive and reactive. *Proactive aggression* is intentional injury to another as a result of a deliber-ate attempt to obtain material gain or to dominate. *Reactive aggression*, also called angry or hostile aggression, is intentional injury to another as a result of an arousal-motivated desire to hurt another. The former, Dodge proposes, logically leads to the recommendation of one set of interventions; the latter, to a quite different prescription.

A second prescriptive proposal is from Goldstein et al. (1995). As men-tioned earlier, to obtain teacher perspectives and experiences relating to

Table 1.4

PRESCRIPTIVE INTERVENTIONS BY TYPE OF AGGRESSION

Proactive Aggression   *Reactive Aggression*

CHARACTERISTICS

- Object oriented
- Goal—to obtain or dominate
- Cold blooded (e.g., bullying)
- Premeditated crimes

- Person oriented
- Goal—to hurt or injure
- Angry, volatile (e.g., temper tantrum)
- Crimes of passion

POSSIBLE INTERVENTIONS

- Consistent punishment for aggressive behavior
- Consistent reward for prosocial behavior
- Social skills training

- Anger control training
- Empathy training

school violence intervention, we conducted a national teacher survey. This survey yielded 1,000 descriptions of incidents of school violence at all grade levels, as well as of the techniques teachers employed for their management. A cluster analysis of these incidents allowed us to group them into categories and list them in order of their increasing severity (see Table 1.5). Horseplay and rules violation, for example, are mild forms; bullying and sexual harassment are at an intermediate level; and attacks on teachers or use of weapons reflect a high level of intensity. Based upon these teacher experiences, particularly those involving successful management of students' aggressive behaviors, our prescriptive recommendation fits neatly the zero-tolerance climate increasingly characteristic of schools in the United States: "Catch it low to prevent it high."

If aggression is primarily a learned behavior, what does the aggressive adolescent learn who receives only positive peer attention and suffers no

Table 1.5

CATEGORIES OF STUDENT AGGRESSION

1. Horseplay	8. Physical threats
2. Rules violation	9. Vandalism
3. Disruptiveness	10. Out-of-control behavior
4. Refusal	11. Fights
5. Cursing	12. Attacks on teachers
6. Bullying	13. Group aggression
7. Sexual harassment	14. Other (e.g., intruders, weapons)

negative consequences for his misbehavior? Such scenarios reinforce the belief that aggression does pay and encourage its continuation and escalation. As noted in Kelling and Coles' (1996) book entitled *Fixing Broken Windows*, a number of police departments in the United States have reported lowered crime rates in their cities as a result of heightened police attention to incivilities and "quality of life crimes"—subway fare-beating, littering, illegal parking, panhandling, and the like. More research is necessary in order to ascertain the effectiveness of applying this concept to the reduction of youth violence in our society.

Additional possible prescriptive bases for intervention development or selection exist. Each one of these holds promise, but none has as yet been examined for its differential potency for differing types of aggression. Such categorizations of aggression include overcontrol versus undercontrol, high intensity versus low intensity, early onset versus later onset, and overt versus covert expression (Feldman, Caplinger, & Wodarski, 1983; Loeber & Dishion, 1983; Shannon, 1988; Wolfgang, Thornberry, & Figlio, 1987).

Situationality

Until the 1950s, psychology's basic assumption was that the primary determinants of human behavior lie within each individual (i.e., personality traits or dispositional tendencies). Understand the personality better, it was held, and the accurate prediction and control of behavior will follow. As psychology moved into the 1960s, this belief was challenged by the fact that consistency of behavior across situations was not often found to occur. Price and Bouffard (1974) comment:

> Several reviews of personality research have made it clear that traditional assumptions concerning the transituational consistency of personality are in need of considerable revision. . . . These studies have made it clear that (a) simple trait-oriented conceptions of personality must be replaced by much more complex conceptualizations and (b) the scope of these conceptualizations must be expanded from exclusively person-oriented conceptions to approaches which include the domains of situations, behavior, and their interactions. (p. 579)

This call has been heeded. Psychology has moved away from the exclusive use of personality indices and now relies more on information about the interaction between person and situation to understand, predict, and control human behavior. This perspective finds expression across many different classes of behavior, including aggression (Campbell, 1986; Cordilia, 1986; Goldstein, 1994).

Personality information still has major value in making lower order predictions about future aggressive behavior—if we know something about the hostility traits of a given student, athlete, or prisoner, for example. But how much deeper our understanding, better our predictions, and more effective our intervention efforts can be when we also factor in the situational research findings. These findings suggest the following:

- Aggression in a school context is greater in some physical locations (cafeteria, stairwells, bathrooms) than others, greater at some times of the year than others (March is the worst month in the U.S.; the last day of school is worst in Japan), greater the larger the school, and greater when the school's governance is either autocratic or laissez-faire, as contrasted to "firm but fair."

- Aggression in an athletic context is greater for members of home teams than visiting teams, greater later in the season than earlier, later in the game than earlier, and when the team is in the middle rather than top or bottom of its league standings.

- Aggression in a prison context is greater the larger the prison, the more external (in and out) traffic, the more internal (within) traffic, and the more racially mixed or gang-dominated.

Considering the influence of specific contextual features on aggressive behaviors can, when combined with personality information, aid our efforts to understand, predict, and control human aggression. These features include location, physical arrangement, entrances and exits, illumination, temperature, noise level, people present, time of day, actions that take place, norms, rules, goals, roles, tasks, themes, expectations, ambiguities, and so on. These and other situational characteristics are antecedents of or correlates to aggressive behavior.

Schools in the United States have implemented violence prevention and reduction interventions reflecting the perspective of situationality. Table 1.6 lists several environmental design methods; the information here is drawn from the work of Brantingham and Brantingham (1991) and Clarke (1992) as well as from a person-environment approach to school vandalism (Goldstein, 1994, 1995). These are the methods of environmental criminologists, who assert that, regardless of the motivations of potential perpetrators, the supply of persons motivated to engage in

Table 1.6

ENVIRONMENTAL METHODS FOR PREVENTING AND REDUCING VANDALISM

1. Target hardening (e.g., security screens, slash-proof seats)
2. Access control (e.g., locked doors, blocked-off streets)
3. Deflecting offenders (e.g., graffiti boards, home activities)
4. Controlling facilitators (e.g., spray paint sales control, plastic "glass")
5. Entry and exit screening (e.g., closed-circuit television, merchandise tags)
6. Formal surveillance (e.g., burglar alarms, tenant patrols)
7. Employee surveillance (e.g., aisle mirrors, more employees)
8. Natural surveillance (e.g., improved lighting, clear store windows)
9. Target removal (e.g., exact change fares, removable car radios)
10. Identifying property (e.g., vehicle parts ID, marking with social security numbers)
11. Removing inducements (e.g., rapid graffiti cleanup, small windowpanes)
12. Rule setting (e.g., drug-free school zones, building design codes)

aggressive and other antisocial behaviors will always outdistance remedial efforts to alter such behaviors and that needed instead (or in addition) are means for altering the opportunity to engage in these behaviors. The dozen strategies listed in Table 1.6 decrease potential perpetrators' opportunity by limiting access to targets of vandalism, by causing them to believe they will be discovered, or by making the consequences of a vandalistic act less attractive.

Aggression as Learned Behavior

As discussed previously, aggression is primarily learned behavior and, for many delinquent youths, it is well learned and generously rewarded over their lifetimes. It is therefore no wonder that short-term, quick-fix programs—a week in the wilderness, wagon trips, maritime experiences, scared straight programs, and boot camps—appear to have little enduring impact. Because diminished use of antisocial behaviors and increased use of their prosocial alternatives are central to successful outcomes for aggressive youths, approaches emphasizing learning, un-learning, and relearning show promise, whereas individual counseling or psychotherapeutic approaches, targeted toward "underlying causes," show little.

In its rationale and procedures, Aggression Replacement Training reflects the four productive intervention strategies we have examined. First, it is complex: The program recognizes that aggressive youths characteristically are weak in or lack many of the personal, interpersonal, and social-cognitive skills that collectively constitute effective prosocial behavior. In addition, their frequent impulsiveness and overreliance on aggressive means to meet their daily needs and longer term goals reflect deficiency in anger control. With respect to values, such adolescents also have been shown to respond at a more egocentric, concrete, and, in a sense, primitive level of moral reasoning. ART addresses each of these concerns, respectively, in its three coordinated components: Skillstreaming, Anger Control Training, and Moral Reasoning Training.

Second, ART is prescriptive in its adaptability to the learning styles of different individuals. Specifically, the program derives from developmental psychological research outlining optimal teaching and learning styles for people from various socioeconomic classes. Mental health and psychoeducational services have traditionally been inadequate for low-income populations, and there has been a comparative scarcity of appropriately tailored interventions for such populations. Since our first published proposal for an ART-like prescription, a book entitled *Structured Learning Therapy: Toward a Psychotherapy for the Poor* (Goldstein, 1973), we have developed and implemented ART to benefit participants from various backgrounds, particularly those from low-income environments.

As numerous application models and evaluations of program effectiveness have shown, ART is situational in its consideration of the importance of the interactions between the aggressive individual and the significant people in his or her life. As detailed in chapter 8, the program has been used not only with youths but also with their families, peers, teachers, and others.

Above all, ART embraces the viewpoint that aggression is primarily learned behavior. Central to its purpose are the ideas that aggressive youths often do not possess the prosocial skills necessary for a nonaggressive yet satisfying and effective life-style and that they must be afforded the opportunity to learn such prosocial alternatives to antisocial behaviors.

CHAPTER TWO

An Overview of ART

Underlying Aggression Replacement Training is the idea that every act of adolescent or child aggression—in school, at home, in the community—has multiple causes, both external and internal to the youth. As discussed in chapter 1, external influences, particularly of parents and peers, are substantial. With regard to internal causes, ample evidence supports the belief that chronically aggressive youngsters possess a series of interlocking and compounding deficiencies. First, these youths characteristically are weak in or lack many of the personal, interpersonal, and social-cognitive skills that collectively constitute effective prosocial behavior. Second, their frequent impulsiveness and overreliance on aggressive means to meet their daily needs and longer term goals reflect deficiency in anger control. Third, with respect to values, such adolescents have been shown to respond at a more egocentric, concrete, and, in a sense, primitive level of moral reasoning.

COMPONENTS OF ART

ART addresses each of these concerns in its three coordinated components: Skillstreaming, Anger Control Training, and Moral Reasoning Training.

Skillstreaming

Skillstreaming is a set of procedures designed to enhance prosocial skill levels (Goldstein, 1973, 1981). It grows from our interpretation of research on optimal teaching styles for certain categories of aggressive youth as well as from the social learning, behavior-deficit model advanced by Bandura (1973). The approach consists of a series of social learning instructional procedures. Concretely, in Skillstreaming, small groups of frequently aggressive or delinquent adolescents are (a) shown several examples of expert use of the behaviors that constitute the skills in which they are deficient (i.e., modeling); (b) given several guided opportunities to practice and rehearse these competent behaviors (i.e., role-playing); (c) provided with praise, reinstruction, and related feedback on how well their role-playing skill enactments match the expert model's portrayals (i.e., performance feedback); and (d) encouraged to engage in a series of activities designed to increase the chances that skills learned in the training setting will endure and be available when needed in school, home, community, institutional, or other real-world settings (i.e., transfer training). By these means—modeling, role-playing, performance feedback, and transfer training—instruction is offered in a curriculum of 50 prosocial skills. The history of Skillstreaming and all procedures necessary for its effective use are described in chapter 3.

Anger Control Training

Anger Control Training, the second component of ART, was developed by Feindler and her research group (Feindler & Ecton, 1986) at Adelphi University and is based in part on the earlier anger control and stress inoculation research of, respectively, Novaco (1975) and Meichenbaum (1977). Skillstreaming, the behavioral component of ART, teaches youths what to do instead of aggression. In a complementary manner, Anger Control Training—ART's emotion-oriented component—teaches trainees what not to do. Its aim is to enhance the self-control, reduction, or management of anger and aggression. Youths are trained to respond to provocations ("hassles") not with anger but with a chain of responses focusing on (a) triggers—the external events and internal appraisals that function as one's anger stimuli; (b) cues—kinesthetic or other physiological sensations or experiences signifying one's anger arousal; (c) reducers—arousal-lowering techniques such as backward counting, deep breathing, peaceful imagery, and reflection on long-term consequences, (d) reminders—self-instructional statements designed to reinterpret and defuse internal triggers; (e) use of the appropriate Skillstreaming alternative to anger or aggression; and (f) self-evaluation—of the use and results obtained in the previous steps in the anger control sequence. The background of Anger Control Training and its procedures are described in chapter 4.

Moral Reasoning Training

Moral Reasoning Training is the third intervention of ART. If armed with the enhanced ability to respond prosocially to the real world and the skills necessary to control or at least diminish impulsive anger and aggression, will the chronically acting-out youth choose to use these skills? To answer this question, one must enter into the realm of moral values. In a long and pioneering series of investigations, Kohlberg (1969, 1973) demonstrated that exposing a youth to a series of moral dilemmas in a discussion-group context, including others with differing levels of moral reasoning, arouses an experience of cognitive conflict whose resolution will advance the youth's moral reasoning to that of the higher level peers in the group. Such moral reasoning advancement is a reliable finding, but as with many other single interventions, efforts to use this intervention alone to enhance overt moral behavior have yielded at best mixed success (Arbuthnot & Gordon, 1983; Zimmerman, 1983). Perhaps, we speculated, such youths did not have in their behavioral repertoires either the actual skill behaviors for acting prosocially or for successfully inhibiting their antisocial behaviors. We thus reasoned that Kohlbergian Moral Reasoning Training could enhance prosocial and reduce antisocial behavior in youths who had successfully undergone both Skillstreaming and Anger Control Training. Chapter 5 examines Moral Reasoning Training in detail, providing a complete description of its procedures, curriculum, and materials.

ART AS A MULTICHANNEL APPROACH

When used separately, each of these three interventions results in substantial change in those to whom it is directed. But in each instance, limitations on the changes obtained exist. Both Skillstreaming and Anger Control Training yield reliable short-term alterations in participants' target behaviors, but neither has been shown to have equally reliable longer term effects. Moral Reasoning Training seems to influence values, but much less frequently can changes in moral behavior be shown. Therefore, the combination of these three interventions might reasonably yield more reliable and longer term positive outcomes than each could individually. Three different but overlapping rationales support this contention. These rationales concern the generally superior potency of multimodal interventions, the utility of constructive treatment strategies, and the likely fruitfulness of incremental prescription building.

With regard to the first of these rationales, the potency of *multimodal interventions,* we have commented elsewhere that

behavior change in our view may result from interventions which are explicitly targeted on overt behavior, or which seek to diminish emotional responses which inhibit use of behaviors already in the person's behavioral repertoire, or which provide information about the consequences of alternative behaviors.

Behavioral, affective, and cognitive interventions each in these differing ways possess potential for altering overt behaviors. Which, and how many of these alternative intervention routes will correspond to any given youngster's channels of accessibility will obviously vary from youngster to youngster. We believe, however, that it generally will prove efficacious to take more than one route simultaneously. The source and maintainers of aggression are diverse and multichanneled. So too must its remediation be. Skillstreaming is our behavioral intervention; Anger Control Training is affective in its substance; Moral Education is cognitive in nature. Guided by our multimodal philosophy, it is our hypothesis that these interventions will yield outcomes superior to those resulting from single-channel interventions. (Goldstein & Glick, 1987, p. 16)

In our development, implementation, and evaluation of ART, we have sought to execute a *constructive treatment* strategy, an approach to intervention research and development described well by Kazdin (1975):

The constructive treatment strategy refers to developing a treatment package by adding components to enhance therapy. . . . With the constructive approach the investigator usually begins with a basic treatment component that is relatively narrow or circumscribed in focus. Research is conducted that adds various ingredients to the basic treatment to determine what enhances treatment effects. As research continues, effective components are retained and a large treatment package is constructed. (p. 87)

Finally, ART is in its development, application, and evaluation an example of *incremental prescription building*. Describing this treatment-enhancing strategy, elsewhere we have observed:

An incremental prescriptive strategy [is] one in which partial or tentative prescriptions are replicated, combined, and empirically examined in such a manner that one can ascertain whether the percent of outcome variance accounted for is, as predicted, progressively increasing. Klett and Moseley (1963) champion a similar incremental strategy. They propose a prescription-building process in which (a) active treatment ingredients are identified, (b) their weighting vis-à-vis outcome variance is determined, (c) ingredients are combined into new sets and combinations, and (d) the new prescriptive combinations are offered, evaluated, reweighted and so forth. (Goldstein & Stein, 1976, p. 19)

Central to the notions of multimodal intervention, constructive treatment, and incremental prescription building is the belief that the development of effective habilitative interventions for aggressive and delinquent youths is a process without end, an ongoing search for more effective solutions. ART is a beginning, not an end, in this search.

A SAMPLE ART CURRICULUM

In this section, we provide an example of an ART curriculum as it is often offered in schools, agencies, and institutions. While program lengths are varied, and to some extent "the more the better," a 10-week format is common (see Table 2.1). In this format, group members attend an ART session three times a week, with one of these sessions respectively devoted to Skillstreaming, Anger Control Training, or Moral Reasoning Training. Typically, a single session lasts 45 to 50 minutes, with Moral Reasoning Training sessions sometimes lasting longer, perhaps up to 1½ hours.

The 10 Skillstreaming skills included in this program are those collectively chosen by the staffs of the two delinquency centers at which we conducted our first ART evaluation studies (Goldstein & Glick, 1987; Goldstein, Glick, Irwin, McCartney, & Rubama, 1989; see chapter 8). They represent those skills judged to be most needed by the youths in their charge. The Anger Control Training component of the ART curriculum is that originated by Feindler (Feindler, 1979; Feindler & Ecton, 1986) and modified by us. The moral problem situations included in the Moral Reasoning Training component are those effectively employed by Gibbs, Potter, and Goldstein (1995) in the EQUIP program, directed toward aggressive youths.

Though we describe a 10-week program here, we do not mean to imply that 10 weeks is optimal, nor that curriculum content should be fixed. Some ART trainers find it useful, for example, to prepare trainees for group participation by beginning the Skillstreaming component with the skills of Listening and Using Self-Control rather than with the skills indicated in Table 2.1 (see Appendix A). Ten weeks is satisfactory in many schools and institutions, but in others—especially those in which the aggressive nature of the youths is chronic and enduring—a longer program, perhaps with a curriculum much different from the one outlined in Table 2.1, may be required. Chapter 8 describes a number of

Table 2.1

TEN-WEEK ART CURRICULUM

Week	Skillstreaming	Moral Reasoning Training	Anger Control Training
1	*Making a Complaint* 1. Decide what your complaint is. 2. Decide whom to complain to. 3. Tell that person your complaint. 4. Tell that person what you would like done about the problem. 5. Ask how he/she feels about what you've said.	*Jim's Problem Situation*	*Introduction* 1. Explain the goals of Anger Control Training and "sell it" to the youngsters. 2. Explain the rules for participating and the training procedures. 3. Give initial assessments of the A-B-Cs of aggressive behavior: A = What led up to it? B = What did you do? C = What were the consequences? 4. Review goals, procedures, and A-B-Cs.
2	*Understanding the Feelings of Others* 1. Watch the other person. 2. Listen to what the other person is saying. 3. Figure out what the person might be feeling. 4. Think about ways to show you understand what he/she is feeling. 5. Decide on the best way and do it.	*Jerry's Problem Situation*	*Triggers* 1. Review the first session. 2. Introduce the Hassle Log. 3. Discuss what makes you angry (triggers). 4. Role-play triggers. 5. Review the Hassle Log and triggers.

3

Getting Ready for a Difficult Conversation

1. Think about how you will feel during the conversation.
2. Think about how the other person will feel.
3. Think about different ways you could say what you want to say.
4. Think about what the other person might say back to you.
5. Think about any other things that might happen during the conversation.
6. Choose the best approach you can think of and try it.

4

Dealing with Someone Else's Anger

1. Listen to the person who is angry.
2. Try to understand what the angry person is saying and feeling.
3. Decide if you can say or do something to deal with the situation.
4. If you can, deal with the other person's anger.

5

Keeping Out of Fights

1. Stop and think about why you want to fight.
2. Decide what you want to happen in the long run.
3. Think about other ways to handle the situation besides fighting.
4. Decide on the best way to handle the situation and do it.

Mark's Problem Situation

Cues and Anger Reducers 1, 2, and 3

1. Review the second session.
2. Discuss how to know when you are angry (cues).
3. Discuss what to do when you know you are angry.
   - Anger reducer 1: Deep breathing
   - Anger reducer 2: Backward counting
   - Anger reducer 3: Pleasant imagery
4. Role-play triggers + cues + anger reducers.
5. Review the Hassle Log; triggers; cues; and anger reducers 1, 2, and 3.

George's Problem Situation

Reminders

1. Review the third session.
2. Introduce reminders.
3. Model using reminders.
4. Role-play triggers + cues + anger reducer(s) + reminders.
5. Review reminders.

Leon's Problem Situation

Self-Evaluation

1. Review the fourth session.
2. Introduce self-evaluation.
   - Self-rewarding
   - Self-coaching
3. Role-play triggers + cues + anger reducer(s) + reminders + self-evaluation.
4. Review self-evaluation.

Table 2.1 (continued))

TEN-WEEK ART CURRICULUM

Week	Skillstreaming	Moral Reasoning Training	Anger Control Training

6	*Helping Others*
	1. Decide if the other person might need and want your help.
	2. Think of the ways you could be helpful.
	3. Ask the other person if he/she needs and wants your help.
	4. Help the other person.
		Sam's Problem Situation	*Thinking Ahead (Anger Reducer 4)*
			1. Review the fifth session.
			2. Introduce thinking ahead.
			  • Short- and long-term consequences
			  • Internal and external consequences
			3. Role-play "if-then" thinking ahead.
			4. Role-play triggers + cues + anger reducer(s) + reminders + self-evaluation.
			5. Review thinking ahead.

7	*Dealing with an Accusation*
	1. Think about what the other person has accused you of.
	2. Think about why the person might have accused you.
	3. Think about ways to answer the person's accusation.
	4. Choose the best way and do it.
		Reggie's Problem Situation	*Angry Behavior Cycle*
			1. Review the sixth session.
			2. Introduce the Angry Behavior Cycle.
			  • Identify your own anger-provoking behavior.
			  • Change your own anger-provoking behavior.
			3. Role-play triggers + cues + anger reducer(s) + reminders + self-evaluation.
			4. Review the Angry Behavior Cycle.

8

Dealing with Group Pressure
1. Think about what the group wants you to do and why.
2. Decide what you want to do.
3. Decide how to tell the group what you want to do.
4. Tell the group what you have decided.

Rehearsal of Full Sequence
1. Review the seventh session.
2. Introduce the use of Skillstreaming skills in place of aggression.
3. Role-play triggers + cues + anger reducer(s) + reminders + Skillstreaming skill + self-evaluation.

Alonzo's Problem Situation

9

Expressing Affection
1. Decide if you have good feelings about the other person.
2. Decide if the other person would like to know about your feelings.
3. Choose the best way to express your feelings.
4. Choose the best time and place to express your feelings.
5. Express your feelings in a friendly way.

Rehearsal of Full Sequence
1. Review the Hassle Logs.
2. Role-play triggers + cues + anger reducer(s) + reminders + Skillstreaming skill + self-evaluation.

Juan's Problem Situation

10

Responding to Failure
1. Decide if you have failed at something.
2. Think about why you failed.
3. Think about what you could do to keep from failing another time.
4. Decide if you want to try again.
5. Try again using your new idea.

Overall Review
1. Review the Hassle Logs.
2. Recap anger control techniques.
3. Role-play triggers + cues + anger reducer(s) + reminders + Skillstreaming skill + self-evaluation.
4. Give reinforcement for participation and encourage trainees to continue.

Antonio's Problem Situation

specific program applications and variations, illustrating the range of ways ART may be prescriptively employed.

IMPLEMENTATION CONCERNS

Trainee Selection and Preparation

In the majority of the school, agency, and residential settings in which ART has been used, youth have been assigned to the program by staff responsible for their education or well-being. Such involuntary trainee involvement has in particular characterized ART programming in special education, juvenile justice, and mental health settings. Youth participation in regular school settings has more typically been voluntary (an "it's up to you" invitation) or quasi-voluntary (with strong teacher encouragement). Whether participation is on a voluntary, quasi-voluntary, or involuntary basis, the criteria for inclusion in ART are substantial deficiencies in the prosocial skill, anger control, and moral reasoning capacities that are the targets of the intervention.

We recommend no more than six to eight trainees per group, although fewer members may be necessary and desirable if the trainees involved are very aggressive and out of control. Under these circumstances, one would start with a smaller group (even as few as two members) and slowly build membership, perhaps at the rate of one additional new trainee per week, as the group comes under control and a group culture begins to build. At other times, the opposite challenge is to successfully manage larger groups. The larger group could be subdivided and smaller groups run concurrently.

Once groups have been formed, the next step is preparing and motivating trainees for ART participation. Ideally, basic program information is provided first to the individual, then to the group when it first convenes. Purposes, procedures, incentives, and group rules are covered.

The *purposes* of ART are presented as they relate to the specific youngster with whom one is meeting. For example, the trainer might say, "Remember last week when you got into a fight with Russ and were suspended for 2 days? Well, in these meetings you'll be taught new ways of thinking and behaving to help you stay out of that kind of trouble." Note how a statement such as this can serve in both group preparation and motivation.

General *procedures* for the ART program are next explained. In the case of the 10-week curriculum, the trainer might say that the group will meet three times a week and that meetings will help trainees learn skill alternatives to aggression, ways to control their anger, and methods for thinking in more effective ways.

An explanation of any *incentives* that are available and the specific rules that govern how they can be earned or lost is given in the meetings with individual youths and spelled out in greater detail at the first group meeting.

Like many other educational and training approaches, ART's ultimate effectiveness depends not only on its teaching procedures and the content of its curriculum, but also on the core qualities of the group. Is it a safe place, free of put-downs, intimidation, and subtle bullying? Are the trainers, in addition to being competent teachers or workers, also competent protectors? Have members formulated a useful set of *group rules*, and are members functioning in accordance with them? It is desirable for each group's rules to be established at least in part by its own members. Ownership enhances compliance. In doing so, the trainer can suggest that rules pertaining to attendance, participation, confidentiality, management of disagreements, and other topics unique to the particular setting be considered. Detailed procedures for preparing and motivating youths for effective participation in the three ART components are presented in chapters 3, 4, and 5.

Trainer Selection and Preparation

Since the inception of ART, hundreds of people with a wide variety of backgrounds and credentials have been effective trainers. Teachers, counselors, school psychologists, youth care workers, social workers, and correctional officers are primary examples of people who become trainers. Three related qualities seem to characterize effective trainers. First, they are at ease with adolescents, individually and in groups. The concerns youngsters share (even their musings) are taken seriously; the youths are listened to respectfully and never belittled. Whether dealing with youngsters individually or as a group, skilled trainers show sensitivity toward the fact that adolescence is a stormy time of life, characterized by unpredictable expressions of both adult and childlike behaviors.

At times this mix of youth behaviors causes problems manifested in ART groups in a variety of aggressive, resistive, or otherwise difficult behaviors. When these behaviors do occur, the skilled trainer is able to respond effectively. Chapter 6 details techniques for moderating, reducing, and even eliminating such problem behaviors. Effective trainers are competent in the use of these techniques, can apply the appropriate consequence for the behavior without demeaning the youth, and are able to maintain the skills-training agenda of the group.

The third quality of effective trainers is that they deliver the training agenda well. They are competent teachers, whether or not their formal credentials are in education. Their teaching is alive, energetic, and responsive to diverse trainee learning abilities and styles. They are able to work with individual trainees during group sessions without losing the group focus. There is little off-task time, transitions are made smoothly from one activity to another, and, in a variety of ways, a "can do" attitude is communicated.

The preparation of trainers follows what may appropriately be called an apprenticeship training sequence. Having been selected for program participation, the next step for the trainer-to-be is to become familiar with the content of and proficient in the procedures that constitute the ART method. Reading this book is a good first step, as it comprehensively describes the background, methods, and materials needed to initiate and sustain high levels of trainee skill. We provide regular trainer preparation workshops at various sites, which beginning trainers may attend to augment the written materials. Many other competent and experienced trainers regularly employ ART program methods in schools and other locations in the United States and beyond, and it is often helpful to visit such sites and observe the program in action.

The next step in trainer preparation is to participate in mock Skillstreaming, Anger Control Training, and Moral Reasoning Training groups, led by experienced trainers, in which the trainers-to-be pretend to be adolescent trainees. After this role-playing, the trainers-to-be observe experienced trainers actually leading ART groups. Then they co-lead groups with experienced trainers. Finally, they lead the groups themselves (or better, as part of a pair of apprentice trainers) while an experienced trainer observes. This incremental training sequence has proven to be a satisfactory means of preparing trainers.

How can we motivate potential trainers to participate in this training sequence? After all, most teachers, delinquency workers, and other professionals who work with unskilled and often aggressive adolescents are frequently overworked, underpaid, and urged to adopt and implement many other interventions. Rarely is a school, facility, agency, or other institution willing or able to pay its staff for participation in activities such as ART. Other forms of external reward or recognition, such as titles, awards, or even compensatory time off, or relief from other duties, are similarly uncommon. Ultimately, volunteering to learn and use this approach is motivated by potential trainers' desire to enhance their own levels of competence and to be more helpful to the adolescents for whom they are responsible. These internal goals and satisfactions are, therefore, the trainers' motivations to participate in ART group leadership.

In addition to prepared and motivated trainers, trainees, and support staff, many effective ART programs include a master trainer in their staff. It is common in schools and other settings to begin programs with appropriate organization, good intentions, and adequate enthusiasm, but to wind up in shambles a few months later because no one is specifically responsible for coordinating and overseeing operations. The barrage of other responsibilities placed on teachers and other staff makes the collapse of programs, if not inevitable, certainly more likely in the absence of a guiding overseer. The master trainer should be knowledgeable in both ART procedures and program management in order to carry out such responsibilities as training and supervising trainers, observing sessions, monitoring progress, and sustaining motivation.

Cultural Compatibility

Whether culture is defined by geography, ethnicity, nationality, social class, gender, sexual orientation, age, or some combination thereof, for ART to be meaningful it must be viewed in a multicultural context and practiced in a manner responsive to such a context. When trainers and trainees are from different cultural groups, definitions and prescriptions may conflict. Training goals may not be met. Cartledge and Johnson (1997) state it well when they assert the following:

> Cultural differences may cause children from diverse back-grounds to respond to environmental events in different or non-productive ways and cause their actions to be misperceived by peers and adults who do not share the same cultural orientation. School personnel are challenged to interpret accurately the behaviors of culturally different learners, to distinguish social skill differences from deficits, and to employ instructional strategies effective in helping those learners maximize their schooling experiences. (p. 391)

ART is most effective when it is delivered in a manner appreciative of and responsive to such culturally relevant notions as skill strengths and differences versus skill deficits, differential or tailored training strategies and instructional tactics, trainee channels of accessibility and communication styles, stereotyping of culturally different trainee populations, and culturally associated qualities of trainees. Trainer knowledge, skill, and sensitivity are required to minimize the influence of cultural differences.

CHAPTER THREE

Skillstreaming: The Behavioral Component of ART

Skillstreaming is a technique for teaching an extended curriculum of interpersonal, aggression management, and related skills to youngsters who are weak or lacking in these competencies. In Aggression Replacement Training, our emphasis is on the use of Skillstreaming with youngsters who are frequently aggressive, but in schools and elsewhere the program has been used successfully with other types of adolescents. These include teenagers who are shy or withdrawn, immature, developmentally delayed, or otherwise nonaggressively deficient in their interpersonal skills.

HISTORY AND DEVELOPMENT

Until the early 1970s, in schools and delinquency and mental health settings, there existed three major psychological approaches designed to alter the behavior of chronically aggressive, unhappy, ineffective, or disturbed youth—psychodynamic, nondirective, and behavioral. Although each differed from the others in several major respects, one thing they held in common was the assumption that the youngster had somewhere within, though unexpressed, effective prosocial or healthy behaviors. The expression of these behaviors was one of the goals of the therapy or counseling. The client could realize such a desirable outcome if the therapist or counselor was able to reduce or remove the obstacles to such a realization. The psychodynamic therapist called forth and interpreted unconscious material that blocked progress-relevant awareness. The nondirective therapist believed that the potential for change resided within the youngster and provided a warm, empathic, accepting environment in which to access these behaviors. The behavioral therapist, by means of one or more contingency management procedures, employed contingent reinforcement for desirable behaviors to increase the probability that these behaviors would reoccur.

All three approaches assumed that somewhere within the individual's repertoire resided the goal behaviors.

In the early 1970s, an important new intervention approach began to emerge—psychological skills training, an approach based on different assumptions. Viewing the individual in therapy more in educational, pedagogic terms than as a client in need of therapy, the psychological skills trainer assumed that the individual was deficient, or at best weak, in the interpersonal, emotional, and cognitive skills necessary for an effective and satisfying life. The task of the skills trainer became, therefore, not to interpret, reflect, or reinforce, but to actively teach the desirable behaviors. Rather than an intervention called *psychotherapy*, between patient and psychotherapist or client and counselor, what emerged was *training*, between trainee and psychological skills trainer.

The roots of the psychological skills training movement lie within both education and psychology. Teaching desirable behaviors has been and is a significant goal of the educational system. The Character Education movement of the 1920s and more contemporary Moral Education, Responsibility Education, and Values Clarification programs are but a few of the interventions with this goal. Add to the educational interest in skills training the hundreds of interpersonal and planning skills courses offered in more than 2,000 community colleges in the United States and the hundreds of self-help books oriented toward similar skill-enhancement goals, and it becomes clear that the formal and informal educational establishment in this country has provided an environment in which the psychological skills training movement could grow.

The same can be said for psychology, as it, too, laid the groundwork for the skills training movement with its prevailing philosophy and interests. The learning process has been the central theoretical and investigative concern of psychology since the late 19th century. This focal point assumed major therapeutic form in the 1950s, as psycho-therapy practitioners and researchers alike came to view psychothera-peutic treatment more and more in terms of learning. The expanding field of behavior modification grew from this joint learning-clinical focus and can be viewed as the immediate precursor to psychological skills training.

Perhaps psychology's most direct contribution to psychological skills training comes from social learning theory—in particular, from the research done by Albert Bandura. His work is based on the same principles of modeling, behavioral rehearsal, and social reinforcement underlying the development of the Skillstreaming approach. Bandura (1973) has commented as follows:

> The method that has yielded the most impressive results with diverse problems contains three major components. First, alternative modes of response are repeatedly modeled, preferably by several people who demonstrate how the new style of behavior can be used in dealing with a variety of . . . situations. Second, learners are provided with necessary guidance and ample opportunities to practice the modeled behavior under favorable conditions until they perform it skillfully and spontaneously. The latter procedures are ideally suited for developing new social skills, but they are unlikely to be adopted unless they produce rewarding consequences. Arrangement of success experiences, particularly for initial efforts at behaving differently, constitutes the third component in this powerful composite method. . . . Given adequate demonstration, guided practice, and success experiences, this method is almost certain to produce favorable results. (p. 253)

We became involved in the early 1970s in the psychological skills training movement with an approach we first referred to as Structured Learning and later renamed Skillstreaming. It was the era of deinstitutionalization, during which tens of thousands of long-term mental hospital patients, who lacked the interpersonal skills necessary for effective daily living, were discharged to their communities. In many areas across the United States, small groups of these skill-deficient adults became our initial Skillstreaming trainees.

In the years following its first use as an intervention strategy targeted toward socially skill-deficient adults, applications of Skillstreaming to other types of populations have grown. These populations include young children (elementary age, preschool), elderly adults, child-abusing parents, industrial managers, police officers, and many others. Applications of Skillstreaming to skill-deficient adolescents appeared early in this time of expansion and dissemination. Over the more than 20 years during which these interventions were initiated and applied in a large number of schools, agencies, and institutions, a considerable amount of evaluation research was conducted and reported, both by us and by numerous other investigators (see Goldstein & McGinnis, 1997, for an annotated review). These studies represent a healthy underpinning in the development of Skillstreaming; their results have been used not only as overall tests of the method's efficacy, but also as guidelines for altering and improving its component procedures and materials.

Of the many changes in Skillstreaming's character and use over the years, clearly the most important has been the decision to combine it with Anger Control Training and Moral Reasoning Training to create the more comprehensive and effective intervention of ART. The rest of this chapter describes the procedures necessary to conduct effective Skillstreaming sessions within the context of the ART program.

THE SKILLSTREAMING CURRICULUM

The Skillstreaming curriculum consists of 50 skills, grouped into six skill categories (see Table 3.1). Each skill is broken down into its behavioral steps, which are modeled by the trainers and role-played by each trainee during the Skillstreaming session. In a real sense, the behavioral steps of any given skill *are* that skill (see Figure 3.1 for a sample skill). The 50 skills and their behavioral steps are provided as Appendix A.

Skill Selection

In a 10-week ART curriculum, skills are predetermined (see Table 2.1). However, if a longer ART program is planned, specific Skillstreaming skills may be selected on the basis of trainees' strengths and weaknesses. Even within the 10-week curriculum, flexibility exists to substitute some skills for others, as well as to present the 10 predetermined skills in a different order. The process of selecting skills for ART can include many assessment techniques—interviews, sociometric procedures, skill games, trial groups, direct observation, and skill checklists. We have found it useful to rely primarily on direct observation and skill checklists.

Direct observation is especially valuable if the people planning to be the group's trainers are the same people (teachers, delinquency workers, etc.) who are with the youngsters all day and who routinely see them in interactions with others. In such circumstances, observations of behavior are frequent, take place in the natural environment, and, since skill deficiencies are often situation specific, reflect each youth's skill competency across various peers, adults, challenges, times, and physical conditions. In other words, when the teacher or youth care worker is also the observer, more opportunities exist to observe in various situations.

Table 3.1

SKILLSTREAMING SKILLS FOR ADOLESCENTS

Group I: Beginning Social Skills
1. Listening
2. Starting a Conversation
3. Having a Conversation
4. Asking a Question
5. Saying Thank You
6. Introducing Yourself
7. Introducing Other People
8. Giving a Compliment

Group II: Advanced Social Skills
9. Asking for Help
10. Joining In
11. Giving Instructions
12. Following Instructions
13. Apologizing
14. Convincing Others

Group III: Skills for Dealing with Feelings
15. Knowing Your Feelings
16. Expressing Your Feelings
17. **Understanding the Feelings of Others**
18. **Dealing with Someone Else's Anger**
19. **Expressing Affection**
20. Dealing with Fear
21. Rewarding Yourself

Group IV: Skill Alternatives to Aggression
22. Asking Permission
23. Sharing Something
24. **Helping Others**
25. Negotiating
26. Using Self-Control
27. Standing Up for Your Rights
28. Responding to Teasing
29. Avoiding Trouble with Others
30. **Keeping Out of Fights**

Group V: Skills for Dealing with Stress
31. **Making a Complaint**
32. Answering a Complaint
33. Being a Good Sport
34. Dealing with Embarrassment
35. Dealing with Being Left Out
36. Standing Up for a Friend
37. Responding to Persuasion
38. **Responding to Failure**
39. Dealing with Contradictory Messages
40. **Dealing with an Accusation**
41. **Getting Ready for a Difficult Conversation**
42. **Dealing with Group Pressure**

Group VI: Planning Skills
43. Deciding on Something to Do
44. Deciding What Caused a Problem
45. Setting a Goal
46. Deciding on Your Abilities
47. Gathering Information
48. Arranging Problems by Importance
49. Making a Decision
50. Concentrating on a Task

Note. Skills in bold type are the ones taught in the 10-week ART curriculum.

Figure 3.1

A SAMPLE SKILLSTREAMING SKILL

Making a Complaint
1. Decide what your complaint is.
2. Decide whom to complain to.
3. Tell that person your complaint.
4. Tell that person what you would like done about the problem.
5. Ask how he/she feels about what you've said.

Adequate assessment is, in addition, both multimodal and multi-source. Multimodal means that more than one type of assessment approach (such as observation) is employed in order to minimize assessment biases associated with the type of measurement being administered. Our choice for this purpose is the Skillstreaming Checklist, offered in versions for teachers/staff, parents, and students (see Appendix B). This checklist is a straightforward screening and selection device, on which all 50 Skillstreaming skills are listed and defined. It employs a frequency-of-use response format, with the person completing it circling *almost never, seldom, sometimes, often,* or *almost always.*

Multisource assessment means that more than one person completes a checklist for each youth to minimize assessment biases associated with the *source* of the measures being administered. In most school-based Skillstreaming programs, teachers, parents, and youth all complete the checklist. In some instances, siblings, peers, or other significant adults may be involved. In delinquency facilities, checklists are typically completed by the youth's counselor, youth care worker, and perhaps teachers. In using multisource assessment, it is common for people such as teachers, youth care workers, and parents to report considerably more (in number and frequency) skill deficiencies for the youth than does the youth. The teacher or worker, or mom or dad, may circle *almost never* or *seldom* for twenty-five skills, whereas the youth does so for only six or seven. Whether such a discrepancy reflects overconfidence, denial, blaming others, or some other distorted process in perception of self, it nonetheless is very important to assess the skill deficiency perspective that each youth personally holds. Teaching trainees the skills in which *they* feel they are deficient has proven to be a successful motivational tactic, discussed at greater length in the following section.

Skill Negotiation

Experience suggests that one of the most potent means for motivating trainees to participate is skill negotiation. Many youths for whom Skillstreaming is appropriate consistently place responsibility for their antisocial acts on others. Rarely is something *their* fault. As noted, teachers, workers, or parents may indicate on the Skillstreaming Checklist that a youngster seldom or almost never uses several of the prosocial skills listed, yet the youth may check only a few of the skills as deficient. Knowing those few self-admitted deficiencies is invaluable information to the trainer. Teaching these particular skills (in addition to those selected by the trainer) has proven to be a positive trainee motivator. In what might be viewed as a consumer model, we give the customer what he or she wants. Thus, we begin the Skillstreaming meeting with "How is it going?" or "What's been happening since our last meeting?" instead of enacting a modeling display for a skill chosen by the trainers. Out of a brief discussion prompted by these openings often comes information about difficulties at home, in school, on the street, in the facility, or elsewhere, difficulties that can be resolved by the skill the trainers and trainees then jointly select and portray. The earlier in the life of the group that negotiation of the curriculum begins, the better. In fact, in the ART group's very first Skillstreaming session, when open discussion may be uncomfortable, the trainer can initiate negotiation by listing on a chalkboard the skills most frequently checked on the Skillstreaming Checklist for all members, without revealing who checked which ones. It can be especially motivating and empowering when trainers follow presentation of this listing by communicating to the group that the first skill to be taught is the one selected most frequently by the members themselves.

IMPLEMENTATION CONCERNS

The mechanics of the Skillstreaming component of ART are important to successful program operation. Specific considerations include trainee selection, trainer collaboration, frequency of sessions, program length, and room arrangement and materials.

Trainee Selection

As discussed in chapter 2, trainees may be assigned to ART groups on the basis of assessed or apparent need for improvement in interpersonal skills, anger control, and/or concern for the rights and needs of others. If more than one ART group will be running concurrently, trainees may be selected on the basis of two other criteria: The first is *shared skill deficiency*. We urge trainers to group together those trainees who share highly similar skill deficiencies and patterns. The Skillstreaming Grouping Chart included in Appendix B can be used to summarize the checklist skill scores of an entire class of students or group of youths living in a residential facility unit and thus identify such shared skill deficiencies. The second grouping criterion is responsive to the generalization-enhancing principle of *identical elements*. This principle states that the greater the similarity between qualities of the training session and the real world, the greater the likelihood that training-to-application transfer will take place. One means of maximizing identical elements is to group similar people together (i.e., adolescents from the same class, living unit, neighborhood, etc). As we like to put it, "If they live together, hang around together, or even fight together, put them in the same group together."

Trainer Collaboration

Though sometimes Skillstreaming groups have been effectively and productively led by one trainer, we strongly recommend that for ART, wherever possible two trainers work together. Skill-deficient adolescents are often quite proficient in generating the behavior management problems that make successful training difficult. To arrange and conduct role-playing between two youths and at the same time oversee six or more other easily distracted youths is a daunting challenge for all but the most experienced trainer. A much better arrangement is to use two trainers, one in front of the group leading the role-playing and the second sitting in the group, preferably next to the individuals most likely to behave disruptively. If two trainers are not available, the use of aides, parents, volunteers, or other adults can be effective.

Frequency of Sessions

In a 10-session ART curriculum, the group convenes for Skillstreaming once a week. In freestanding Skillstreaming programs—that is, Skillstreaming without Anger Control Training or Moral Reasoning Training—we have found a schedule of two sessions per week to be optimal. In brief, trainees must have the time and opportunity use the skills in their everyday lives. These practice attempts (or homework) are more likely to occur if sufficient time is provided between sessions.

Length of Program

Freestanding Skillstreaming programs have lasted as briefly as 2 days, as long as 3 years, and just about every length in between. The 2-day programs are in in-school detention centers, in which detained students are taught a single skill during their brief stay. Three-year and other lengthy programs—in maximum security delinquency centers, for example—are open Skillstreaming groups, adding new members as older members "graduate" or drop out. A more typical program length for Skillstreaming alone is a school year.

In ART, the 10-session curriculum provides an arbitrary beginning and end to the Skillstreaming effort. If a more open-ended ART arrangement is possible, another way of defining length of program is by the number of skills taught. The goal of the Skillstreaming component is to teach skills so they are not only learned (acquired) but also used (performed) in an effective manner in a variety of situations for the rest of the trainee's life. Skillstreaming is not a curriculum to rush through. While the full curriculum contains 50 skills, there is no expectation that every one of them will be taught to any given ART group. Since, ideally, the goal is to teach the skills in which the youths in the group are deficient, a full curriculum for some groups may be only a few skills; for other groups, it may be several skills.

Whether few or many skills are to be taught, trainers should not move on to a second skill until the first is learned (as evidenced by successful role-playing within the group) and regularly performed (as evidenced by successful homework outside the group). This training goal usually requires that the same skill be taught (modeled, role-played, etc.) for more than one Skillstreaming session. In fact, even at the price of trainee boredom with repetition, skills should be taught until they are automatic or "overlearned," a process that we and others have demonstrated to increase generalization substantially.

Room Arrangement and Materials

Figure 3.2 depicts a common horseshoe-shaped furniture arrangement often used in conducting the Skillstreaming component of ART. In this group arrangement all observing trainees and the main actor can watch the trainer point to the given skill's behavioral steps, written on a chalkboard or easel pad, while the role-play is taking place.

Materials for Skillstreaming are inexpensive and readily available: a chalkboard or easel pad and a set of skill cards for each participant

Figure 3.2

ROOM ARRANGEMENT FOR SKILLSTREAMING

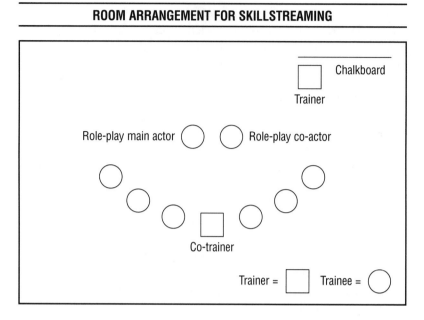

(cards on which individual skill names and their steps are listed). Pre-printed skill cards are available as part of the *Skillstreaming the Adolescent* curriculum (Goldstein & McGinnis, 1997). However, hand-printed versions on index cards will work quite well. Skill step posters to hang around the classroom, school, or institution are also helpful, both for reminding trainees of skill content and for sensitizing school and institutional staff not directly involved in the ART effort to opportunities to observe, reward, and, when needed, coach. These posters can be made by trainers, trainees, or both.

SKILLSTREAMING TRAINING PROCEDURES

In order to carry out the four core training procedures that constitute Skillstreaming—modeling, role-playing, performance feedback, and generalization training—trainers lead the group through the nine steps listed in Table 3.2.

Step 1: Define the Skill

This session-opening activity is a brief, trainer-led group discussion of the skill to be taught during that meeting. Whether the skill is selected

Table 3.2

SKILLSTREAMING TRAINING STEPS

Step 1: Define the skill.
Step 2: Model the skill.
Step 3: Establish trainee skill need.
Step 4: Select a role-player.
Step 5: Set up the role-play.
Step 6: Conduct the role-play.
Step 7: Provide performance feedback.
Step 8: Assign skill homework.
Step 9: Select the next role-player.

by the trainers, or by negotiation between trainers and trainees, this beginning activity is necessary. Its purpose is to orient group members by conveying both the abstract meaning and concrete examples of the chosen skill. The training goal here is to make certain that group members understand the skill to be taught. In actual practice, this goal can be met quickly—in perhaps a few minutes—avoiding a long lecture or a protracted group discussion over inconsequential details.

Trainer: OK, let's get started. Today's skill is an important one which many people have trouble doing well, or even at all. It's called Expressing Affection. Can anyone tell me what expressing affection means? Latoya, what do you think?

Latoya: Like, when you love somebody.

Trainer: Good, a good part of it. Anyone else? Chico, you had your hand up.

Chico: Kissing, hugging.

Trainer: OK again. Those are two ways of expressing affection. Good examples. What is the general idea of expressing affection, its definition? Emily?

Emily: Letting someone know how you feel about them, when you feel really good about them.

Trainer: I agree. You've given good definitions, all of you. That's the skill we're going to learn today. Ann [second trainer], would you mind handing out the skill cards while I write the skill steps on the board?

Step 2: Model the Skill

Definition

Modeling is defined as learning by imitation. Imitation has been examined in much research and under many names: copying, empathic learning, observational learning, identification, vicarious learning, matched-dependent behavior, and, most frequently, modeling. This research has consistently shown that modeling is an effective and reliable technique for both the rapid learning of new behaviors and the strengthening or weakening of previously learned behaviors. Three types of learning by modeling have been identified.

Observational learning refers to the learning of new behaviors, or behaviors the person has never performed before. Adolescents are great imitators. Almost weekly, new idioms, new clothing styles, new ways of walking, dancing, and doing emerge, and, with fad-like swiftness, take hold. Many of these events are clear examples of observational learning effects.

Inhibitory and *disinhibitory effects* involve the strengthening or weakening of behaviors previously performed only rarely by the person due to a history of punishment or other negative consequences. Modeling offered by peers is, again, a major source of inhibitory and disinhibitory effects. Youngsters who know how to be altruistic, sharing, caring, and the like may inhibit such behaviors in the presence of models who are behaving more egocentrically and who are being rewarded for their egocentric behavior. Aggressive models may also have a disinhibitory effect and cause the observing youngster to engage in aggressive behavior. Skillstreaming skills such as Standing Up for Your Rights and Dealing with Group Pressure help youngsters avoid such disinhibitory effects.

Behavioral facilitation refers to the performance of previously learned behaviors that are neither new nor a source of potential negative reactions from others. One person buys something he seems to enjoy, so a friend buys one, too. A child deals with a recurring household matter in an effective manner, so a sibling imitates her behavior. A classmate tries talking over a class problem with his teacher; when he succeeds, a second student decides to approach the teacher in a similar way. These are all examples of behavioral facilitation effects.

Research has demonstrated that a wide variety of behaviors can be learned, strengthened, weakened, or facilitated through modeling. These include acting aggressively, helping others, behaving independently, planning careers, becoming emotionally aroused, interacting socially, displaying dependency, exhibiting certain speech patterns, behaving empathically, self-disclosing, and many more. It is clear from such research that modeling can be an important tool in teaching new behaviors and strengthening or weakening existing ones.

Modeling Enhancers

Most people observe dozens and perhaps hundreds of behaviors every day that they do not imitate. Many people are exposed (by television, radio, magazines, and newspapers) to very polished, professional modeling displays of someone's buying one product or another, but they do not later buy the product. And many people observe expensively produced and expertly acted instructional films but remain uninstructed. Apparently, people learn by modeling under some circumstances but not others. Laboratory research on modeling has successfully identified *modeling enhancers*, or circumstances that increase modeling. These modeling enhancers are characteristics of the model, the modeling display, or the trainee (the observer) that have been shown to significantly affect the degree to which learning by imitation occurs.

Model characteristics

More effective modeling will occur when the model (the person to be imitated) (a) seems to be highly skilled or expert; (b) is of high status; (c) controls rewards desired by the trainee; (d) is of the same sex, approximate age, and social status as the trainee; (e) is friendly and helpful; and, of particular importance, (f) is rewarded for the given behaviors. That is, we are all more likely to imitate expert or powerful yet pleasant people who receive rewards for what they are doing, especially when the particular rewards involved are something that we too desire.

Modeling display characteristics

More effective modeling will occur when the modeling display shows the behaviors to be imitated (a) in a clear and detailed manner; (b) in the order from least to most difficult behaviors; (c) with enough repetition to make overlearning likely; (d) with as little irrelevant (not to be learned) detail as possible; and (e) when several different models, rather than a single model, are used.

Trainee characteristics

More effective modeling will occur when the person observing the model is (a) told to imitate the model; (b) similar to the model in background or in attitude toward the skill; (c) friendly toward or likes the model; and, most important, (d) rewarded for performing the modeled behaviors.

Stages of Modeling

The effects of these modeling enhancers, as well as of modeling itself, can be better understood by examining the three stages of learning by modeling.

Attention

Trainees cannot learn from watching a model unless they pay attention to the modeling display and, in particular, to the specific behaviors being modeled. Such attention is maximized by pointing to each step on the chalkboard or easel pad as it is being modeled, eliminating irrelevant detail in the modeling display, minimizing the complexity of the modeled material, making the display vivid, and implementing the modeling enhancers previously described.

In order to help trainees attend to the skill enactments, skill cards, which present the name of the skill being taught and its behavioral steps, are distributed prior to the modeling displays. Trainees are told to watch and listen closely as the models portray the skill. Particular care should be given to helping trainees identify the behavioral steps as they are presented in the context of the modeling vignettes. Trainers should also remind group members that in order to depict some of the behavioral steps in certain skills, the actors will "think out loud" statements that ordinarily would be thought to oneself, and that this process is used to facilitate learning.

Retention

In order to reproduce later the behaviors he or she has observed, the trainee must remember or retain them. Since the behaviors of the modeling display itself are no longer present, retention must occur by memory. Memory is aided if the behaviors displayed are classified or coded by the observer. Such coding is facilitated by covert rehearsal (i.e., reviewing in one's mind the performance of the displayed behaviors). Research has shown, however, that an even more important aid to retention is overt, or behavioral, rehearsal. Such practice of the specific behavioral steps is crucial for learning and, indeed, is the second major procedure of Skillstreaming. This is role-playing, to be examined in depth shortly. It should be noted at this point, however, that the likelihood of retention via either covert or overt rehearsal is greatly aided by rewards being provided to both the model and/or the trainee.

Reproduction

Researchers interested in human learning have typically distinguished between learning (acquiring or gaining knowledge about how to do something) and performance (doing it). If a person has paid attention and remembered the behaviors shown in the modeling display, it may be said that the person has learned. The main interest, however, is not so much in whether the person *can* reproduce the behaviors that have been seen, but whether he or she *does* reproduce them. As with retention, the likelihood that a person will actually perform the behavior that has been learned will depend mostly on the expectation of a reward for doing so. Expectation of reward has been shown to be determined by the amount, consistency, recency, and frequency of the reward that the trainee has observed being provided to the model for performing the desired behavior. The crucial nature of reward for performance will be further examined in later discussion of trainee motivation (see chapter 6).

Step 3: Establish Trainee Skill Need

Before the group members commence their role-playing of the skill they have seen demonstrated by the trainers, it is necessary to openly identify each trainee's *current* need for the skill. After all, it is behavioral rehearsal that is the purpose of the role-play—that is, enactment of the skill as it serves to deal with a contemporary or anticipated situation or relationship in the trainee's present life, not a fictitious situation provided by the trainers or a reenactment of a past problem or circumstance no longer relevant to the trainee.

Skill need may have been established earlier. Nonetheless, its open discussion *in the group* is required as part of the sequence of steps necessary to establish relevant and realistic role-plays. Each trainee, therefore, is asked in turn briefly to describe where, when, and especially with whom he or she would find it useful to employ the skill the trainers have modeled. In order to make effective use of such information, it is often valuable to list group members' names on the chalkboard or easel pad at the front of the room and to record next to each member's name the name of the target person with whom the skill will be used and the theme of the role-play associated with that person. Since an ironclad rule of Skillstreaming is that every trainee must perform a role-play for every skill, with no exceptions, having such information at hand will be of considerable use should a given trainee express reluctance to participate.

Step 4: Select a Role-Player

Since all members of the Skillstreaming group will be expected to role-play each skill, in most instances it is not of great concern who does so first. Typically, especially after the teaching of one or two skills has made clear that all must role-play, the selection process determining the sequence of trainee role-playing can proceed by the use of volunteers. If for any reason there are group members for whom the act of role-playing a particular skill on a particular day seems threatening, it may be helpful not to ask them to role-play first or second. Their seeing other trainees do so first can be reassuring and help ease them into the activity. For some, reluctance may turn into outright resistance and refusal. Means for dealing with such problematic behaviors are described at length in chapter 6. For the present, it is useful to indicate that although we maintain our "no exceptions" rule, we try to involve trainees in role-playing by means of support, encouragement, reassurance, and highlighting the usefulness of the skill for their own personal needs, rather than by making use of penalties, heavy-handed persuasion, or overly authoritarian means.

Step 5: Set Up the Role-Play

Once a trainee has described a real-life situation in which skill use might be helpful, that trainee is designated the main actor. He or she chooses a second trainee (the co-actor) to play the role of the other person (e.g., mother, peer, etc.) relevant to the skill problem. The trainee should be urged to pick a co-actor who resembles the real-life person in as many ways as possible. The trainer then elicits from the main actor any additional information needed to set the stage for role-playing. In order to make role-playing as realistic as possible, the trainer obtains a description of the physical setting, events immediately preceding the role-play, the mood or manner the co-actor should portray, and any other details of apparent value.

Step 6: Conduct the Role-Play

Before the role-playing begins, the trainer should remind all of the participants of their roles and responsibilities: The main actor is told to follow the behavioral steps; the co-actor, to stay in the role of the other person; and the other trainees, to watch carefully for the enactment of the behavioral steps. It is often useful to assign one specific behavioral step to each observing trainee and to have that trainee track it during the role-play and report on its content and quality during the subsequent feedback session. For the first several role-plays, observers can be coached as to what kinds of cues to observe (e.g., posture, tone of voice, content of speech, etc.). Then the actors are instructed to begin. At this point it is the responsibility of the trainer to provide the main actor with whatever help or coaching is required to keep the role-playing going according to the behavioral steps. Trainees who "break role" and begin to explain their behavior or make other comments should be urged to get back into the role and explain later. If the role-play is clearly going astray from the behavioral steps, the scene can be stopped, instruction provided, and the role-play restarted. One trainer should be positioned near the chalkboard and point in turn to each of the behavioral steps as the role-play unfolds, thus helping the main actor (as well as the other trainees) to follow the steps in order.

The role-playing should be continued until all trainees have had an opportunity to participate in the role of main actor at least once and, depending on the quality of the role-plays and related skill homework, perhaps two or more times. Sometimes this will require two or three sessions for a given skill. We suggest that each session begin with two modeling vignettes for the chosen skill, even if the skill is not new to the group. It is important to note that while the framework (behavioral steps) of each role-play in the series remains the same, the actual content can and should change from role-play to role-play. It is the problem as it actually occurs, or could occur, in each youngster's own environment that should be the content of the role-play. When the role-play is completed, each trainee will thus be better armed to act appropriately in a real-life situation requiring skill use.

There are a few further procedural matters relevant to role-playing that will serve to increase its effectiveness. Role reversal is often a useful role-play procedure. A trainee role-playing a skill may occasionally have a difficult time perceiving the co-actor's viewpoint and vice versa. Having the two exchange roles and resume the role-play can be most helpful in this regard.

On occasion the trainer can also assume the co-actor role in an effort to give youngsters the opportunity to handle types of reactions not otherwise role-played during the session. For example, it may be crucial to have a difficult adult role realistically portrayed. The trainer as co-actor may also be particularly helpful when dealing with less verbal or more hesitant trainees.

Step 7: Provide Performance Feedback

A brief feedback period follows each role-play. This helps the main actor find out how well he or she followed or departed from the behavioral steps, examines the psychological impact of the enactment on the co-actor, and provides the main actor with encouragement to try out the role-played behaviors in real life. To implement this process, the trainer asks the main actor to wait until he or she has heard everyone else's comments before responding to them.

The co-actor is asked about his or her reactions first. Next the other observing trainees comment on how well the behavioral steps were followed and on other relevant aspects of the role-play. Then the trainers comment on how well the behavioral steps were followed and provide social reinforcement (praise, approval, encouragement) for close following. To use reinforcement most effectively, trainers should follow these guidelines:

1. Provide reinforcement only after role-plays that follow the behavioral steps.

2. Provide reinforcement at the earliest appropriate opportunity after role-plays that follow the behavioral steps.

3. Always provide reinforcement to the co-actor for being helpful, cooperative, and so on.

4. Vary the specific content of the reinforcements offered (e.g., praise particular aspects of the performance, such as tone of voice, posture, phrasing, etc.).

5. Provide enough role-playing activity for each group member to have sufficient opportunity to be reinforced.

6. Provide reinforcement in an amount consistent with the quality of the given role-play.

7. Provide no reinforcement when the role-play departs significantly from the behavioral steps (except for "trying" in the first session or two).

8. Provide reinforcement for an individual trainee's improvement over previous performances.

After hearing all the feedback, the main actor is invited to make comments regarding the role-play and the comments of others. In this way the main actor can learn to evaluate the effectiveness of his or her skill enactment in light of feedback from others.

In all aspects of feedback, it is crucial that the trainer maintain a behavioral focus. Trainer comments must point to the presence or absence of specific, concrete behaviors and not take the form of broad generalities. Feedback, of course, may be positive or negative in content. Negative comments should always be followed by constructive comments as to how a particular fault might be improved. At minimum, a "poor" performance (a major departure from the behavioral steps) can be praised as "a good try" at the same time it is being criticized for its real faults. If at all possible, youngsters failing to follow the behavioral steps in their role-play should be given another opportunity to role-play these same behavioral steps after receiving corrective feedback. At times, as a further feedback procedure, we have audiotaped or video-taped entire role-plays. Giving trainees the opportunity to observe themselves on tape can help them reflect on their own verbal and non-verbal behavior.

Since a primary goal of Skillstreaming is skill flexibility, role-play enactment that departs somewhat from the behavioral steps may not be "wrong." That is, a different approach to the skill may in fact work in some situations. Trainers should stress that they are trying to teach effective alternatives and that the trainees would do well to have the behavioral steps being taught in their repertoires of skill behaviors, available for use when appropriate.

Step 8: Assign Skill Homework

Following successful role-plays, trainees are instructed to try in their own real-life settings the behaviors they practiced during the session. For incarcerated trainees, the homework setting is inside the institution but outside the ART group. For trainees in school, homework may be done elsewhere in the school, out of the school with peers, at home, or elsewhere. The name of the person(s) with whom the trainee will try the skill, the day, the place, and so on are all discussed and entered on the Homework Report 1 form (see Figure 3.3). Latter sections of the report request information about what happened when the trainee attempted

Figure 3.3

HOMEWORK REPORT 1

Name: _____ Date: _____

FILL IN DURING THIS CLASS

1. What skill will you use?

2. What are the steps for the skill?

3. Where will you try the skill?

4. With whom will you try the skill?

5. When will you try the skill?

FILL IN AFTER DOING YOUR HOMEWORK

1. What happened when you did the homework?

2. What skill steps did you really follow?

3. How good a job did you do in using the skill? *(circle one)*

      excellent   good   fair   poor

4. What do you think should be your next homework assignment?

the homework assignment, how well he or she followed the behavioral steps, and the trainee's view of performance quality and thoughts about the content of the next assignment.

It is often useful to start with relatively simple homework behaviors and, as mastery is achieved, work up to more complex and demanding assignments. This provides the trainer with an opportunity to reinforce each approximation of the more complex target behaviors. Successful experiences at beginning homework attempts are crucial in encouraging the trainee to make further attempts in real-life situations.

The first part of each Skillstreaming session is devoted to presenting and discussing the homework reports. When trainees have made an effort to complete their homework assignments, trainers should provide social reinforcement. Failure to do homework should be met with the trainers' expressions of disappointment. If the ART group's functioning is tied to the school or institution's incentive or level system, successful homework should be generously rewarded. It is important to stress that without these or similar attempts to maximize transfer, the value of the entire training session is in jeopardy.

When most of the group's trainees are demonstrating proficiency in the skill being taught—gauged by their successful role-plays in the group and skill use outside the group—it is time for the group as a whole to move on to another skill. But what of the trainees not yet up to speed, not yet competent in the skill most others have mastered? Such trainees move on with the rest of the group to the new skill but continue their homework efforts on the old skill. Homework Report 2 (Figure 3.4) is used for this purpose. Trainees submit these reports to the trainers, who react verbally or jot a feedback note on the form, in either case using little or no group time in the process. By the time a group is a few months old, all its members will be doing homework on whatever new skill is being addressed, but most will also be working to master one or another old skill.

Step 9: Select the Next Role-Player

The next trainee is selected to serve as main actor, and the training sequence previously described is repeated until all members of the group are consistently demonstrating in-group and out-of-group skill proficiency.

Figure 3.4

HOMEWORK REPORT 2

Name: _____ Date: _____

FILL IN BEFORE DOING YOUR HOMEWORK

1. What skill will you use?

2. What are the steps for the skill?

3. Where will you try the skill?

4. With whom will you try the skill?

5. When will you try the skill?

6. If you do an excellent job, how will you reward yourself?

7. If you do a good job, how will you reward yourself?

8. If you do a fair job, how will you reward yourself?

FILL IN AFTER DOING YOUR HOMEWORK

1. What happened when you did the homework?

2. What steps did you really follow?

3. How good a job did you do in using the skill? *(circle one)*

        excellent   good   fair   poor

4. What do you think should be your next homework assignment?

CHAPTER FOUR

Anger Control Training: The Emotional Component of ART

We all feel anger at times; anger is a natural human emotion. For most of us the outlet for our anger is something other than aggression. Sometimes we pout; sometimes we withdraw, perhaps muttering to ourselves; sometimes we allow the anger to spur us to constructive problem solving. Perhaps only 10% of the time for the majority of people, anger leads to aggression in the form of verbal or physical attempts to hurt the person with whom we are angry. But for chronically aggressive youths, the opposite is true. Seldom do they merely pout, withdraw, or constructively problem solve. Instead they often lash out with intent to harm—sometimes with words, commonly with fists, and increasingly with weapons.

The Anger Control Training component of Aggression Replacement Training is designed to serve two related purposes: (a) to help make the arousal of anger in chronically aggressive youths a less frequent occurrence and (b) to provide such youths with the means to learn self-control when their anger is aroused. In essence, just as Skill-streaming is designed to teach youths what they *should do* in problematic situations, Anger Control Training teaches them what they *should not do*.

ORIGINS OF ANGER CONTROL TRAINING

We begin this chapter in what at first may seem to be a setting distant from the study of anger management—the experimental laboratory of the Russian psychologist Luria. In an extended series of investigations, Luria (1961) explored the manner in which children learn to regulate their external behavior by means of internal speech. Little and Kendall (1979) succinctly describe this unfolding pattern:

The process of development of verbal control of behavior . . . seems to follow a standard developmental sequence. First, the initiation of motor behavior comes under control of adult verbal cues, and then the inhibition of responses is controlled by the speech of adults. Self-control emerges as the child learns to respond to his own verbal cues, first to initiate responses and then to inhibit them. . . . The 3- or 4-year-old child normally can follow rather complicated instructions given by an adult, and it is at this age that the child is said to begin to regulate his own behavior on the basis of verbal self-instructions. . . . Between the ages of 4½ and 5½, the child's self-verbalizations shift from overt to covert (primarily internal) speech. (p. 101)

In addition to Luria's seminal research, a number of other investigators have examined and confirmed this verbal meditation, self-control process. But as with all normative developmental processes, in some children the expected sequence fails to occur, occurs only in part, or occurs in distorted form. Yes, "there is considerable evidence to support the belief that self-control develops largely as a function of a child's development of [internal] language mechanisms" (Little & Kendall, 1979, p. 104). But what of the youngster in whom this sequence fails to fully or correctly unfold? As we shall see, it is precisely such youngsters who—deficient in the ability to regulate overt behavior by internal speech—display the behaviors associated with terms such as *hyperactivity, impulsivity, poor self-control, acting out,* and the like. However, as we shall also see, impulsive behavior in these youngsters may be reduced by externally imposed interventions that closely replicate the normal developmental sequence described by Luria. This is precisely what Anger Control Training does.

Donald Meichenbaum and his research group have been active in this area of study. Their initial investigations sought to establish further the relationship between impulsivity and poor verbal control of overt behavior. Meichenbaum and Goodman (1969), using Kagan's (1966) Matching Familiar Figures Test, now a standard measure for determining impulsivity/reflectivity, found that those youngsters who respond on the test quickly and make many errors (the impulsive youngsters) indeed exercise diminished verbal control over their overt behavior as compared to youngsters who take their time and make fewer errors (the reflective youngsters). But just what do reflective and impulsive youngsters say to themselves, and how does their self-directed speech differ? To answer such questions, Meichenbaum and Goodman (1971) observed and recorded the play behavior and private speech of sixteen 4-year-olds who were matched for age, intelligence, and socioeconomic status. Half of the children were reflective and half of the children were impulsive, as indicated by the Kagan measure. Results indicated that the private speech of the cognitively impulsive preschoolers was largely comprised of the most immature, self-stimulatory content. Reflective preschoolers, in comparison, manifested significantly more outer-directed and self-regulatory speech and significantly more inaudible mutterings. The investigators concluded from their observational studies that cognitively reflective preschoolers use their private speech in a more mature, instrumental, and self-guiding fashion than impulsive preschoolers do.

The nature of the normative developmental sequence described by Luria and found wanting in impulsive youngsters by Meichenbaum and others led Meichenbaum (1977) to duplicate the sequence as a remedial intervention for youngsters deficient in such self-regulatory skills. He comments:

> Could we systematically train hyperactive, impulsive youngsters to alter their problem-solving styles, to think before they act, in short, to talk to themselves differently? Could we, in light of the specific mediational deficits observed, teach the children how to (a) comprehend the task, (b) spontaneously produce mediators and strategies, and (c) use such mediators to guide, monitor, and control their performances? This was the challenge that sparked the development of self-instructional training. (p. 31)

Self-Instructional Training for the Impulsive Youngster

In research on self-instructional training, the typical sequence of instructional procedures is as follows:

1. The trainer models task performance and self-instructs aloud while the child observes.

2. The child performs the task, self-instructing aloud as he or she does so.

3. The trainer models task performance and whispers self-instructions while the child observes.

4. The child performs the task, self-instructing in a whisper while doing so.

5. The trainer performs the task using covert self-instructions, with pauses and behavioral signs of thinking such as raising the eyes toward the ceiling or stroking the chin.

6. The child performs the task using covert self-instructions.

Meichenbaum and Goodman's (1971) initial use of these procedures yielded decreased impulsivity and enhanced reflectiveness (i.e., increased response time and decreased error rate) in samples of hyperactive youngsters in comparison to appropriate controls. The children could indeed learn, as the investigators put it, "to stop, look, and listen." This early research also showed that observing a model using covert self-instructions was insufficient to obtain the desired outcome; the youngster had to covertly self-instruct also.

Other investigators reported essentially confirming results vis à vis impulsiveness and hyperactivity, and extended self-instructional training to other, often related, types of problem behaviors. These included problematic classroom behaviors, tolerance for resisting temptation, and, as we shall now examine, anger and aggression.

Self-Instructional Training for the Aggressive Youngster

In 1975, Novaco sought to apply the self-instructional training approach to the management of anger. By way of definition, he comments:

> The arousal of anger is here viewed as an affective stress reaction. That is, anger arousal is a response to perceived environmental demands—most commonly, aversive psychosocial events. . . . Anger is thought to consist of a combination of physiological arousal and cognitive labeling of that arousal as anger. . . . Anger arousal results from particular appraisals of aversive events. External circumstances provoke anger only as mediated by their meaning to the individual. (pp. 252–253)

As Novaco also states: "A basic premise is that anger is fomented, maintained, and influenced by the self-statements that are made in provocation situations" (p. 17). And, indeed, in his own research involving people with chronic anger problems, use of self-instructional training was shown to substantially decrease anger arousal levels in comparison to control groups not provided this intervention.

Meichenbaum viewed the remediation of impulsivity in the light of Luria's insights about the normal development of self-regulation, and Novaco needed Meichenbaum's impulsivity research results in order to extend self-instructional training to chronically angry individuals. Similarly, the work of Eva Feindler built upon the substantial foundation provided by Novaco. Feindler and her research group have contributed greatly to the development of Anger Control Training, both with important research findings and with substantial refinements in technique (Feindler, 1979; Feindler & Fremouw, 1983; Feindler, Latini, Nape, Romano, & Doyle, 1980; Feindler, Marriott, & Iwata, 1984). This series of investigations provided elaboration of Novaco's intervention sequence into a chain in which clients learn (a) *triggers*—the external events and internal appraisals that serve as provocations to anger arousal; (b) *cues*—the physiological and kinesthetic sensations that signal to the individual the level of anger arousal; (c) *reminders*—the self-instructional statements that may function to reduce anger arousal; (d) *reducers*—techniques that in combination with reminders may reduce anger arousal (e.g., deep breathing, backward counting, peaceful imagery, and consideration of long-term consequences); and (e) *self-evaluation*—the opportunity to self-reinforce and/or self-correct depending on how well or poorly the previous steps have been implemented.

In our work on Anger Control Training and our use of it as one of the three components of ART, we stand on the foundation built by Luria, Meichenbaum, Novaco, Feindler, and others. We hope our own efforts to refine the technology of anger control have proven worthy additions to the ongoing progress of research and development.

In brief, Anger Control Training is a multistep sequence in which trainees are first helped to understand how they typically perceive and interpret (or, better, misperceive and misinterpret) the behavior of others in ways that arouse anger. Therefore, attention in the first lesson is given to identifying the outside occurrences (external triggers) and inner interpretations (internal triggers) that initiate the anger experience. Though anger is indeed elicited by one's cognitions and self-statements, its main emotional feature is a high level of arousal. Before trainees can be taught more productive, less provocative, and less arousing ways of interpreting the world and in fact reducing their distortions, their arousal levels must be reduced. Attention to cues and reducers accomplishes this task.

Impulsive youths frequently confuse the bodily signs or cues that reflect specific emotions—fear, anxiety, anger. Accurate interpretation of such signs in the anger control process can signal to the youths that it is time to make use of one or more techniques to reduce their own levels of anger arousal. Once successful in this regard, with the potential interference of their emotional states substantially reduced, the youths can proceed to employ more accurate, more benign, and less anger-arousing cognitions and interpretations of the world around them. This stage of the process, learning to use reminders, is critical to the anger control outcome. Chronically aggressive youths are exceedingly well-practiced in conjuring up anger-arousing perceptions and interpretations (i.e., internal triggers) and often have made meager use of anger-avoiding self-instructions (i.e., reminders). If they do well at this difficult and, for them, often novel task, it is important that they feel the effort is worthwhile. The self-evaluation lesson in the Anger Control Training sequence teaches the youths how to praise or reward successful accomplishment.

IMPLEMENTATION CONCERNS

The following discussion gives specific details on how Anger Control Training sessions would be employed with a group of chronically aggressive youths. These sessions are part of the 10-week ART curriculum described in chapter 2 (see Table 2.1). It is important to repeat that, although the sessions described here follow the 10-week curriculum, any instructional plans for teaching Anger Control Training will need to be developed prescriptively, with the needs of the trainees and constraints of the setting in mind.

Anger Control Training teaches trainees what not to do (be aggressive) and how not to do it (the anger control techniques). While these are important accomplishments, trainees also need to know how to meet the demands of life situations without resorting to aggression—in other words, how to use the appropriate Skillstreaming skill in a provocative situation. As a result, we have added the opportunity to practice a relevant Skillstreaming skill to the procedures of the last three Anger Control Training sessions.

Anger Control Training is an active process for the trainer. The trainer is required to model (demonstrate) the proper use of the anger reduction techniques that are the core of the program, guide trainees' practice of the program's anger management steps (i.e., lead role-playing), provide feedback about how successful this practice was in matching the trainer's modeling, and supervise trainees' practice outside the ART group (i.e., homework).

Modeling

For an in-depth discussion of modeling principles, the reader may wish to review the section from chapter 3 on modeling Skillstreaming skills. For our purpose here, it is helpful to summarize aspects of the modeling process as they apply to Anger Control Training.

All modeling begins with the trainer's stating the particular anger control technique or chain of techniques that will be demonstrated and then describing a conflict situation in which the technique(s) may be used. If two trainers are available, they should both participate in modeling, with one trainer as the main actor, demonstrating the technique(s), and the other as the co-actor, representing the person provoking the main actor. If two trainers are not available, a group member may serve as the co-actor. In such cases it is important to rehearse briefly with the co-actor in order to provide a realistic portrayal of provocation in a conflict situation.

Once the conflict situation has been briefly described, the two leaders then act out the scene, with the main actor carefully and clearly using the anger control technique(s). Following the completion of the scene, the trainer summarizes the technique(s) used and briefly discusses them with the trainees.

The following general guidelines are helpful in modeling:

1. Use at least two examples for each demonstration.

2. Select scenes that are relevant to the trainees.

3. Arrange for all scenes to result in positive outcomes, never in aggressive acts.

4. Portray the main actor as a person reasonably similar in age, socioeconomic background, verbal ability, and other characteristics salient to the members of the Anger Control Training group.

Role-Playing

Following each modeling presentation, trainees are asked to take part in role-plays in which they practice the just-modeled anger control technique or chain of techniques in situations they have recently encountered or expect to encounter in the near future. Once a trainee has described a conflict situation, he or she becomes the main actor in the role-play and chooses a second trainee (the co-actor) to play the part of the other person in the conflict. The trainer then asks for enough information (time, place, etc.) from the main actor to set the stage for the role-play. The scene is then played out with the main actor's applying the anger control technique(s) as accurately as possible.

Following are some general role-playing guidelines:

1. Just before beginning the role-play, remind the trainees of their parts: The main actor must use the anger control technique(s), and the co-actor should stay in the described role in the scene.

2. Instruct the observing group members to pay attention to whether the main actor is using the anger control technique(s) properly.

3. As the role-play unfolds, if either actor "breaks role," stop the scene and encourage that trainee to get back into role.

4. If the role-play is clearly departing from the anger control technique(s) to be practiced, stop the role-play, give whatever instructions are needed, and then restart the role-play.

5. Role-playing should continue until all trainees have had the opportunity to be the main actor and practice using the technique(s) in a situation they have really encountered or are about to encounter.

Performance Feedback

After each role-play, there is a brief feedback period, during which others point out to the main actor how well he or she used the anger control technique(s). Feedback also provides the main actor with a chance to see how the use of the technique(s) affected the co-actor and provides encouragement to try the technique(s) outside the training sessions. The feedback is sequenced in the following manner: (a) The co-actor is asked to give his or her reactions; (b) the observers are asked to comment on how well the technique(s) were used; (c) the trainers comment on how well the technique(s) were used and provide reinforcement (praise, approval, encouragement); and (d) the main actor makes comments on both the role-play and the feedback he or she received.

There are several guidelines for providing reinforcement:

1. Provide reinforcement only after role-plays in which the technique(s) were used properly.

2. Provide reinforcement to the co-actor for his or her help and cooperation.

3. Provide a degree of reinforcement that matches the quality of the role-play.

4. Provide no reinforcement when the role-play departs significantly from the specific technique.

5. Provide reinforcement for a trainee's improvement over previous role-plays.

Homework

The program requires active participation by trainees, both during the training sessions and afterward, in the form of assigned homework between sessions. Homework assignments are recorded on a "Hassle Log," next described. Once trainees have begun using the Hassle Log, it becomes an ideal source for problem situations to role-play.

The Hassle Log shown in Figure 4.1, developed initially for youthful offenders in residential settings, is the version most commonly used in ART practice. The reader is encouraged to adapt it for his or her particular school, agency, or other facility context. For youths who read poorly or not at all, a pictorial form of the Hassle Log, developed for clinical use by James Gilliam and shown in Figure 4.2, is available.

ANGER CONTROL TRAINING PROCEDURES

Table 4.1 summarizes the content of the 10-session Anger Control Training sequence.* The remainder of this section gives a detailed description of the contents of each of these sessions.

---

*The procedures described in this section follow, in general outline, *The Art of Self-Control* by E.L. Feindler, 1981, unpublished manuscript, Adelphi University, Garden City, NY.

Figure 4.1

HASSLE LOG

Name: _____ Date: _____

☐ Morning   ☐ Afternoon   ☐ Evening

Where were you?

☐ Classroom   ☐ Bathroom   ☐ Off grounds
☐ Dorm   ☐ Team office   ☐ Hall
☐ Gym   ☐ Dining room   ☐ On a job
☐ Recreation room ☐ Outside/grounds ☐ Other

What happened?

☐ Somebody teased me.
☐ Somebody took something of mine.
☐ Somebody was doing something I didn't like.
☐ I did something wrong.
☐ Somebody started fighting with me.
☐ Other

Who was the other person?

☐ Another youth   ☐ Aide   ☐ Teacher   ☐ Counselor   ☐ Other

What did you do?

☐ Hit back   ☐ Told peer or adult
☐ Ran away   ☐ Ignored it
☐ Yelled   ☐ Used anger control technique
☐ Cried   _____
☐ Walked away calmly   _____
☐ Broke something   ☐ Talked it out
☐ Was restrained   ☐ Used Skillstreaming skill *(identify)*
☐ Told aide or counselor _____

How angry were you?

☐ Burning   ☐ Really   ☐ Moderately   ☐ Mildly angry   ☐ Not angry
              angry   angry   but still OK   at all

How did you handle yourself?

1	2	3	4	5
Poorly	Not so well	OK	Good	Great

Figure 4.2

NONREADER'S HASSLE LOG

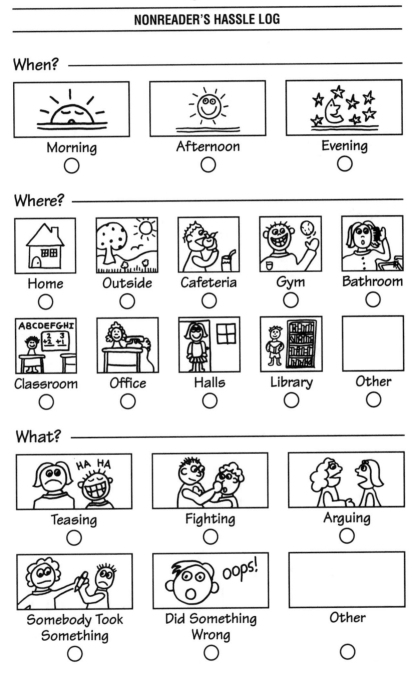

When?

Morning   Afternoon   Evening

Where?

Home   Outside   Cafeteria   Gym   Bathroom

Classroom   Office   Halls   Library   Other

What?

Teasing   Fighting   Arguing

Somebody Took Something   Did Something Wrong   Other

Figure 4.2 (continued)

NONREADER'S HASSLE LOG

Who?

Friend ○ Parent ○ Teacher ○ Brother or Sister ○ Other ○

Action?

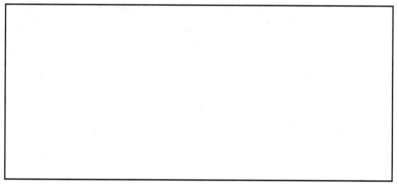

How did you feel afterwards?

Happy ○ OK ○ Sad ○ Mad ○ Scared ○

How did you handle yourself?

| E | S⁺ | S | S⁻ | I | U |

○   ○   ○   ○   ○   ○

Table 4.1

OVERVIEW OF A 10-WEEK ANGER CONTROL TRAINING SEQUENCE

Week 1: Introduction
1. Explain the goals of Anger Control Training and "sell it" to the youngsters.
2. Explain the rules for participating and the training procedures.
3. Give initial assessments of the A-B-Cs of aggressive behavior:
   A = What led up to it?
   B = What did you do?
   C = What were the consequences?
4. Review goals, procedures, and A-B-Cs.

Week 2: Triggers
1. Review the first session.
2. Introduce the Hassle Log.
3. Discuss what makes you angry (triggers).
4. Role-play triggers.
5. Review the Hassle Log and triggers.

Week 3: Cues and Anger Reducers 1, 2, and 3
1. Review the second session.
2. Discuss how to know when you are angry (cues).
3. Discuss what to do when you know you are angry.
   Anger reducer 1: Deep breathing
   Anger reducer 2: Backward counting
   Anger reducer 3: Pleasant imagery
4. Role-play triggers + cues + anger reducers.
5. Review the Hassle Log; triggers; cues; and anger reducers 1, 2, and 3.

Week 4: Reminders
1. Review the third session.
2. Introduce reminders.
3. Model using reminders.
4. Role-play triggers + cues + anger reducer(s) + reminders.
5. Review reminders.

Week 5: Self-Evaluation
1. Review the fourth session.
2. Introduce self-evaluation.
   Self-rewarding
   Self-coaching
3. Role-play triggers + cues + anger reducer(s) + reminders + self-evaluation.
4. Review self-evaluation.

Table 4.1 (continued)

OVERVIEW OF A 10-WEEK ANGER CONTROL TRAINING SEQUENCE

Week 6: Thinking Ahead (Anger Reducer 4)
1. Review the fifth session.
2. Introduce thinking ahead.
   Short- and long-term consequences
   Internal and external consequences
3. Role-play "if-then" thinking ahead.
4. Role-play triggers + cues + anger reducer(s) + reminders + self-evaluation.
5. Review thinking ahead.

Week 7: Angry Behavior Cycle
1. Review the sixth session.
2. Introduce the Angry Behavior Cycle.
   Identify your own anger-provoking behavior.
   Change your own anger-provoking behavior.
3. Role-play triggers + cues + anger reducer(s) + reminders + self-evaluation.
4. Review the Angry Behavior Cycle.

Week 8: Rehearsal of Full Sequence
1. Review the seventh session.
2. Introduce the use of Skillstreaming skills in place of aggression.
3. Role-play triggers + cues + anger reducer(s) + reminders + Skillstreaming skill + self-evaluation.

Week 9: Rehearsal of Full Sequence
1. Review the Hassle Logs.
2. Role-play triggers + cues + anger reducer(s) + reminders + Skillstreaming skill + self-evaluation.

Week 10: Overall Review
1. Review the Hassle Logs.
2. Recap anger control techniques.
3. Role-play triggers + cues + anger reducer(s) + reminders + Skillstreaming skill + self-evaluation.
4. Give reinforcement for participation and encourage trainees to continue.

Week 1: Introduction

Explain Goals of Anger Control Training

In the first session the trainer introduces the program, "sells it" to the trainees, and gets their commitment to participate. The basic introduction involves talking with the trainees about how being angry and aggressive can lead to trouble for them with authorities (police, school), with peers, and even with regard to how they feel about themselves.

To communicate to trainees that learning to achieve greater control of anger is a worthwhile task, the trainer can give examples of people the trainees admire who have excellent self-control—for example, Jackie Chan and Evander Holyfield. Giving real-life examples and stressing that these people would not be successful if they were out of control helps make the point that having more self-control does not mean the trainees will be pushed around or be "wimps."

After providing these examples, the trainer explains how greater self-control means greater personal power: Trainees are more powerful when they are in control of their reactions to others despite the attempts of others to provoke them. By being aggressive, trainees allow others to control them.

Explain Rules and Procedures

It is essential to describe how the group works and what is expected of each trainee at the outset of the program. The trainer begins by explaining that meetings last about an hour and are held once a week for 10 weeks on a specific day and time (or any other program structure, if the 10-week curriculum does not apply). At these meetings, each trainee is expected to participate actively, cooperatively, and with respect for the other trainees. Homework will be given and used as the material for the next session; therefore, completion of homework is required for success in the program. The homework requires each trainee to complete one or more Hassle Logs each week, to record details about conflict situations in which they are involved.

The trainer next explains that a sequence of different techniques for anger reduction are taught by (a) explanations and demonstrations by the trainer and (b) practice in the form of role-playing by trainees. Trainees will role-play the anger control techniques for the situations on their Hassle Logs so that the next time the situation or a similar one occurs, they will have the choice to do something other than get angry.

Explain the A-B-Cs of Anger

The trainer explains to the group how each conflict situation has three steps:

A = What triggered the problem? What led up to it?

B = What did you do (the actual response to *A*)?

C = What were the consequences (to you and to the other person)?

The trainer then gives examples of how he or she has handled some personal conflicts, being sure to point out the *A, B,* and *C* steps. Finally, trainees give examples, while the trainer helps them identify the *A, B,* and *C* steps operating in these situations.

Review

A brief review of the reasons for developing greater self-control, the rules and procedures of the group, and the A-B-Cs ends the meeting.

Week 2: Triggers

Review the First Session

Trainees are reminded that they increase their personal power by having control over their reactions to others. Again, providing examples of popular sports figures or others who demonstrate exceptional self-control is helpful. The trainer reviews the rules and procedures, emphasizing that anger control involves learning techniques by watching them being demonstrated and then practicing them. Then the trainer goes over the A-B-C model, reminding the group of the three steps in each conflict. The trainer gives an example and asks a few trainees for examples that occurred in their lives during the past week.

Introduce the Hassle Log

The trainer next shows the group an example of the Hassle Log (see Figure 4.1) and asks a different trainee to read each item. Then he or she explains the importance of the log: (a) It provides an accurate picture of conflicts that occur during the week; (b) It helps trainees learn about what makes them angry and how they handle these situations (so they can work to change behaviors that cause them trouble and leave them feeling bad about themselves); and (c) It provides material for role-playing in future sessions (using situations that really happen is much more effective than using made-up situations). The Hassle Log is filled out for situations that trainees handle well as well as for those in which they become angry or aggressive.

At this point, the trainer shows how to fill out the Hassle Log using a sample conflict. The trainer makes sure each trainee understands how to complete the Hassle Log by having each of them fill out a log for a recent hassle. Then the trainer checks the logs and corrects any misunderstanding of instructions. Trainees are given a folder or binder containing several Hassle Logs and are instructed to fill out a log as soon as possible after an incident.

Discuss Triggers

The trainer reviews the idea that each conflict situation has an *A* (trigger), a *B* (behavior), and a *C* (consequence). In this session, the focus is on the *A* step, or trigger. The goal is to help trainees identify things that arouse their anger. Both external and internal triggers are described.

External triggers are things done by one person that make another person angry. They may be verbal (e.g., telling a trainee what to do or calling him or her a name) or nonverbal (e.g., pushing the trainee or making an obscene gesture). The trainer helps trainees identify the external triggers (verbal or nonverbal) that led them to become angry or aggressive during the last few weeks. Almost always, it takes more than just an external trigger to lead to anger arousal and aggressive behavior: Internal triggers, or what youngsters think or say to themselves when faced with an external trigger, are crucial to whether or not they become angry. Youngsters often say things to themselves such as "That S.O.B. is making fun of me"; "He's making me look like a wimp"; or "I'm going to tear that guy's head off." These distorted self-statements are the internal triggers that combine with external triggers to lead to high levels of anger arousal and aggressive behavior. Helping trainees identify their internal triggers sets the stage for later sessions, in which they learn how to replace internal triggers that make them angry with positive self-statements or reminders that reduce their anger in conflict situations.

Role-Play

The trainers model, help the trainees role-play, and give feedback on the trainees' use of triggers (external and internal). For these role-plays, situations from the Hassle Logs are used. In this session's role-playing, the emphasis is on identifying internal triggers. Some useful situations for this role-play include being deliberately tripped or fouled during an athletic competition, getting into trouble for something one didn't do, and feeling lied to by a peer or adult.

Review

The trainer reviews the use of the Hassle Log and reminds trainees of the importance of completing it, then goes over the topics taught so far—namely, external and internal triggers.

Week 3: Cues and Anger Reducers 1, 2, and 3

Review the Second Session

The trainer reviews the triggers taught in Session 2 by going over the completed Hassle Logs. The trainer checks to be sure the Hassle Logs are filled out properly; reinforcement is provided for those trainees who have successfully identified their internal triggers.

Discuss Cues

All people have physical signs that let them know they are angry—for example, muscle tension, a knot in the stomach, clenched fists, grinding teeth, or a pounding heart. The trainer gives some personal examples of these signs and explains that individuals must know they are angry before they can use self-control to reduce the anger. Next trainees try to identify their own and others' warning signs by role-playing short conflict situations. The trainer gives feedback on how well each trainee has identified the warning signs or cues. In some Anger Control Training groups, trainees have found it helpful to communicate their cues to the group in pictures they draw of themselves, rather than in verbal reports (M. Ptacek, personal communication, October 10, 1997). Figure 4.3 is a sample drawing generated in this way.

Discuss Anger Reducers 1, 2, and 3

Now that the trainees are beginning to identify their anger warning signs (cues), they can start to make use of anger reduction techniques to lower their arousal levels and increase their self-control and personal power when they notice themselves getting angry. Any or all of the three anger reducers can be a first step in a chain of new behaviors giving the trainees greater self-control and more time to decide how

Figure 4.3

SAMPLE DRAWING OF PARTICIPANT'S ANGER CUES

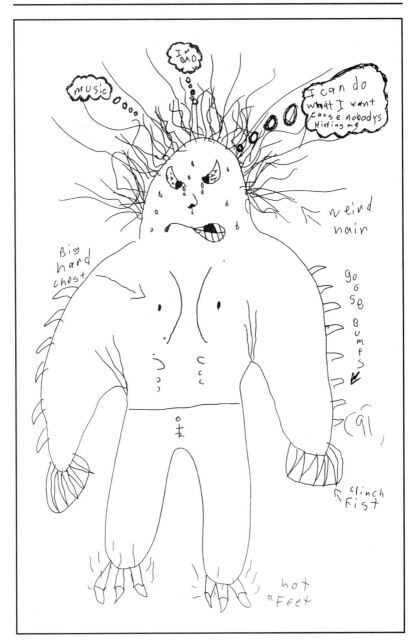

to respond effectively. The key sequence here is identification of physical cues of anger followed by the use of one or more anger reducers. As the trainer presents each of the three anger reducers, he or she models its use, has the trainees role-play the sequence "triggers + cues + anger reducer," then gives feedback on the role-plays.

Anger reducer 1: Deep breathing

Taking a few slow, deep breaths to which trainees pay full attention can help them make a more controlled response in a pressure situation. Examples from sports of taking a few deep, focusing breaths (e.g., in basketball, before taking an important foul shot, and in boxing) can be presented. Trainees are reminded about their signs of being angry and told how deep breathing can reduce tension by relieving physical symptoms of tension. Then the trainer models, has trainees role-play, and gives feedback on the sequence of "triggers + cues + deep breathing."

Anger reducer 2: Backward counting

A second method of reducing tension and increasing personal power in a pressure situation is to count backward silently (at an even pace)—for example, from 20 to 1. Trainees are instructed to turn away from the provoking person or situation, if appropriate, while counting. Counting backward is a way of simultaneously lowering arousal level and gaining time to think about how to respond most effectively. The trainer models, helps trainees role-play, and gives feedback on the sequence of "triggers + cues + backward counting."

Anger reducer 3: Pleasant imagery

A third way to reduce tension in an anger-arousing situation is to imagine being in a peaceful scene (e.g., "You are lying on the beach. The sun is warm, and there is a slight breeze"). Trainees are encouraged to think of scenes they find peaceful and relaxing. Then the trainer models, helps the trainees role-play, and gives feedback on the sequence of "triggers + cues + pleasant imagery."

Review

Each member's identification of triggers and physical signs of anger (cues) are reviewed, along with the three anger reducers. Homework involves having trainees attempt to use each of the three anger reducers in the coming week in situations where they notice they are getting angry. On their Hassle Logs for each situation, trainees note which anger reducer(s) they use.

Week 4: Reminders

Review the Third Session

The trainer reviews the cues and anger reducers taught during the previous session by going over the Hassle Logs assigned as homework. Reinforcement is provided for reports of successful use, or attempted use, of one or more of the three anger reducers.

Introduce Reminders

Reminders are self-instructional statements used to help increase success in pressure situations of all types. Some examples of reminders that can be used during pressure situations in sports are (a) "Bend your knees and follow through" when making a foul shot in basketball and (b) "Watch out for his left" or "Jab and then hook" in boxing. Trainees suggest several reminders of this type that they use or could use. The trainer describes and gives several examples of how reminders can also be very helpful in situations in which trainees must try very hard to keep calm (e.g., confrontations with police, court appearances). Finally, trainees generate a list of reminders they have used or could have used in recent pressure or conflict situations (drawn from the Hassle Logs). Some reminders are in a sense generic (i.e., they fit almost any anger experience). Examples include such self-instructional statements as "Take it easy," "Relax," "Calm down," "Chill out," and "Cool off." Some reminders are benign reinterpretations of the anger-arousing internal trigger (e.g., "He didn't bump me on purpose. The hall is really crowded between classes").

Novaco (1975) has provided a useful pool of reminders, to be employed before, during, or after the anger-arousing experience (see Table 4.2). A second valuable set of reminders has been provided by Deffenbacher (1996), subgrouped into cool thoughts (e.g., "Just stay cool," "This battle isn't worth it"); problem-solving thoughts (e.g., "OK, develop a plan," "What's the first thing I want to do?"); control and escape thoughts (e.g., "I can always just walk away," "It's OK to take time out"); and self-rewarding thoughts ("Good, I'm hanging in there," "I feel great—I'm dealing with it and not yelling"). In addition to these choices, and more effective than any selected from a list, are those reminders created by trainees themselves.

Table 4.2

SELF-INSTRUCTIONAL REMINDERS FOR
USE BEFORE, DURING, AND AFTER PROVOCATION

Preparing for Provocation

- This is going to upset me, but I know how to deal with it.
- What is it that I have to do?
- I can work out a plan to handle this.
- I can manage the situation. I know how to control my anger.
- If I find myself getting upset, I'll know what to do.
- There won't be any need for an argument.
- Don't take this too seriously.
- This could be a testy situation, but I believe in myself.
- Time for a few deep breaths of relaxation. Feel comfortable, relaxed, and at ease.
- Easy does it. Remember to keep your sense of humor.

Impact and Confrontation

- Stay calm. Just continue to relax.
- As long as I keep my cool, I'm in control.
- Just roll with the punches; don't get bent out of shape.
- Think of what you want to get out of this.
- You don't need to prove yourself.
- There is no point in getting mad.
- Don't make more out of this than you have to.
- I'm not going to let him get to me.
- Look for the positives. Don't assume the worst or jump to conclusions.
- It's really a shame she has to act like this.
- For someone to be that irritable, he must be awfully unhappy.
- If I start to get mad, I'll just be banging my head against the wall. So I might as well just relax.
- There is no need to doubt myself. What he says doesn't matter.
- I'm on top of this situation and it's under control.

Coping with Arousal

- My muscles are starting to feel tight. Time to relax and slow things down.
- Getting upset won't help.
- It's just not worth it to get so angry.
- I'll let him make a fool of himself.
- I have a right to be annoyed, but let's keep the lid on.
- Time to take a deep breath.
- Let's take the issue point by point.
- My anger is a signal of what I need to do. Time to instruct myself.
- I'm not going to get pushed around, but I'm not going haywire either.

- Try to reason it out. Treat each other with respect.
- Let's try a cooperative approach. Maybe we are both right.
- Negatives lead to more negatives. Work constructively.
- He'd probably like me to get really angry. Well, I'm going to disappoint him.
- I can't expect people to act the way I want them to.
- Take it easy, don't get pushy.

Reflecting on the Provocation
When conflict is unresolved:
- Forget about the aggravation. Thinking about it only makes you upset.
- These are difficult situations, and they take time to straighten out.
- Try to shake it off. Don't let it interfere with your job.
- I'll get better at this as I get more practice.
- Remember relaxation. It's a lot better than anger.
- Can you laugh about it? It's probably not so serious.
- Don't take it personally.
- Take a deep breath.

When conflict is resolved or coping is successful:
- I handled that one pretty well. It worked!
- That wasn't as hard as I thought.
- It could have been a lot worse.
- I could have gotten more upset than it was worth.
- I actually got through that without getting angry.
- My pride can sure get me into trouble, but when I don't take things too seriously, I'm better off.
- I guess I've been getting upset for too long when it wasn't even necessary.
- I'm getting better at this all the time.

Model the Use of Reminders

The trainer models the use of appropriate reminders to increase self-control and personal power in conflict situations, as opposed to using internal triggers (e.g., "Cool it" versus "I'll kill him"). At first it is useful for the trainer to say the reminders aloud, but over time and practice, the goal is for trainees to be able to "say" them silently—that is, to think them. This goal can be accomplished by gradually decreasing the frequency of saying a reminder and increasing the frequency of saying it in a whisper, then saying it silently.

Role-Play

The trainer models the chain "triggers + cues + anger reducer(s) + reminders." Then trainees role-play conflict situations from their Hassle

Logs in which the main actors (a) identify the external and internal triggers, (b) identify the cues of anger, (c) use anger reducers 1, 2, and 3 (any or all), and (d) use reminders. If the main actor has trouble using the reminders, it may be helpful for the trainer to quietly give examples at the proper time. Focus in the role-play is on moving from "out loud" reminders, through whispered reminders, to silent ones. The trainer gives feedback on the role-plays, particularly on the use of the anger reducers and reminders.

Review

The trainer summarizes the use of reminders, their timing, and the rationale for their use. Then each trainee is given three index cards and asked to select and write down three reminders that might be useful in the coming week. As homework, trainees are instructed to use each of these reminders during hassles that arise during the week and to note in the Hassle Log for that situation the reminder they used.

Week 5: Self-Evaluation

Review the Fourth Session

The trainer reviews reminders by having each trainee relate a hassle from the past week in which a reminder was used and recorded as homework. The group is reminded of the A-B-C model, and each trainee is asked about the consequences to self and to others of having used the reminder. Again, "out loud," whispered, and silent reminders are distinguished. The outcome of using the reminder is evaluated: Did the reminder work? If not, what went wrong?

Introduce Self-Evaluation

Self-evaluation is a way for trainees to (a) judge for themselves how well they have handled a conflict, (b) reward themselves for handling it well (self-rewarding), or (c) help themselves find out how they could have handled it better (self-coaching). Basically, self-evaluation is conducted by using a set of reminders relevant to feelings and thoughts *after* a conflict situation. The trainer presents some statements that trainees can use to reward themselves (e.g., "I really kept cool" or "I was really in control") and to coach themselves when they fail to remain in control in a conflict situation (e.g., "I need to pay more attention to my cues"). Then each trainee generates a list of self-rewarding and self-coaching statements to use in the situations taken from the Hassle Logs. These statements are discussed individually and in the group.

Role-Play

The trainer models the chain "triggers + cues + anger reducer(s) + reminders + self-evaluation." In this modeling, both self-rewarding and self-coaching statements are emphasized. Next the trainer conducts role-plays from Hassle Log situations in which the main actors carry out all the following steps: (a) identify external and internal triggers, (b) identify cues of anger, (c) use any or all of the anger reducers, (d) use reminders, and (e) evaluate their performances, either rewarding or coaching themselves. The trainer provides feedback on the role-plays with an emphasis on self-evaluation.

Review

The two types of self-evaluation are reviewed. Then the trainer assigns homework requiring trainees to list on their Hassle Logs self-evaluation statements following conflicts (resolved or unresolved) that occur in the coming week.

Week 6: Thinking Ahead (Anger Reducer 4)

Review the Fifth Session

The trainer reviews self-evaluation by going over the Hassle Logs for the self-rewarding and self-coaching statements written down as homework from the last session.

Introduce Thinking Ahead

Thinking ahead is another way of controlling anger in a conflict situation by judging the likely future consequences of current behavior. The trainer refers to the A-B-C model and explains that thinking ahead helps trainees figure out what the C (consequence) will probably be before they decide what to do (i.e., the B step). The sentence "If I do this now, then this will probably happen later" guides trainees' estimation of consequences.

The trainer distinguishes between short- and long-term consequences, encouraging trainees to consider the long-term results over the short-term ones (e.g., the short-term "If I slug him now, he'll shut up" versus the long-term "If I slug him now, I'll be put on in-school suspension for a week"). Trainees are asked to list short- and long-term consequences, for both themselves and others, of specific aggressive acts they have engaged in during the last 2 months.

Finally, the trainer explains the difference between the internal and external consequences of being aggressive. For example, external consequences might include going back to court and having to serve a week of in-school suspension, whereas internal consequences might be feeling terrible about oneself or losing self-respect. The trainer also talks about social consequences, such as losing friends or being excluded from a group. Each group member lists negative external, internal, and social consequences of being aggressive and enumerates the positive consequences of using self-control.

Role-Play: "If-Then" Thinking Ahead

Using situations from the Hassle Logs, the trainer models, helps trainees role-play, and gives feedback on using the "if (I act aggressively), then (this will probably be the consequence)" thinking ahead procedure. Negative consequences are emphasized as additional reminders not to act aggressively.

Role-Play: Anger Control Chain

The trainer models the chain presented so far: "triggers + cues + anger reducer(s) + reminders + self-evaluation." Then role-plays are conducted using situations from the Hassle Logs in which the main actors follow all of the above steps and use any or all of the anger reducers, plus thinking ahead. The trainer gives feedback on the role-plays.

Review

The reasons to use thinking ahead, the different types of consequences of aggression, and the "if-then" statements are reviewed. Then the trainer assigns the homework: to use thinking ahead in two conflict situations in the coming week and to write "if-then" statements on the Hassle Log for those situations.

Week 7: Angry Behavior Cycle

Review the Sixth Session

The trainer reviews thinking ahead by going over with the group the completed Hassle Logs, in which the trainees wrote down "if-then" statements used in conflict situations in the past week.

Introduce the Angry Behavior Cycle

Until this point, the focus has been on what to do when other people make trainees angry. This session focuses on the Angry Behavior Cycle, or what trainees do to make other people angry with them.

Personal examples are given of things the trainer does that are likely to make others angry (e.g., calling someone a name, making fun of a person's appearance). Each trainee then thinks about and lists three things he or she does to make other people angry. If the group can handle some confrontation, trainees can respectfully take turns telling one another about behaviors that make them angry.

The trainer gets an agreement from each trainee to try to change these problematic behaviors in the coming week, perhaps by using the thinking ahead procedure ("If I do this, then this person may get angry and the situation may get out of hand"). Changing even one behavior may prevent some conflicts and lead to trainees' being better liked or having more friends.

Role-Play

This role-play is again designed to allow practice of all the anger control techniques taught so far. The trainer models the chain of "triggers + cues + anger reducer(s) + self-evaluation." Then the trainer conducts role-plays of this chain from trainees' Hassle Logs, with the main actors using any or all of the anger reducers in addition to all the other steps. The trainer then gives feedback on the role-plays.

Review

The trainer reviews the behaviors each trainee has identified as often making other people angry. Trainees are reminded of their agreement to try in the coming week to change at least one of the three behaviors they have identified as being part of their Angry Behavior Cycle.

Week 8: Rehearsal of Full Sequence

Review the Seventh Session

The trainer reviews the Angry Behavior Cycle—the idea that in addition to getting angry at what other people do, trainees do things that make other people angry. The trainer discusses with the trainees their attempts to change their own anger-provoking behavior, as agreed upon in the last session.

Introduce Skillstreaming Skills

At this point, the trainer explains to the group that this week and the next 2 weeks will be devoted to role-plays that use all the anger control techniques and some of the skills they have already learned in the Skillstreaming sessions.

Role-Play

The trainer conducts role-plays from situations in trainees' Hassle Logs that follow the entire sequence: "triggers + cues + anger reducer(s) + reminders + Skillstreaming skill + self-evaluation." Then feedback is given on the role-plays, focusing on how well all the steps were put together.

Week 9: Rehearsal of Full Sequence

Review the Hassle Logs

The trainer goes over the completed Hassle Logs to reinforce how well the trainees are using all of the anger control techniques and beginning to use the Skillstreaming skills.

Role-Play

Role-playing and feedback are continued using the entire series of steps: "triggers + cues + anger reducer(s) + reminders + Skillstreaming skill + self-evaluation."

Week 10: Overall Review

Review the Hassle Logs

The trainer goes over the completed Hassle Logs to continue reinforcing the trainees' new ways of handling conflict situations. It may be helpful to bring some of each trainee's Hassle Logs from very early in the program to compare against those filled out for the last week.

Recap Anger Control Techniques

All of the anger control techniques taught in the program are briefly recapped: (a) increasing personal power through self-control; (b) using the A-B-C model; (c) identifying internal and external triggers; (d) using anger reducers; (e) recognizing anger cues; (f) using reminders; (g) using self-evaluation; (h) thinking ahead; (i) recognizing the Angry Behavior Cycle; and (j) using Skillstreaming skills.

Role-Play

The trainer conducts role-plays and gives feedback using the full chain: "triggers + cues + anger reducer(s) + reminders + Skillstreaming skill + self-evaluation."

Reinforce and Encourage Continuation

If appropriate, the trainer lets the group know they have learned how to control their anger, increase their personal power, be better liked and respected, and stay out of trouble caused by aggression. Each trainee now has a choice to make—whether or not to use what has been learned.

CHAPTER FIVE

Moral Reasoning Training: The Values Component of ART

In order to be effective, treatment programs for antisocial youths must have a moral component (Gibbs, Potter, & Goldstein, 1995). Surprisingly, almost all antisocial youths affirm the importance of moral values such as keeping promises, telling the truth, helping others, saving a life, not stealing, and obeying the law (Gregg, Gibbs, & Basinger, 1994). Given a choice of possible worlds, they prefer one that is nonviolent and caring. Most also can propose responsible decisions to hypothetical social problem situations (Gibbs, Potter, & Goldstein, 1995).

Aggression Replacement Training addresses the limitations of antisocial youths—limitations that keep them from fulfilling this positive potential. For example, when asked *why* moral values such as honesty and property are important, a distressingly high percentage of antisocial youths give reasons that are developmentally delayed or immature (e.g., Gregg et al., 1994).

In this chapter, we provide the background and procedures for the Moral Reasoning Training component of ART. Specifically, we introduce the cognitive-developmental theory of sociomoral development and delay, briefly review moral reasoning programs that have attempted to remediate this delay, and provide the ART program's Moral Reasoning Training procedures and curriculum.

BACKGROUND: SOCIOMORAL DEVELOPMENT AND DELAY

According to Piaget and Kohlberg, children in the natural course of interacting with others develop more mature social perspective taking and moral reasoning. Whether a youth's moral reasoning is mature or delayed is important because "as you think, so you act." Delay in thought and behavior means two problems: prolonged immaturity in the stage of moral reasoning and persistent and pronounced cognitive distortions. Both of these aspects of delay are remediated in the moral developmental teaching component of ART.

Delay as Prolonged Immaturity in the Stage of Moral Reasoning

We conceptualize Kohlberg's (1969, 1973, 1984) main stages as developmental levels of moral immaturity and maturity. Stages 1 and 2 represent immature or superficial moral judgment; an adolescent or adult operating at these stages has a developmental delay in moral reasoning. Stages 3 and 4 represent mature or profound moral reasoning and should be the norm for any culture. These four stages are summarized in Table 5.1.

Generally, superficiality is the mark of sociomoral immaturity. Stage 1 is superficial insofar as concrete or physical appeals are made in justifying moral values—for example, "The father's the boss because he's bigger." Saving the life of more than one person is especially important because, in the words of one of Kohlberg's (1984) young subjects, "One man has just one house, maybe a lot of furniture, but a whole bunch of people have an awful lot of furniture" (p. 192). Stage 2 is more psychological but is still superficial in a pragmatic way. For example, Stage 2 youths justify keeping promises to ensure that others keep their promises to them and do nice things for them, and to keep others from getting

Table 5.1

STAGES OF MORAL REASONING

IMMATURE MORALITIES: STAGES 1 AND 2

Stage 1: Power—"Might Makes Right"

- Morality is whatever big or powerful people say that you have to do. If you are big or powerful, whatever you say is right, and whatever you want to do or get is fair.
- If you don't get punished for what you do or no one powerful sees it, whatever you do is OK. It is wrong if you do get punished; the punishment makes it wrong.
- Physical damage or other obvious injury—but not psychological suffering—is noticed and acknowledged to be wrong.
- Individuals tend to spout clichés ("You should never tell a lie") without much understanding of what they mean.

Critique

- A Stage 1 individual doesn't understand the moral reasons for rules, has trouble with reciprocity if it requires taking more than one perspective at a time, and is best at taking the perspective of someone physically powerful.

Stage 2: Deals—"You Scratch My Back, I'll Scratch Yours"

- Morality is an exchange of favors ("I did this for you, so you'd better do that for me") or of blows (misunderstanding of the Golden Rule as "Do it to others before they do it to you" or "Pay them back if they've done it to you").

- You should ask or figure, "What's in it for me?" before you help or obey others.
- The main reason for not stealing, cheating, and so on is that you could get caught.
- Individuals may assert that nobody (even those in legitimate positions of authority) should "boss anybody around," that people should mind their own business, that everybody has his or her own point of view as to what's right, and that everybody should have the right to think and do whatever he or she wants.
- Individuals may suggest that you should "fix things" if somebody gets more than you do.

Critique
- Stage 2 individuals have trouble understanding the ideal of mutuality in a relationship. Also, they tend to be self-centered: better at detecting how others are unfair to or don't do things for them than how they are unfair to or don't do things for others.

MATURE MORALITIES: STAGES 3 AND 4
Stage 3: Mutuality—"Treat Others as You Would Hope They Would Treat You"
- In mutual morality, the relationship itself becomes a value: "Trust" and "mutual caring," although intangible, are real and important.
- People can really care about other people, can have trust in them, and can feel part of a "we."
- You should try to understand if your friend is acting hostile or selfish.
- You should try to make a good impression so others understand that you are a well-intentioned person and so you can think well of yourself.

Critique
- Stage 3 thinking can entail caring about the preciousness of human life. However, Stage 3 thinkers can care so much about what others think of them that they turn into "moral marshmallows" in difficult situations.

Stage 4: Systems—"Are You Contributing to Society?"
- This morality involves interdependence and cooperation for the sake of society: Society can't make it if people don't respect others' rights and follow through on their responsibilities.
- Honoring your commitments is a sign of good character.
- If you are in the position of judge, teacher, or some other social authority, you should uphold consistent and fair standards (but also consider extenuating circumstances).
- In difficult situations, retaining integrity and self-respect may mean becoming unpopular.

Critique
- Stage 4 thinking can entail appeals to moral law and to respect for rights and responsibilities as the basis for society. However, Stage 4 societal morality is more a supplement to than a replacement of Stage 3 interpersonal morality.

mad at them. With the advent of Stage 3, moral judgment advances beyond superficiality to a beginning mature understanding of moral norms and values. Stage 3 goes beyond pragmatic thinking to achieve a mutuality of perspectives. Piaget (1932/1965) characterizes this transition as one from "reciprocity as a fact" to "reciprocity as an ideal" or "do as you would be done by" (p. 323). As the adolescent interacts in the larger world—campus, workplace, travel, and so on—the Stage 3 understanding of the need for mutual trust expands into an appreciation of the need for commonly accepted, consistent standards and interdependent requirements: Stage 4. As one of Kohlberg's older adolescent subjects put it, "You've got to have certain understandings in things that everyone is going to abide by or else you could never get anywhere in society, never do anything" (Colby et al., 1987, p. 375).

In summary, then, youths normally progress from a relatively superficial (physical, pragmatic) level to a more profound or mature level of interpersonal and sociomoral reasoning. Youths who even in the adolescent years show little or no moral reasoning beyond Stage 2 are considered to be developmentally delayed. At home, school, or in the community they have not had enough opportunities to take on the roles or consider the perspectives of others (Gibbs, 1995). In a study analyzing moral judgment delay by area of moral value, we find delay in *every* area (Gregg et al., 1994). The area of greatest delay concerns the reasons for obeying the law. Nondelinquents generally give Stage 3 reasons— for example, people's mutual expectations of adherence to the law; the selfishness of lawbreaking; and the resulting chaos, insecurity, or loss of trust in the world. By contrast, delinquent youths generally use reasoning that appeals to the risk of getting caught and going to jail (Stage 2).

Delay as Persistent and Pronounced Cognitive Distortions

The works of Yochelson and Samenow (1976, 1977) and Gibbs and Potter (1992) have identified a particularly frequent series of cognitive distortions regularly made by easy-to-anger and chronically aggressive youths. Chief among these are *self-centered* thinking errors reflecting a singularly egocentric bias. Gibbs, Potter, and Goldstein (1995) define such thinking as "according status to one's own views, expectations, needs, rights, immediate feelings, and desires to such an extent that the legitimate views, etc., of others . . . are scarcely considered or are disregarded altogether" (p. 108). On Gibbs, Barriga, and Potter's (1995) *How I Think*

Questionnaire, a device designed to measure cognitive distortions, youths seeing their worlds through distinctly self-centered, egocentric lenses agree to such items as the following:

- If I see something I like, I take it.
- If I lie to people, that's nobody's business but my own.
- If I really want to do something, I don't care if it is legal or not.
- When I get mad, I don't care who gets hurt. (p. 227)

As these scale items reflect, egocentric bias is a me-first, me-only stance to life experiences. Such bias is a natural feature of thought and behavior in childhood; a young child may declare, "I should get it because I want to have it!" or "Whatever I want is what's fair!" Lickona (1983) describes this "me-centeredness" as follows:

Especially when Stage 2 is first breaking through, kids' energy tends to go into asserting *their* needs and desires and making the world accommodate to them. They have a supersensitive Unfairness Detector when it comes to finding all the ways that people are unfair to them. But they have a big blind spot when it comes to seeing all the ways they aren't fair to others and all the ways parents and others do things for them. (p. 149)

Normally, egocentric bias declines with experience as children see their self-interest in light of the welfare of others. Of course, all of us continue to have some bias. Even as mature adults "we experience our own points of view more or less directly, whereas we must always attain the other person's view in more indirect ways. . . . We are usually unable to turn our own viewpoints off completely, when trying to infer another's viewpoints" (Flavell, Miller, & Miller, 1993, p. 181). "Not turning one's own viewpoint off completely" is an understatement in the case of antisocial youths, whose egocentric bias typically remains at the pronounced levels characteristic of childhood. Incarcerated juvenile felons in our groups, when reflecting on their shoplifting and other offenses, have recollected that their thoughts at the time concerned whether they could do what they wanted and get away successfully. Spontaneous references to the victims of the offenses are totally absent.

Assuming the worst is a second frequently occurring cognitive distortion characteristic of aggressive youths. It is a distortion evident in a number of ways—belief that one's own behavior or that of others cannot change, belief in the worst about people and their motivations, and, more generally, belief in worst-case scenarios in life. However, its main anger-arousal feature is, as Dodge and his research team (Dodge, 1980; Dodge, Price, Bachorowski, & Newman, 1990) have consistently shown, attribution of hostile intent. Ambiguous behaviors by others are interpreted as deliberately hostile acts. A look from another youth in the school cafeteria or facility yard is perceived as a stare-down, a challenge, and a threat rather than the simple glance it often is. The bump in the school corridor between classes is experienced as an intentional "dissing," a put-down, and rarely a mere accident. Youngsters prone to assuming the worst, as measured by the *How I Think Questionnaire,* agree that

- You might as well steal. If you don't take it, somebody else will.

- I might as well lie—when I tell the truth, people don't believe me anyway.

- People are always trying to hassle me.

- You should hurt people first, before they hurt you. (p. 227)

Both self-centeredness and assuming the worst are made more comfortable and acceptable distortions when they are accompanied by an externalizing view of the world in which little or "nothing is *my* fault!" Thus, a third chronic cognitive distortion of angry, aggressive youths is *blaming others.* Gibbs, Barriga, and Potter (1995) describe this misperception as

> misattributing blame for one's harmful actions to outside sources, especially to another person, a group, or a momentary aberration (one was drunk, high, in a bad mood, etc.), or misattributing blame for one's victimization or other misfortune to innocent others. The burglarizing youth who neutralized his conscience by blaming his victims (they were negligent in protecting their homes and so deserved whatever happened to them) was engaging in Blaming Others. (p. 111)

Blaming others is shown by agreement with such scale items as the following:

- If people don't cooperate with me, it's not my fault if someone gets hurt.

- People force me to lie when they ask me too many questions.

- When I lose my temper, it's because people try to make me mad.

- If someone is careless enough to lose a wallet, they deserve to have it stolen.

There is also the thinking error of *minimizing/mislabeling,* an error "depicting antisocial behavior as causing no real harm or as being acceptable or even admirable" (Gibbs, Barriga, & Potter, 1995, p. 113). As these authors note, such thinking serves and abets egocentricity by weakening inhibitions to aggress and by neutralizing pangs of conscience. Here, youths subscribe to such *How I Think Questionnaire* items as these:

- Everybody lies. It's no big deal.

- If you know you could get away with it, only a fool wouldn't steal.

- People who get beat up badly probably don't suffer a lot.

- You have to get even with people who don't show you respect.

In addition to these four major errors in perception and cognition, chronically aggressive youths not infrequently rationalize a type of *false consensus,* in which they believe others act as they do. They also display a strong resistance to change, or *anchoring,* even in the face of substantial contrary evidence.

Cognitive distortions are not easily changed. Typically, they have been well practiced, finely honed, and from the youth's perspective, have worked well, often for many years. Techniques that may usefully be employed for the purpose of what has been termed *cognitive restructuring* are indicated in Table 5.2. Their most effective use, as Gibbs, Barriga, and Potter (1995) demonstrate, appears to occur in a group context, one in which leaders and members join constructively in the restructuring effort.

MORAL REASONING TRAINING PROCEDURES

To the extent that antisocial behavior reflects a delay of mature moral reasoning and egocentric bias, the aim of an effective program is to remediate that developmental delay. In effect, antisocial youths need a concentrated dose of social perspective taking opportunities. This is the focus of a number of interventions for troubled youths. For example, in Just Community programs, the school or treatment facility is built on the principles of democracy and justice. Students or residents participate in making and enforcing the rules that govern their community life (Hickey & Scharf, 1980; Higgins, 1995; Power, Higgins, & Kohlberg, 1989).

Table 5.2

COGNITIVE RESTRUCTURING STRATEGIES FOR
SELF-INSTRUCTION TRAINING

1. Question the evidence.
2. Dispute irrational beliefs.
   - Reversing: Placing responsibility for change back on the perpetrator while not permitting projection of blame onto others
   - Relabeling: Countering the use of self-serving, positive labels on negative behaviors
   - Confronting: Making perpetrators aware of the effect of their actions on others
3. Redirect attention to nonhostile cues.
4. Decatastrophize. (What is the worst that can happen?)
5. Examine options and alternatives: Generate *several* solutions.
6. Generate assertive rather than aggressive responses.
7. Reduce imaginal ruminating about the anger-inducing event.
8. Reduce imaginal exaggeration of the anger-inducing event.
9. Consider both short- and long-term consequences of both aggressive and prosocial responses.
10. Plan and rehearse prosocial response, step by step.

On a smaller scale, some programs use peer group discussion, posing relevant sociomoral dilemmas or problem situations to stimulate perspective taking. Participants must justify their problem-solving decisions in the face of challenges from more developmentally advanced peers and from adult leaders (e.g., Gibbs, Arnold, Ahlborn, & Cheesman, 1984).

Sociomoral developmental delay is a serious handicap for youths attempting to help one another. For example, a youth with a lying and stealing problem can scarcely be helped by a group whose moral judgment with respect to such problems is at Stage 2. In such a group, social decision making meetings are needed to stimulate a more mature understanding of the value of truth and respect for property. Other social decision making meetings might deal with a variety of value themes, such as peer or family relationships, resisting drugs, and preventing suicide.

The Social Decision Making Meeting

ART promotes the development of sociomoral reasoning through social decision making meetings. The substance of these meetings constitutes Moral Reasoning Training. Our goal is to facilitate progress along the natural stage-sequential trajectory of moral-cognitive development so that youths will make more mature decisions in social situations. This does not mean interfering with private morals or dictating a group's morality.

Problem Situations for Teaching Mature Moral Reasoning

In these social decision making meetings, the group strives to develop the capacity to make mature decisions concerning specific problem situations, presented in Appendix C. These 10 problem situations, derived from various sources and appearing in Gibbs, Potter, and Goldstein's (1995) book *The EQUIP Program,* are designed to create opportunities for participants to take the perspectives of others.

The settings represented by the situations range from the home to the school or correctional facility to the workplace. Each situation depicts an adolescent with a problem, typically one created by someone *else* with a problem (an effective way to induce a nondefensive and more objective discussion). In terms of cognitive distortions, all of the problem friends are self-centered. Probe questions following each situation promote examination of other cognitive distortions (blaming others, minimizing/mislabeling, assuming the worst). These questions tend to bring out the implications of the problem situations in terms of such moral values as keeping a promise or telling the truth, helping others, saving a life/living even when you don't want to, not stealing, obeying the law, or sending lawbreakers to jail. Controversial questions can evoke active challenges from peers (or, if necessary, from the group leader). A sample problem situation, including accompanying questions, is shown in Figure 5.1.

Even among antisocial adolescents, group majority positions and reasoning on the problem situation questions tend to be positive, responsible, and mature. A student who makes a negative decision and justifies it at Stage 1 or 2 may lose to a more mature challenge and experience the conflict or "disequilibration" of having to acquiesce to the majority. Disequilibration may be crucial if a group member using predominantly immature stages of moral reasoning is to achieve more mature sociomoral development.

Although the problem situations (e.g., deciding to try to persuade a friend against stealing a car) generally do have "right" or responsible answers, the right answer may not be immediately apparent (e.g., the group may decide to take the ride if it is mislabeled and minimized with the cognitive distortion of "doing fun things with a friend"). Similarly,

Figure 5.1

JERRY'S PROBLEM SITUATION

Jerry had just moved to a new school and was feeling pretty lonely until one day a guy named Bob came up and introduced himself. "Hi, Jerry. My name is Bob. I heard one of the teachers say you're new here. If you're not doing anything after school today, how about coming over to shoot some baskets?" Pretty soon Jerry and Bob were good friends.

One day when Jerry was shooting baskets by himself, the basketball coach saw him and invited him to try out for the team. Jerry made the team, and every day after school he would practice with the rest of the team. After practice, Jerry and his teammates would always go out together to get something to eat and sit around and talk about stuff. On weekends they would sometimes take trips together.

As Jerry spends more time with the team, he sees less and less of Bob, his old friend. One day, Jerry gets a call from Bob. "Say, I was wondering," says Bob, "if you're not too busy on Thursday, my family is having a little birthday party for me. Maybe you could come over for dinner that night." Jerry tells Bob he'll try to come to the party. But during practice on Thursday, everyone tells Jerry about the great place they're all going to after practice.

What should Jerry say or do?

1. Should Jerry go with the team?

   go with team / go to Bob's party / can't decide *(circle one)*

2. What if Jerry calls Bob from school and says he's sorry, but something has come up and he can't come over after all? Then would it be all right for Jerry to go with the team?

   go with team / go to Bob's party / can't decide *(circle one)*

3. What if Jerry considers that his teammates may be upset if Jerry doesn't come— that they may start to think Jerry's not such a good friend? Then would it be all right for Jerry to go with the team?

   go with team / go to Bob's party / can't decide *(circle one)*

4. What if Jerry thinks that, after all, Bob came along and helped Jerry when Jerry was lonely. Then should Jerry go with the team?

   go with team / go to Bob's party / can't decide *(circle one)*

5. Let's change the situation a bit. Let's say that before Bob asks Jerry to come over, the teammates ask if Jerry will be coming along on Thursday. Jerry says he thinks so. Then Bob asks Jerry. Then what should Jerry do?

   go with team / go to Bob's party / can't decide *(circle one)*

6. Which is more important: to have one close friend or to have a group of regular friends?

    one close friend / group of regular friends / can't decide *(circle one)*

7. Let's change the situation a different way. What if Jerry and Bob are not good friends but instead are just acquaintances? Then should Jerry go with the team?

    go with team / go to Bob's party / can't decide *(circle one)*

---

problem situations in which the right answer is to tell on a friend (e.g., if the friend is dealing in drugs) may at first be experienced as dilemmas because the peer norm against "ratting" or "narking" is so strong.

The problem situations are written for male adolescents; however, they are readily adapted for female group members by substituting girls' names and by modifying the circumstances, as appropriate. The probe questions are then revised accordingly.

Preparations for the Social Decision Making Meeting

Preferably, a copy of the problem situation is given to each group member before the session begins. Based on the members' responses to the situations, the group leader prepares a chart to be used at the meeting. Jerry's Problem Situation (Figure 5.1) calls for a positive decision (loyalty to an old friend, Bob) but presents a temptation against doing the right thing (to have fun with more exciting new friends, Jerry's high school basketball teammates). The positive (responsible, fair, caring) decision is to go to Bob's party. Figure 5.2 displays a representative set of decisions for Jerry's Problem Situation. Note that not all responses are positive ("Bob's party"); some are "can't decide," and some are "go with team." Such a collection of decisions is good—diversity fosters lively discussion and creates the developmentally stimulating disequilibration that delayed group members need.

After preparing a chart similar to that shown in the example, the group leader writes at the bottom the most likely group decisions—those favored by the greatest number of group members. These decisions, followed by question marks, are good candidates for becoming official group decisions—that is, positions endorsed by the entire group. Once the chart has been prepared, the group leader studies it to identify the relatively positive group members; as we shall see, they play a crucial role in the cultivation of mature morality. In the example, Robert, Earl, Jonathan, and Brian show overwhelmingly positive decisions.

Figure 5.2

RESPONSES TO JERRY'S PROBLEM SITUATION

Name	QUESTION NUMBER						
	1	2	3	4	5	6	7
Dante	party	team	party	party	team	close friend	team
David	team	team	team	party	team	close friend	team
Tommy	can't decide	party	team	party	team	close friend	can't decide
Robert	party	party	party	party	can't decide	close friend	team
Andy	team	party	team	team	team	can't decide	team
Daniel	party	team	party	party	team	close friend	team
Earl	party	party	party	party	party	close friend	party
Jonathan	party	party	party	party	party	close friend	team
Brian	party	party	party	party	party	close friend	party
Group decision	Bob's party?	Bob's party?	Bob's party?	Bob's party?	go with team?	close friend?	go with team?

POSSIBLE GROUP DECISION OUTCOMES

Group decision	Bob's party	Bob's party	Bob's party	Bob's party	go with team?	Close friend	go with team?

If responses to the problem situation cannot be obtained in advance, group members are asked to respond at the beginning of the meeting (although then the trainer doesn't have the advantage of advance preparation).

At the start of the session, the group leader also displays some simple rules:

1. Never put down or threaten anyone.

2. Listen to what others have to say.

3. If you criticize another group member, give that person a chance to answer.

4. Stay on the subject when you disagree.

5. Never talk to anyone outside the group about what is said in the group.

Four Phases of Sociomoral Development

The group leader next promotes sociomoral development in four phases: (a) introducing the problem situation, (b) cultivating mature morality, (c) remediating moral developmental delay, and (d) consolidating mature morality. At the close of each session, the group leader conducts a self-evaluation using a checklist corresponding to the four phases (see Figure 5.3).

Phase 1: Introduce the Problem Situation

To have an effective social decision making session, all group members must understand clearly what the problem situation is and how it relates to their lives. If members have read the problem situation and answered the related questions before the meeting begins, the leader can bring copies of their responses to the meeting and ask a group member to hand them back. (If group members answer the questions at the beginning of the meeting, they simply hold their own papers.) The leader then asks another group member to read the problem situation to refresh everyone's memory, then raises questions to stimulate discussion. This phase does not consume more than 10 to 15 minutes in a 1- to 1½-hour meeting.

Possible questions

- Who can tell the group just what Jerry's problem is?

- Why is that a problem?

Figure 5.3

SOCIAL DECISION MAKING MEETINGS:
GROUP LEADER REVIEW/SELF-EVALUATION CHECKLIST

Group: _____ Date: _____

Problem Situation: _____

In the various phases, did I ask questions to:

Phase 1: Introduce the Problem Situation

_____ 1. Remind the group of the ground rules for discussion?

_____ 2. Make sure the group understood the problem situation (e.g., "Who can tell the group just what Jerry's problem is? Why is that a problem?")?

_____ 3. Relate the problem situation to the group members' everyday lives (e.g., "Do problems like this happen? Who has been in a situation like this? Tell the group about it.")?

Phase 2: Cultivate Mature Morality

_____ 4. Establish mature morality as the tone for the meeting (e.g., eliciting, reconstructing, and listing on easel pad or chalkboard mature reasons for each positive majority decision)?

Phase 3: Remediate Moral Developmental Delay

_____ 5. Use more mature group members and the list of reasons (Phase 2) to challenge the hedonistic or pragmatic arguments of some group members?

_____ 6. Create role-taking opportunities in other ways as well (e.g., "What would the world be like if everybody did that?" "How would you feel if you were Bob?")?

Phase 4: Consolidate Mature Morality

_____ 7. Make positive decisions and mature reasons unanimous for the group (e.g., "Are there any strong objections if I circle that decision as the group decision/underline that reason as the group's number one reason?")?

_____ 8. Praise the group for its positive decisions and mature reasons (e.g., "I'm really pleased that the group is able to make so many good, strong decisions and back them up with good, strong reasons." "Would the group like to tape this sheet onto the wall?")?

In general:

_____ 9. *(Prior to the session)* Did I review the leader notes?

_____ 10. Did the group members follow the ground rules (concerning listening, confidentiality, etc.)?

_____ 11. Were all group members interested and involved? (If not, list the names of uninvolved group members.)

_____ 12. Was some constructive value found in every serious group member comment?

_____ 13. Was the *should* supported and relabeled as strong (e.g., "Yes, it does take guts to do the right thing . . .")?

After the meeting:

_____ 14. Did I make notes regarding the meeting and individual group members?

- Do problems like this happen?
- Who has been in a situation like this? Tell the group about it.

Phase 2: Cultivate Mature Morality

Once the group understands the problem situation, Moral Reasoning Training begins. If all antisocial adolescents were totally lacking in mature moral judgment, this work would be very difficult indeed. As noted earlier, however, many antisocial adolescents do show some potential to make positive decisions or evaluations on the basis of mature moral reasons. In responding to Jerry's Problem Situation, many group members tend to indicate positive decisions—for example, "go to Bob's party" for Questions 1 through 4 and "one close friend" for Question 6 (see Figure 5.1). Furthermore, the reasons for these decisions tend to be mature.

The group leader during this phase exploits this potential for mature morality—that is, cultivates a group atmosphere of mature morality characterized by both positive decisions and mature moral reasoning. The makings of a mature moral climate are typically available from the group members themselves (at least from the majority). The group leader's job is to exploit the resources available in the class in order to render mature morality prominent and to set the tone for the remainder of the meeting. The group leader highlights mature morality by asking group members who indicated positive decisions about the reasons for those decisions and then writing those reasons on an easel pad or chalkboard for the group to consider. (The leader writes down reasons offered for negative decisions separately—after the reasons for the positive choices have been listed.)

For Jerry's Problem Situation, then, the leader elicits the reasons for the majority "go to Bob's party" decision for Questions 1 through 4 and the "close friend" decision for Question 6. Although some of these reasons are pragmatic, many of them are typically mature, showing Stage 3 or even transitional reasoning between Stages 3 and 4. Granted, it is often necessary to suggest to group members more mature reconstructions of their thoughts. For example, a rejoinder to "Jerry might still want to have Bob around" might be "So you're saying Jerry might still want to keep up his friendship with Bob?"

Possible questions

- Those who chose "Bob's party" for Questions 1 through 4, like Earl and Brian, are the majority. Brian, why did you decide that Jerry should go to Bob's party? What are the reasons for your decision?

- Those who chose "close friend" for Question 6, like Dante and Tommy, are the majority. Dante, why did you decide it is more important to have one close friend? Tommy?

Phase 3: Remediate Moral Developmental Delay

If a mature moral atmosphere is cultivated in the class, the group leader has made crucial preparation for the next phase, which shifts the focus to the youths with delayed reasoning. These group members can seriously undermine the group culture and will do so if allowed. The mature moral atmosphere established at the outset is a necessary defense against the onslaught of these group members as they are brought into the discussion and challenged.

In theoretical terms, remediating moral developmental delay means creating social perspective taking opportunities or challenging individuals to consider other—especially other more mature—viewpoints. Such opportunities can reduce self-centered cognitive distortion by engendering disequilibration and stimulating more mature moral judgment. Exposure to mature moral reasons for positive decisions has already provided delayed group members with an opportunity or a challenge to grow. But mere exposure is insufficient. The group leader must (a) invite the negative group members to explain their views, (b) publicly record on an easel pad or chalkboard the explanations or reasons for their decisions, and (c) invite members of the majority to respond.

Possible questions

- David, you're one of the group members who chose "go with team" instead of "Bob's party." What are your reasons for that decision? *(After hearing these reasons, point to easel pad or chalkboard.)* Is that still your decision? Why? How will you answer these arguments made by the group majority?

- *(To the group)* Do David's reasons persuade the group to change to "go with team"? Why or why not?

Particular types of probe questions are especially helpful in creating perspective-taking opportunities. Self-centered reasoners are challenged to generalize ("What would the world be like if everybody did that?") or to consider the point of view or feelings of another party in the problem situation. Group members with puzzling or contradictory answers are asked to clarify: "Dante, your decision is 'Bob's party' on Question 1, but 'go with team' on Question 2. How come?" Quiet group members are brought out, and members with "can't decide" responses are probed for both sides of their thinking: "Tommy, you're quiet today. Are you still undecided? Why do you partly think Jerry should go to Bob's party? *(List the reason[s] on the easel chart or chalkboard.)* Why do you partly think he should go with the team?" *(List the reason[s].)*

The favored tactic of pragmatic-level group members is to argue that their reasons are more realistic and hence more compelling. For example, they may say that their decision and reasoning ("Jerry should go with the team because he'd have more fun") is superior because, after all, that is what Jerry would probably really do. The strategy for handling this tactic is twofold. First, clarify the distinction between *would* and *should*: "Are you saying this is what Jerry *would* be likely to do or that this is what he *should* do? If it's true he'd be likely to go with the team, does that mean he *should* go with the team?" Second, relabel—specifically, counterattack the positive labeling of the *would* as "only realistic" with a positive characterization of the *should*: "That's true, it would take real guts for Jerry not to give in to what he feels like doing and instead do what a lot of people might not be strong enough to do—the right thing."

Phase 4: Consolidate Mature Morality

Once mature morality has been cultivated and challenged, it needs to be consolidated. The group's mature morality is consolidated—and the group's culture becomes more positive and cohesive—as the group leader seeks consensus for positive decisions and mature reasons. In the process, group members with initially immature moral judgment continue to feel pressure to defer to and even reconstruct for themselves mature morality. In the discussion of the problem situation, the goal is to convert as many of the positive majority positions as possible into unanimous group decisions. As the discussion moves toward the majority position, the group leader asks whether any members object strongly to declaring the majority decision to be the group's official decision on a given question. Similarly, the leader asks whether there are any strong objections to the group's official decision. If none is stated, the leader deletes the question mark and circles the decision on the bottom row of the chart (see Figure 5.2). If objections are voiced, the decision remains merely a majority position. (This outcome is almost as valuable because the frustration from a deadlock also stimulates group members developmentally.) In either event, the group is praised or encouraged at the conclusion of the social decision making meeting.

Possible questions

- Is the group ready to agree that Jerry should go to Bob's party? Any strong objections?

- It sounds like one of the most positive reasons for why Jerry should go to Bob's party is that it is a chance to renew the friendship. Are there any strong objections to my circling that reason as the group's number one reason? (*Alternative selections are not problematic as long as a pragmatic reason is not selected.*)

- (*If there are objections and the discussion deadlocks*) Well, I guess we just aren't able to come up with a group decision/number one reason on this question.

- (*Encouragement at the end of a successful meeting*) I'm really pleased that the group is able to make so many good, strong decisions and back them up with good, strong reasons. This group has shown again what it can do.

- (*If not so successful*) Is the group satisfied with what was accomplished today? I know the group can do better next time because it did before. (*Recollect positive example, if available.*) What plans will the group make right now before leaving so that more good decisions are accomplished at the next social decision making meeting?

- *(To build positive group identity)* Would the group like to put the sheet(s) showing its decisions/reasons on the wall? Here's some masking tape.

YOUTH PERCEPTIONS OF MORAL REASONING TRAINING

When program youths are asked about their impressions of the ART curriculum, the Moral Reasoning Training sessions often prove to be the most popular. Group members sometimes even request such sessions or ask when the next one will be. Why is this component of ART so popular? One possible reason may be that situation content is inherently interesting to the youths. Another may involve the fact that even those Moral Reasoning Training groups with initially immature moral judgment generally make positive, responsible, and mature decisions about the problem situations, especially as cultivated by the group leader. Through responsible decision making, the group not only develops more mature moral judgment but also discovers common moral values underlying their decisions. In the course of these sessions, then, many group members discover that mature morality is the majority position and that a positive potential exists in themselves and others. Perhaps they develop legitimate self-respect as they contribute to a group striving for dedication to more mature moral considerations and ideals.

CHAPTER SIX

Trainee Motivation and Resistance

Problems can and do occur in Aggression Replacement Training groups. Trainees may not want to attend, or their attendance may be sporadic. Once in the training room, they may be unmotivated to participate as requested. They may fail to see the relevance of the curriculum to the demands of their everyday lives. In a variety of ways, they may actively resist meaningful group involvement. Their resistive behavior may interfere not only with their own skill acquisition, anger control, or enhanced moral reasoning, but also with the learning of others in the group. This chapter addresses such matters and offers suggestions for increasing trainee motivation and reducing trainee resistance.

INCREASING TRAINEE MOTIVATION

What means do we have at our disposal, or can we create, in order to increase the likelihood that trainees will actually (a) show up for planned ART sessions (i.e., attendance motivation), (b) take part as requested in all group training procedures (i.e., participation motivation), and (c) use what they learn on a continuing basis in their lives (i.e., generalization motivation)? Generalization motivation is the topic of chapter 7. Here, our focus is on the identification and use of various tactics to motivate regular attendance and active and appropriate participation.

This motivational task often is not an easy one. Many of the youths who are offered the opportunity to participate in ART—a technique for training *prosocial* behaviors—are highly competent in the regular use of *antisocial* behaviors. Furthermore, this predilection is frequently encouraged, supported, and generously rewarded by many of the significant people in these youngsters' lives—family, peers, and others.

In the final analysis, two types of motivational strategies are available: extrinsic and intrinsic. Extrinsic motivators are tangible rewards provided contingent upon performance of desirable behaviors. These kinds of rewards take many forms and constitute a long menu of reinforcers. In the early years of the behavior modification movement, the use of extrinsic motivators was often denounced as "bribery." It was asserted that youths should *want* to engage in desired behaviors, for their own sake, and not for the external rewards these rewards would bring. Some detractors still offer similar protests (e.g., Kohn, 1986), but most agree that the use of a combination of extrinsic and intrinsic motivators is typically the most effective motivational strategy.

Tangible motivators are, in fact, widely used in contemporary U. S. schools and in other institutions for adolescents. The points, checks, stars, and stickers of elementary schools give way to pizza parties, movie privileges, club clothing, special activities, or other similar perks at the secondary level and in delinquency centers. The use of extrinsic rewards, in whatever forms, is a widespread motivational approach. Such rewards seem especially useful in eliciting initial involvement in ART program activities.

It is the consistent experience of many ART trainers, however, that resting one's motivational effort strictly on a foundation of external rewards—whether in the form of tangible reinforcers, token economy, level system, or other extrinsic incentives—is insufficient to sustain motivation. There must be substantial payoffs inherent in the activity itself. In ART, and especially its Skillstreaming component, such intrinsic motivators reside within the skills, especially those trainees select and use successfully in their real-world contexts. Our discussion in chapter 3 of negotiating the skill curriculum is central here. According youths the opportunity to select the skills *they* feel they need is a major step toward positive attendance and participation motivation. When these trainee-selected (or, to a somewhat lesser degree, trainer-selected) skills actually yield positive outcomes in the trainees' interactions with their families, peers, or significant others, further motivational reinforcement takes place.

In addition to regular skill negotiation with participating trainees, another tactic can be used to augment intrinsic motivation—to communicate to trainees in the initial structuring of the Skillstreaming component of ART and throughout the sessions that the goal of Skillstreaming is to teach alternatives, not substitutes. Many of the youths who are referred to an ART program have been admonished, reprimanded, and punished literally hundreds of times for behaviors their parents, teachers, or others have deemed inappropriate. In one way or another, they have been told to "stop doing that." We agree that it is certainly a desirable goal to decrease antisocial behaviors (largely the goal of the Anger Control Training component of ART). At the same time, we believe it is important to provide alternatives to the undesirable behaviors by expanding the range of available responses. This is the goal of Skillstreaming. If, for example, a youth is falsely accused of stealing, and the only response to such an accusation that he or she previously has learned, practiced, and been rewarded for is to lash out, the youth will do so again. The youth has, in effect, no choice because he or she has no alternatives from which to choose. If, however, the youth learns through Skillstreaming that accusations can be handled by explaining, investigating, negotiating, or walking away, he or she can choose an alternative to counterattack. The very fact that reprimands and punishments have had to be used hundreds of times is testimony to their lack of effectiveness. If given appropriate skill response choices, youths will likely use these responses at least some of the time.

The following dialogue shows how a trainer might convey the concept of skill alternatives to a trainee.

Trainee: This won't work.

Trainer: What do you mean, it won't work?

Trainee: Come on, get real, get out of that university, get out on the street more. You can negotiate up the wazoo in here, but you can't negotiate out on the street. Out on the street you got to hit the guy before he hits you.

Trainer: Now wait a second, what do you think we're doing in here? We're not teaching substitutes—we're teaching alternatives.

Trainee: I don't understand those words.

Trainer: All right, I'll give you a sports example. There's a team with a good quarterback, the only quarterback on the team, but for some reason, injury or whatever, one Sunday he can't throw long and he can't run. All he's got working for him is his short pass, and he's good at it. So on the first down, he goes out and throws that short pass, and it's good. Same thing on the second down, another good short pass. After the second pass the

defense in the huddle says, "Two short passes on two
plays—maybe that's all the guy's got today. Let's look for
it." Third down he throws the ball again, and the
defense knocks it down. Fourth down, it's his only play,
he throws it again, and they intercept it.

You're like that quarterback. You have only one play—
your fist. You've got a fist in every pocket. Others look
at you, you hit them. They don't look at you, you hit
them. They talk to you, you hit them. They don't talk
to you, you hit them. That's why you get into so much
trouble. How about we help you become like a skilled
quarterback, who has a variety of plays? You keep your
fists, and if you need to hit someone, you hit them. I
don't want you to, but I can't follow you around to stop
you, and I'm not going to teach you how to hit. You're
already better at that than I am. But keep the fist in one
pocket only, instead of in every pocket. In the back
pocket put a different play. It's called negotiation. We'll
teach you how to do it, and as a group we'll figure out
where and when it fits. And in the other back pocket,
keep a miracle play. I think you're going to call it a miracle play, but I actually wouldn't. I think you'll call it a
miracle play because once I tell you what it is, you're
going to say to me it's a miracle if you can do that. But
you know what? I've seen kids do it, and like any good
football play, it fits some situations, and it doesn't fit
others. It's called walking away without losing face.
There are times adolescents like yourself can do it. Let's
figure out together where and when. And in the fourth
pocket, put yet another play. So like a good quarterback
you have a variety of plays.

So far we have suggested that a trainee's motivation to attend regularly
and participate appropriately in ART sessions is enhanced by the use of
both extrinsic and intrinsic motivators, as well as by helping participants
understand that the core goal of the program is to provide them with behavioral options—alternative responses to be used at their discretion. There
is one other motivational concern to be addressed here: Youngsters who
frequently exhibit angry, aggressive, intimidating, bullying, domineering,

and threatening behaviors toward others in their everyday lives often display the same behaviors in the ART group. If these behaviors are not dealt with immediately, the trainees toward whom these behaviors are aimed may show up for sessions, but their participation may be guarded and minimal. The skilled ART trainer functions not only as a competent teacher, model, and role-play/feedback guide for the group, but also as a protector. As part of the central training goal of creating a safe learning environment, the trainer must be vigilant for problem behaviors and act immediately to correct any participant efforts to bully, intimidate, dominate, or otherwise treat co-trainees in an inappropriate, aggressive manner. Such vigilance and responsiveness serve to protect the one being attacked; they also provide an additional skill lesson for the attacker.

The following excerpt from an ART trainer workshop illustrates this twofold benefit of a protective trainer response. In this situation, the trainer has just modeled a new skill with the co-trainer, and the trainee, Carolyn, has just completed the group's first role-play of that skill. Since the trainer personally thinks she did a fine job in following the skill's steps during her role-play, he hopes she will get the kind of positive performance feedback from her peers that will motivate her to use the skill where and when it is helpful to her.

Trainer: *(To the first trainee)* Karen, could you tell us what Carolyn did to carry out the first skill step, and how well you think she did it?

Karen: It was really nice what she said. When she said, "I appreciate the invitation a lot, but I can't go," it was right on target—firm but friendly.

Trainer: Thanks, Karen. *(The trainer thinks, "Good, this is just the kind of feedback I hoped Carolyn would get.")*

Trainer: *(To a second trainee observer)* Bill, how do you think Carolyn handled Step 2 of the skill?

Bill: Pretty good. The step was clear. She did good.

Trainer: Pam, how do you think Step 3 went in the role-play?

Pam: It was so bad I thought I would puke as she did it.

Pam's statement instantly initiates three problems, and they all revolve around the issue of protection. The first problem concerns Pam. Pam is exhibiting the type of aggressive behavior that made her a part of the ART group in the first place. Her behavior is threatening to another group member and must be dealt with, but dealt with in a manner that is instructive, constructive, and protective to her as well as to Pam. The second problem relates to Bill and Karen. They haven't role-played yet, so they are likely wondering, "When I get up to role-play, will Pam stick it to me the way she just stuck it to Carolyn?" The third problem is Carolyn. Carolyn is getting the kind of feedback that discourages rather than encourages her to use the skill. The trainer's response must consider the needs of all of these participants. One way to do this is to say to Pam, "Look, Pam, it's good that you gave Carolyn frank feedback, but the way you said it is not going to help her. Can you say it in a more constructive way?" If that behavior is not in Pam's repertoire, the trainer could stand behind her and whisper in her ear: "Pam, I'm going to say certain things to you, and you say them to Carolyn." That teaches Pam about giving constructive feedback and lets her know that threatening comments are not acceptable. Carolyn gets the feedback, and this encourages real-world skill use. Bill and Karen get the message that if Pam "sticks it to them" the trainer will come to their aid. In an active manner, the trainer has provided protection plus instruction to all four group members. In brief, if the trainer fails to protect group members from intimidation, the group will be unproductive no matter how skilled the modeling, role-playing, and so forth. The protector role must be invoked at any and all times it is needed as the program progresses.

REDUCING TRAINEE RESISTANCE

Though not infinite (it just seems that way on occasion), the variety of ways trainees seek to thwart, circumvent, object to, or resist participation in the ART group in the manner requested by the trainer is substantial. Table 6.1 lists the more frequently observed types of trainee resistance; the following discussion provides a brief description of each.

Types of Trainee Resistance

Inactivity

Minimal participation involves trainees who seldom volunteer, provide only brief answers, and in general give trainers a feeling that they are "pulling teeth" to keep the group at its various learning tasks.

A more extreme form of minimal participation is *apathy*, in which nearly everything the trainer does to direct, enliven, or activate the group

Table 6.1

TYPES OF TRAINEE RESISTANCE

Inactivity
- Minimal participation
- Apathy
- Falling asleep

Hyperactivity
- Digression
- Monopolizing
- Interruption
- Excessive restlessness

Active Resistance
- Participation but not as instructed
- Passive-aggressive isolation
- Negativism, refusal
- Disruptiveness

Aggression
- Sarcasm, put-downs
- Bullying, intimidation
- Use of threats
- Assault

Cognitive Inadequacies and Emotional Disturbances
- Inability to pay attention
- Inability to understand
- Inability to remember
- Bizarre behavior

is met with a lack of interest and spontaneity and little if any progress toward group goals.

While it is rare, *falling asleep* does occur from time to time. Sleepers need to be awakened, and the trainer should inquire into the cause of the tiredness. Boredom in the group, lack of sleep, and physical illness are all possible reasons, each requiring a different response.

Hyperactivity

Digression is a repetitive, determined, and strongly motivated movement away from the purposes and procedures of ART. Here the trainee feels some emotion strongly, such as anger or anxiety or despair, and is determined to express it. Or the brief lecture given or the skill, anger control step, or moral problem situation being focused on may set off associations with important recent experiences, which the trainee feels the need to present and discuss. Digression is also often characterized by "jumping out of role." Rather than merely wandering off track, in digression the trainees drive the train off its intended course.

Monopolizing involves subtle and not-so-subtle efforts by trainees to get more than a fair share of time during an ART session. Long monologues sharing a moral reasoning perspective, unnecessary requests by trainees to repeat an anger control step, overly elaborate feedback in a Skillstreaming session, and other attention-seeking efforts to "remain on stage" are examples of such monopolizing behaviors.

Similar to monopolizing, but more intrusive and insistent, *interruption* is literally breaking into the ongoing flow of a trainer's Hassle Log modeling display, a Skillstreaming role-play or feedback period, or other ART activity with comments, questions, suggestions, observations, or other statements. Interruption may be overly aggressive or angry, or it may take the pseudobenevolent form of "help" to the trainer. In either event, such interruptions more often than not retard the group's progress toward its goals.

Excessive restlessness is a more extreme, more physical form of hyperactivity. The trainees may fidget while sitting; rock their chairs; get up and pace; or display other nonverbal, verbal, gestural, or postural signs of restlessness. Excessive restlessness is typically accompanied by digression, monopolizing, or interrupting behavior.

Active Resistance

Trainees involved in *participation but not as instructed* are off target. They may be trying to present a moral reasoning perspective, role-play a Skillstreaming skill, serve as an anger control co-actor, give accurate feedback, or engage in other tasks required in a given ART session, but their own personal agendas or misperceptions interfere, and they wander off course to irrelevant or semirelevant topics. As such, this problem behavior is related to digression, although digression is perhaps a more intense manifestation of off-task behavior.

Passive-aggressive isolation is not merely apathy, in which trainees are simply uninterested in participating. Nor is it participation but not as instructed, in which trainees actively go off task and raise personal agendas. Passive-aggressive isolation is the purposeful, intentional withholding of appropriate participation, an active shutting down of involvement. It can be thought of as a largely nonverbal "crossing of one's arms" in order to display deliberate nonparticipation.

When displaying *negativism* and *refusal,* trainees signal more overtly, by word and deed, the desire to avoid participation in the ART group. They may openly refuse to be part of a role-play, listen to trainer instructions, or complete homework or Hassle Log assignments. Or they may miss sessions, come late to sessions, or walk out in the middle of a session.

Disruptiveness encompasses active resistance behaviors more extreme than negativism, such as openly and perhaps energetically ridiculing the trainer, other trainees, or aspects of the ART procedures. Or disruptiveness may be shown by gestures, movements, noises, or other distracting, nonverbal behaviors characteristically symbolizing overt criticism and hostility.

Aggression

Sarcasm and *put-downs* are denigrating trainee comments, made to ridicule the skill enactment or other behaviors of a fellow group member. The intent of such caustic evaluations is to criticize and diminish the appraised worth of such performances.

Bullying and *intimidation* are common problem behaviors, as they are modes often characteristic of the youngsters selected for ART participation. We distinguish these problems from the use of sarcasm and put-downs in that the behaviors in this category are more severe in intent and consequences.

Continuing along the severity continuum, the overt use of explicit *threats* is the next category of ART group management problems. One youth may threaten another with embarrassment, revelation of confidences, or even bodily harm if his or her demands are not met.

Finally, on rare occasions, actual physical *assault* may occur in an ART group. This serious breach of group safety can have long-term, negative consequences for group functioning. The negative implications for the group's skill training agenda do not easily dissipate.

Cognitive Inadequacies and Emotional Disturbances

Closely related to excessive restlessness, the *inability to pay attention* is often an apparent result of internal or external distractions, daydreaming, or other pressing agendas that command trainees' attention. Inability to pay attention, except for brief time spans, may also be due to one or more forms of cognitive impairment.

Cognitive deficits due to developmental disability, intellectual inadequacy, impoverishment of experience, disease processes, or other sources may result in trainees' *inability to understand* aspects of the ART curriculum. Failure to understand can, of course, also result from lack of instructional clarity or excess complexity.

Material presented in the ART group may be attended to and understood by the trainees, but not remembered. *Inability to remember* may result not only in problems of transfer, but also in group management problems when what is forgotten includes rules and procedures for trainee participation, homework assignments, and so forth.

Bizarre behavior is uncommon, but when it does occur, it can be especially disruptive to group functioning. This type of group management problem may not only pull other trainees off task, it may also frighten them or make them highly anxious. The range of bizarre behaviors possible is quite broad, including talking to oneself or inanimate objects, offering incoherent statements to the group, becoming angry for no apparent reason, hearing and responding to imaginary voices, and exhibiting peculiar mannerisms.

MINIMIZING NEGATIVE BEHAVIORS

How can such behaviors be dealt with constructively and their negative impact on the training goals of the ART group minimized? We provide three answers to this crucial question. The first concerns the notion that diagnosis of the resistive behavior will help point to and, at times, determine its cure. The second answer focuses on behavior modification techniques that can be employed successfully to reduce problem behaviors. The third answer we term "capturing the teachable moment," a resistance-reducing strategy in which problem behaviors occurring during the ART session are employed as stimuli for selecting and teaching Skill-streaming and anger control skills that are directly relevant for resolving the problems displayed.

Diagnosis Determines Cure

As the ART session unfolds, trainees may display resistive behavior. One trainee starts engaging in horseplay with another trainee. In another group, when a trainee is asked to set the stage for an anger control role-play or to share her reasoning regarding a given moral dilemma, that trainee begins delivering a long monologue about irrelevant matters. In a third group, a trainee laughs at another trainee's role-play and shouts demeaning evaluations of the effort. In yet another group, a trainee sits, arms folded and silent, shaking his head "no" time and time again as he refuses the trainer's request that he come up front for his turn at role-playing.

As a first step in managing such resistive behaviors we urge trainers to ask themselves *why?* Why at this moment is this trainee engaging in that particular behavior? Trainers need to make a guess, a hypothesis, a diagnosis. The diagnosis often suggests the cure. Perhaps one's hypothesis is that the trainee is displaying the particular resistive behavior at that moment because what is being asked is too complicated (too many steps, too complex a challenge, too demanding a requirement). If so, resistance reduction would take the form of simplifying—decreasing demands on the youth's abilities. Following are some steps trainers can take during the Skillstreaming or Anger Control Training component to simplify what is asked of trainees when it appears that procedural requests are too complicated:

1. Reward minimal trainee accomplishment.

2. Shorten the role-play.

3. "Feed" sentences to the trainee.

4. Have the trainee read a prepared script portraying the behavioral steps.

5. Have the trainee play the co-actor role first.

Alternatively, assume a different trainer hypothesis for the behavior. Perhaps the trainer thinks, "No, it's not too complicated. Helen has handled even more difficult demands before. Perhaps she's feeling threatened. The feedback to Sarah from Charlie and Ed on her anger control role-play was really tough. She had a hard time dealing with it. Maybe Helen is afraid she's about to become their next target." If, as in this example, threat and intimidation are the trainer's diagnosis, steps to reduce the threat must be taken immediately. Following are several suggestions for reducing threatening behavior:

1. Employ additional live modeling.

2. Postpone the trainee's role-playing until the last.

3. Provide reassurance to the trainee.

4. Provide empathic encouragement to the trainee.

5. Clarify aspects of the trainee's task experienced as threatening.

6. Restructure aspects of the trainee's task experienced as threatening.

The goals in seeking to reduce these problematic behaviors are straightforward: (a) to maximize the youth's involvement, on-task time, and potential learning and (b) to minimize the time spent in distraction, aggression, or other off-task behaviors.

Behavior Modification Techniques

We believe that trainee behaviors that promote learning in the ART group, as well as behaviors that inhibit the learning process, can be managed optimally through the use of behavior modification techniques. The effectiveness of behavior modification technology rests upon a firm experimental foundation. Beyond the repeated demonstration that "they work," behavior modification techniques are relatively easy to learn and use; can be self-administered or administered by teachers, youth care workers, peers, and parents; are generally cost effective; yield tangible behavior changes; have a long history of successful application (with aggressive youngsters in particular); and, for these reasons, can maximize trainers' time doing what trainers do best: train! The following discussion offers an overview of major behavior-change procedures and the rules optimally governing their use, especially regarding aggression reduction and the enhancement of prosocial behaviors. These procedures can be readily employed in classroom, agency, and institutional settings.

Behavior modification is a set of techniques, derived from formal learning theory and rigorously evaluated by experimental research, that is systematically applied in an effort to change observable behavior. Almost all of these techniques are derived from the basic premise developed by Skinner and his followers (Ferster & Skinner, 1957; Skinner, 1938, 1953) that behavior is largely determined by its environmental consequences. In a broadly operational sense, this premise finds expression in techniques that employ rewards or punishments (i.e., environmental consequences) to alter the behaviors that precede the consequences. It is this contingent quality that leads to the use of the term *contingency management* to describe the activities in which the one who applies the techniques (the behavior modifier) engages. Specifically, if the goal is to increase the likelihood that a given (i.e., prosocial) behavior will reoccur, instances of its occurrence are followed by positive consequences—presenting a reward or removing an aversive event. In contrast, if the goal is to decrease the likelihood that a given (i.e., antisocial) behavior will reoccur, instances of its occurrence are followed by negative consequences—presenting an aversive event or removing a rewarding event. To decrease a youngster's disruptiveness, aggression, or acting-out behavior and to increase the chances of his or her behaving in a constructive, attentive, and prosocial manner, the skilled behavior modifier often uses a combination of aversive or reward-withdrawing techniques (for the aggressive behaviors) and aversiveness-reducing or reward-providing techniques (for the constructive behaviors). The following definitions help further clarify the substance of the contingency management process.

A *reinforcer* is an event that increases the subsequent frequency of any behavior it follows. When the presentation of an event following a behavior increases the frequency of the behavior, the event is referred to as a *positive reinforcer.* Praise, special privileges, tokens or points exchangeable for material goods, or snacks are a few examples of positive reinforcers. When the removal of an event following a behavior increases the subsequent frequency of the behavior, the event is referred to as a *negative reinforcer.* When a youngster ceases to behave in a disruptive manner following a teacher's yelling at him or her to do so, we say that the youngster has negatively reinforced the teacher's yelling, thus increasing its future likelihood. When the presentation of an event following a behavior decreases its subsequent frequency, the event is referred to as a *punisher.* In the preceding example, the teacher's yelling, which is negatively reinforced by the student's decrease in disruptive behavior, functions as a punishment to the student to the extent that it decreases the likelihood of subsequent student disruptiveness. Another way to decrease the probability of a given behavior is to remove positive reinforcers each time the behavior occurs. Ignoring the behavior or removing the reinforcer of attention (i.e., extinction), physically removing the person from important sources of reinforcement (i.e., time-out), and removing the reinforcer from the person (i.e., response cost) are three means of contingently managing behavior by *removing positive reinforcers.* To repeat, these four groups of techniques—positive reinforcement, negative reinforcement, punishment, and the removal of positive reinforcers—are the core methods of contingency management, from which stem all the specific contingency management techniques next described.

It helps in describing the relationship among these four procedures, as well as their characteristic implementation in classroom and other settings, to point out that they are all means for either presenting or removing positive reinforcers or presenting or removing aversive stimuli. The various procedures for presenting or removing positive reinforcement are by far the more common uses of contingency management in school contexts. We will first examine these two sets of procedures. Procedures for the presentation of aversive stimuli (i.e., punishment) or for their removal (i.e., negative reinforcement) are employed less frequently in school and agency settings, and we will briefly examine them following the discussion of positive reinforcement.

ART's use of contingency management optimally begins with the development of behavioral *rules* to be followed in order to create a safe and effective learning environment in the group. Then necessary behavior-change procedures (the presentation or removal of positive reinforcement or the presentation or removal of aversive stimuli) are applied in order to change undesirable behaviors into desirable behaviors.

Communicating Behavioral Rules

A number of effective "rules for the use of rules" have emerged in the contingency management literature (Greenwood, Hops, Delquadri, & Guild, 1974; Walker, 1979), including the following:

1. Define and communicate rules for trainee behaviors in clear, specific, and especially behavioral terms. As Walker (1979) notes, it is better (more concrete and behavioral) to say, "Raise your hand before asking a question" than "Be considerate of others." Similarly, "Listen carefully to trainer instructions" or "Pay attention to the feedback procedure" are statements more likely to serve as rules that actually find expression in student behavior than the more ambiguous statements "Behave in class" or "Do what you are told."

2. It is more effective to tell trainees what to do, rather than what not to do. This accentuation of the positive, for example, finds expression in rules about taking turns, talking over disagreements, or working quietly, rather than in rules directing students not to jump in, not to fight, or not to speak out.

3. Communicate rules in such a manner that trainees are assisted in memorizing them. Depending on the age of the trainees

and the complexity and difficulty of enacting the rules the trainer is presenting, such memorization aids may include keeping rules short and few in number, repeating the rules several times, and posting the rules in written form where they can be seen readily.

4. Rule adherence is likely to be more effective when trainees have a substantial role in rule development, modification, and implementation. This sense of participation is brought about by explicit trainee involvement in rule development, thorough discussion of rules with the entire group, having selected trainees explain to the group the specific meaning of each rule, and trainee role-playing of the behaviors identified by the rules.

5. In addition to the foregoing, further effective rules for the use of rules are that they be developed at the start of the group; that they be fair, reasonable, and within the trainees' capacity to follow; that all members of the group understand them; and that they be applied equally and fairly to all trainees.

ART group rules developed in this manner enhance the likelihood that the group will be a safe and productive place for its members.

Identifying Positive Reinforcers

Our overall purpose is to substitute appropriate behaviors for inappropriate behaviors by means of skilled management of contingencies. As noted earlier, one major way of doing this is to present positive reinforcement to the trainee following and contingent upon the occurrence of an appropriate behavior. Before discussing procedures for presenting positive reinforcers, however, we must first consider the process of identifying—both for a given youngster and for youngsters in general—events that may in fact function as positive reinforcers.

Teachers and other school-based contingency managers have worked successfully with four types of positive reinforcers: material, social, activity, and token. *Material reinforcers* (sometimes called *tangible reinforcers*) are actual goods or objects presented to the individual contingent upon enactment of appropriate behaviors. One important subcategory of material reinforcement, *primary reinforcement,* occurs when the contingent event presented satisfies a basic biological need. Food is one such primary reinforcer.

Social reinforcers—most often expressed in the form of attention, praise, or approval—are particularly powerful and are frequently used in the ART group. Both schoolhouse and delinquency-facility lore and extensive experimental research testify to the potency of social reinforcement in influencing a broad spectrum of personal and interpersonal behaviors.

Activity reinforcers are those events the youngster freely chooses when an opportunity exists to engage in several different activities. Given freedom to choose, many youngsters watch television rather than complete their homework. The parent who uses this activity reinforcer specifies that the youngster may watch television for a given time period contingent upon the prior completion of homework. Stated otherwise, the opportunity to perform a higher probability behavior (given free choice) can be used as a reinforcer for a lower probability behavior.

Token reinforcers, usually employed when other more easily implemented social reinforcers prove insufficient, are symbolic items or currency (chips, stars, points, etc.) provided to the youngster contingent upon the performance of appropriate or desirable behaviors. Tokens thus obtained are exchangeable for a wide range of material or activity reinforcers. The system by which specific numbers of tokens are contingently gained or lost, and the procedures by which they may be exchanged for backup materials or activity reinforcers, is called a *token economy.*

In making decisions about which type of reinforcer to employ with a given youngster, the trainer must keep in mind that social reinforcement (e.g., attention, praise, approval) is easiest to implement on a continuing basis and is most likely (for reasons discussed in chapter 7, dealing with transfer and maintenance) to lead to enduring behavior change. Thus, it is probably the type of reinforcement the trainer will wish to use most frequently. Unfortunately, in the initial stages of a behavior-change effort—especially when aggressive, disruptive, and other inappropriate behaviors are probably being richly rewarded by the social reinforcement of trainer and peer attention as well as by tangible reinforcers—greater trainer reliance on material and activity reinforcers for desirable behaviors may be necessary. Alternatively, a token reinforcement system may prove most effective as the initial reinforcement strategy. Youngsters' reinforcement preferences change over time, and trainer perspectives of the appropriate reward value of desirable behaviors also change over time; both variables are easily reflected in token-level adjustments. For these and other reasons related to ease of administration and effectiveness of outcome, the skilled contingency manager must be intimately acquainted with the full range of token-economy procedures (see Ayllon & Azrin, 1968; Kazdin, 1975). Again, however, it is crucial to remember that, with few exceptions, use of material, activity, or token reinforcement eventually should give way to use of more "real-lifelike" social reinforcement. Table 6.2 lists specific examples of commonly used material (edible and nonedible), social, activity, and token reinforcers, for use both at school and at home.

Given this wide though nonexhaustive array of potential reinforcers and the fact that almost any event may serve as a reinforcer for one individual but not another, how can the trainer decide which reinforcer(s)

Table 6.2

COMMONLY USED REINFORCERS

Material
- Favorite snack
- Clothes
- Books
- Radio or stereo
- Bicycle
- Own room, telephone, TV
- Watch
- Make-up
- Tapes or CDs
- Jewelry
- Musical instrument

Social
- Smiles
- Hugs
- Attention when talking
- Being asked for opinion
- Winks
- Verbal praise
- Head nods
- Thumbs-up sign

Activity
- Having an extended lunch period
- Participating in school trips
- Being in charge of class discussion
- Serving as hall monitor
- Having a homework pass
- Tutoring another student
- Developing a school radio show
- Being on a sports team
- Being dismissed early from class
- Running errands
- Playing a favorite game
- Having time for a hobby
- Watching films or videotapes
- Listening to CDs or tapes
- Playing an instrument
- Playing a video game
- Having free activity time

Token
- Points or coupons (redeemable for other reinforcers)
- Extra money
- Own checking account
- Allowance
- Gift certificate

are best used with a particular youngster at a given point in time? Most simply, the youngster can be asked which items he or she would like to earn. Often, however, this approach proves insufficient because the youngster is not fully aware of the range of reinforcers available, or, when aware, may discount in advance the possibility that the given reinforcer will actually be forthcoming. When this is the case, other identification procedures must be employed. Carr (1981) and others report three procedures typically used for this purpose.

First, the trainer can often make an accurate determination of whether a given event is in fact functioning as a reinforcer by carefully *observing effects* on the youngster. The event probably is reinforcing if the youngster (a) asks that the event be repeated, (b) seems happy during the event's occurrence, (c) seems unhappy when the event ends, or (d) works in order to earn the event. If any of these reactions is observed, the chances are good that the event is a positive reinforcer and that it can be contingently provided to strengthen appropriate, nonaggressive, or interactive behaviors.

Observing choices can also be helpful. As noted earlier in connection with activity reinforcers, when a youngster is free to choose among several equally available activities, which one he or she chooses and how long he or she engages in the chosen activity are readily observed clues to whether an event is reinforcing.

A few *questionnaires* exist that are effectively used in identifying positive reinforcers. Tharp and Wetzel's (1969) Mediation-Reinforcer Incomplete Blank is one often used for this purpose. It consists of a series of incomplete sentences that the youngster must complete by specifying particular reinforcers: for example, "The thing I like to do best with my mother/father is _____" or "I will do almost anything to get _____." Most of the items help specify not only the nature of the events the youngster perceives as positive reinforcers, but also who functions as a mediator of such reinforcers. This is important information in carrying out a contingency management effort. Going to a ball game may be a powerful reinforcer if one is accompanied by peers, a weak one if accompanied by one's teacher or mother. Praise from a respected teacher may be a potent reinforcing event, whereas the same praise delivered by a peer considered by the youngster to be ignorant makes the praise ineffective. The response format of this questionnaire also asks the youngster to indicate his or her sense of the potency of the reinforcer. Thus, the measure provides a self-report of *which* events are reinforcing for the youngster, when delivered or mediated by *whom*, as well as the youngster's perception of just *how* reinforcing each event is.

A different type of questionnaire-like instrument for identifying positive reinforcers, especially appropriate for younger children and children with limited verbal abilities, is Homme, Csanyi, Gonzales, and Rechs's (1969) Reinforcing Event Menu. This measure is essentially a collection of pictures showing a variety of material and activity reinforcers as well as pictures of potential reinforcement mediators. It is the youngster's task to select from these pictures those reinforcers for which he or she would most like to work.

This process of identifying positive reinforcers for given youngsters completes the series of steps a trainer must undertake prior to actually presenting such events contingently upon the occurrence of appropriate behaviors.

Presenting Positive Reinforcers

The basic principle of contingency management is that the presentation of a reinforcing event contingent upon the occurrence of a given behavior functions to increase the likelihood of the reoccurrence of that behavior. Research demonstrates a substantial number of considerations that influence the success of this reinforcement effort and that are thus optimally reflected in the actual presentation of reinforcers.

Contingency

Although this rule for reinforcer presentation may seem obvious at this point, it is one that is sometimes forgotten or inadequately implemented. The connection between the desirable behavior and the subsequent provision of reward must be made explicit to the youngster. As is true for all aspects of the contingency management effort, this description must be behaviorally specific. Descriptions such as "good behavior," "being a good boy or girl," "being well-behaved," or the like are ambiguous and ineffective.

Immediacy

Related to the communication of the reinforcement's contingency is the fact that the more immediately the reinforcer follows the desirable behavior, the more likely is its effectiveness. Not only does rapid reinforcement augment the message that the immediately preceding behavior is desirable, but delayed reinforcer presentation increases the risk that a sequence will occur of *A* (desirable behavior), *B* (undesirable behavior), and *C* (reinforcement for *A* that in actuality reinforces *B*).

Consistency

The effects of positive reinforcement on behavior are usually gradual, not dramatic, working slowly to strengthen behavior over a period of time. Thus, it is important that positive reinforcement be presented consistently. Consistency here means not only that the trainer must be consistent, but also that the trainer must make certain, as best he or she can, that the reinforcement delivery efforts are matched by similar efforts from as many other important people in the youngster's life as possible. This means that, when the youngster enacts the behavior to be reinforced—on the unit in a delinquency facility in the presence of staff other than the trainers, in school in the presence of other teachers, at home in the presence of parents or siblings, or at play in the presence of peers—such reinforcement will be forthcoming.

Frequency

When first establishing a new behavior, the trainer seeks to reinforce all or almost all instances of that behavior. This high frequency of reinforcement is necessary initially to establish the behavior in the individual's behavioral repertoire. Once it seems clear that the behavior has actually been acquired, it is appropriate for the trainer to thin the reinforcement, decreasing the presentation of reinforcement so that only some of the youngster's desirable behaviors are followed by reinforcement. This thinner reinforcement schedule, known as *partial reinforcement,* is an important contribution to the continued likelihood of the appropriate behavior because such a schedule closely parallels the sometimes reinforcing/sometimes not reaction the youngster's appropriate behavior will elicit in other settings from other people. Partial reinforcement of the youngster's appropriate behaviors may be on a fixed time schedule (e.g., at the end of each ART session), on a fixed number of response schedule (e.g., every fifth instance of the appropriate behavior), or on variable time or number of response schedules. In any event, the basic strategy for reinforcement frequency remains a rich level for initial learning and partial reinforcement to sustain performance.

Amount

In the preceding discussion of frequency of reinforcement, we began to distinguish between learning (i.e., acquiring knowledge about how to perform new behaviors) and actual performance (i.e., overtly using these behaviors). The amount of reinforcement provided influences performance much more than learning. Youngsters learn new appropriate behaviors in the same amount of time for a small reward as for a large reward, but they are more likely to perform the behaviors on a continuing basis when large rewards are involved. Yet rewards can be too large, causing a *satiation effect* in which the youngster loses interest in the reinforcement because it is "too much of a good thing." Or rewards can be too small: too little time on the playground, too few tokens, too thin a social reinforcement schedule. The optimal amount can be determined empirically. If a youngster has in the past worked energetically to obtain a particular reinforcer but gradually slacks off and seems to lose interest in obtaining it, a satiation effect has probably occurred, and the amount of reinforcement should be reduced. On the other hand, if a youngster seems unwilling to work for a reinforcer believed desirable, it can be given once or twice for free—that is, not contingent on a specific desirable behavior. If the youngster seems to enjoy the reinforcer and even wants more of the same, the amount used may have been too little. The amount can be increased and made contingent; observations will then show whether it is yielding the desired behavior modification effect. If so, the amount of reinforcement offered is appropriate.

Variety

As noted, reinforcement satiation may occur as a result of an excessive amount of reinforcement. A parallel type of satiation of reinforcement occurs when the trainer uses the same approving phrase or other reward over and over again. Youngsters may perceive such reinforcement as mechanical, and they may thus lose interest in or decrease responsiveness to it. By varying the content of the reinforcer, the trainer can maintain its potency. Thus, instead of repeating "Nice job" four or five times, using a mix of comments (e.g., "I'm really proud of you," "You're certainly doing fine," or "Well done") is more likely to yield a sustained effect.

Pairing with praise

Earlier we emphasized that social reinforcement is most germane to enduring behavioral change, though there are circumstances under which an emphasis upon material, activity, or token reinforcers is (at least initially) more appropriate. To aid in the movement toward social reinforcement, the trainer should pair all presentations of material, activity, or token rewards with some expression of social reinforcement:

an approving comment, a pat on the back, a wink, a smile, and so forth. A major benefit of this tactic is noted by Walker (1979):

By virtue of being consistently paired with reinforcement delivery, praise can take on the reinforcing properties of the actual reinforcer(s) used. This is especially important since teacher praise is not always initially effective with many deviant children. By systematically increasing the incentive value of praise through pairing, the teacher is in a position to gradually reduce the frequency of [material, activity, or token] reinforcement and to substitute praise. After systematic pairing, the teacher's praise may be much more effective in maintaining the child's appropriate behavior. (p. 108)

The aforementioned rules for maximizing the effectiveness of the presentation of positive reinforcement are all essentially remedial in nature. They are efforts to substitute appropriate prosocial behaviors for aggressive, disruptive, antisocial, withdrawal, or asocial behaviors that are already present in specific youngsters. It is worth noting, however, that the presentation of positive reinforcement may also be used for preventive purposes. Sarason, Glaser, and Fargo (1972) urge teachers to present positive reinforcement openly so the entire class is aware of it. As they comment:

Positive reinforcement for productive activity for the whole group is a powerful preventive technique. It can eliminate or reduce the great majority of behavior problems in classrooms. Try to praise the children who are paying attention. Attend to those who are sitting in their seats, doing their work in a nondisruptive manner. "That's right, John, you're doing a good job." "You watched the board all the time I was presenting the problem. That's paying attention." . . . These responses not only reinforce the child to whom they are directed, but they also help to provide the rest of the class with an explicit idea of what you mean by paying attention and working hard. Young children especially . . . learn to model their actions after the positive examples established and noted by the teacher. (p. 18)

Open attempts to "catch them being good" are strongly recommended for the ART group.

Removing Positive Reinforcers

The ART trainer's behavior modification goal with youngsters displaying aggressive or other problematic behaviors is, in a general sense, twofold. Both sides of the behavioral coin—appropriate and inappropriate, prosocial and antisocial, desirable and undesirable—must be given attention. In a proper behavior-change effort, procedures are simultaneously or sequentially employed to reduce and eliminate the inappropriate, antisocial, or undesirable components of a youngster's behavioral repertoire and to increase the quality and frequency of appropriate, prosocial, or desirable components. This latter task is served primarily by the direct teaching of prosocial behaviors via Skillstreaming and by the contingent presentation of positive reinforcement following such behaviors' occurrence. Conversely, the contingent removal of positive reinforcement in response to aggressive, disruptive, or similar behaviors is—along with participation in the Anger Control Training component of ART—the major behavior modification strategy for reducing or eliminating these behaviors. Therefore, in conjunction with the procedures discussed previously for presenting positive reinforcement, the trainer should also simultaneously or consecutively employ one or more of the following techniques for removing positive reinforcement.

Extinction

Extinction is the withdrawal or removal of positive reinforcement for aggressive or other undesirable behaviors that have been either deliberately or inadvertently reinforced in the past. This technique can be thought of as the procedure of choice with milder forms of aggression (e.g., sarcasm, put-downs, or other forms of low-level verbal aggression). Determining when the use of extinction is appropriate is, of course, in part a function of each trainer's guiding group management philosophy and tolerance for deviance. Each trainer must decide individually the range of undesirable behaviors that can be safely ignored. Taking a rather conservative stance, Walker (1979) suggests that extinction "should be applied only to those inappropriate behaviors that are minimally disruptive to classroom atmosphere" (p. 40). Others are somewhat more liberal in its application (e.g., Carr, 1981). In any event, it is clear that the first step in applying extinction is knowing when to use it.

As noted earlier, attempts to reduce inappropriate behavior by withdrawing reinforcement should always be accompanied by efforts to increase appropriate behavior by providing reinforcement. This combination of efforts succeeds especially well when the appropriate and inappropriate behaviors involved are opposite from, or at least incompatible with, each other (e.g., reward in-seat behavior, ignore out-of-seat behavior; reward talking at a conversational level, ignore yelling).

The reinforcers maintaining inappropriate behaviors are the ones to be withheld. The trainer discerns what the youngster is working for; what payoffs are involved; and what reinforcers are being sought or earned by aggression, disruptiveness, and similar behaviors. Very often, the answer is attention. Laughing, looking, staring, yelling at, talking to, or turning toward are common trainer and peer reactions to a youngster's aggression. The withdrawal of such positive social reinforcement by ignoring the behaviors (by turning away and not yelling, talking, or laughing at the perpetrator) are the teacher and peer behaviors that effect extinction. Ignoring someone who would normally receive one's attention is itself a talent, as the following guidelines for using extinction illustrate (Carr, 1981):

1. Do not comment to the child that you are ignoring him or her. Long (or even short) explanations provided to youngsters about why trainers, peers, or others are not attending to given behaviors provide precisely the type of social reinforcement that extinction is designed to withdraw. Ignoring the behavior simply occurs with no forewarning, introduction, or prior explanation.

2. Do not look away suddenly when the child behaves aggressively or inappropriately. Jerking one's head away suddenly so as not to see the continuation of the aggressive behavior, or otherwise behaving abruptly, may communicate the message "I really noticed and was impelled to action by your behavior," the exact opposite of an extinction message. As Carr recommends, "It is best to ignore the behavior by reacting to it in a matter of fact way by continuing natural ongoing activities" (p. 38).

3. Protect the victims of aggression. If one youngster actually strikes another, the trainer must intervene. One may do so without subverting the extinction effort by providing the victim with attention, concern, and interest and by ignoring the perpetrator of the aggression.

As is true for the provision of reinforcement, its removal must be consistent. Within a given ART group, this rule of consistency means that the trainer and trainees must act in concert and that the trainer must be consistent across time. Within a given school, agency, or institution, consistency means that, to the degree possible, all trainers working with a given youngster must strive to ignore the same inappropriate behaviors. In addition, to avoid the youngster's making a type of "I can't act up here, but I can out there" discrimination, parent conferences should be held to bring parents, siblings, and other significant real-world figures in the youngster's life into the extinction effort. As Karoly and Steffen (1980) note, when consistency on nonattending is not reached, the aggressive behavior is intermittently or partially reinforced, a circumstance that leads to its becoming highly resistant to extinction.

Aggressive behaviors often have a long history of positive reinforcement and, especially if much of that history is one of intermittent reinforcement, efforts to undo them must be sustained. Trainer persistence in this regard usually succeeds. There are, however, two types of events to keep in mind when judging the effectiveness of extinction efforts. The first is what is known as the *extinction burst*. When extinction is first introduced, it is not uncommon for the rate or intensity of the aggressive behavior to increase sharply before it begins its more gradual decline toward a zero level. It is important that the trainer persist during this short detour. Its meaning, in fact, is that extinction is beginning to work. In addition, inappropriate behaviors that are successfully extinguished reappear occasionally for reasons difficult to determine. Like the extinction burst, this *spontaneous recovery* is transitory and disappears if the trainer persists in the extinction effort.

Time-out

In time-out, a youngster who engages in aggressive or other inappropriate behaviors is physically removed from all sources of reinforcement for a specified time period. As with extinction, the purpose of time-out is to reduce the (undesirable) behavior that immediately precedes it and on which its use is contingent. It differs from extinction in that extinction involves removing reinforcement from the perpetrator, whereas time-out usually involves removing the perpetrator from the reinforcing situation.

In school-based and facility-based practice, time-out typically takes three forms. *Isolation time-out,* the most common form, requires the youngster to be physically removed from the classroom unit or other location to a time-out room according to specific procedures (described later in this section). *Exclusion time-out* is somewhat less restrictive but also involves physically removing the youngster from sources of reinforcement. Here the youngster is required to go to a corner of the room in which he or she acted out and perhaps to sit in a "quiet chair" (Firestone, 1976), which is sometimes behind a screen. The youngster is not removed from the classroom but is excluded from ongoing activities for a specified time period. *Nonexclusion time-out* (also called *contingent observation*), the least restrictive time-out variant, requires the youngster to sit and watch on the periphery of class or group activities, to observe the appropriate behaviors of other youngsters. This variant combines time-out with modeling opportunities and thus may be the preferred approach for the ART group. It essentially excludes the youngster from a participant role for a specified time period while leaving intact the opportunity to function as an observer. All three of these variants of time-out may be employed effectively to deal with problematic behavior in the ART group.

Extinction, it will be recalled, is the recommended procedure for those aggressive or otherwise undesirable behaviors that can be safely ignored. Behaviors potentially injurious to other youngsters require a more active trainer response, possibly time-out. In the case of many youngsters at the middle school and high school levels, or in delinquency facilities, physical removal by the trainer may not be wise, appropriate, or even possible. For such youngsters, procedures other than extinction or time-out, discussed later in this chapter, are to be employed. Thus, to reflect both the potential injuriousness of the youngster's behavior and the youngster's age and associated physical status, time-out is recommended as the technique of choice for youngsters ages 2 to 12 years who are displaying high rates of potentially dangerous, aggressive, or other disruptive behaviors. It is also the procedure to use for less severe forms of problematic behavior, when the combination of extinction and positive reinforcement for other, more positive behaviors has been attempted and failed.

As is the case for extinction, positive reinforcement for appropriate behaviors accompanies time-out. When possible, the behaviors positively reinforced should be opposite to, or at least incompatible with, those for which the time-out procedure is instituted. Furthermore, there is an additional basis for recommending the combined use of these two techniques. As Carr (1981) observes:

> Although one important reason for using positive reinforcement is to strengthen nonaggressive behaviors to the point where they replace

aggressive behaviors, there is a second reason for using reinforcement procedures. If extensive use of positive reinforcement is made, then time out will become all the more aversive since it would involve the temporary termination of a rich diversity of positive reinforcers. In this sense, then, the use of positive reinforcement helps to enhance the effectiveness of the time out procedure. (pp. 41–42)

The time-out setting is also of concern. The general principles pertaining to an isolation time-out, next discussed, also pertain to exclusion and nonexclusion time-out environments. Essentially, two general principles are involved. The first concerns the youngster's health and safety. The time-out setting should be a small, well-lit, and well-ventilated room that provides a place for the youngster to sit. The second principle reflects the fact that the central quality of this procedure is time out from positive reinforcement. Time-out must be a boring environment, with all reinforcers removed. There should be no distracting objects or opportunities—no television, radio, books, posters, people, windows to look out of, sounds to overhear, or other obvious or not-so-obvious potential reinforcers. A barren isolation area is the optimal time-out environment.

A number of actions can be taken by the teacher when initiating time-out to increase the likelihood of its effectiveness. As with the immediate presentation of positive reinforcement contingent upon appropriate behaviors, time-out is optimally instituted immediately following the aggressive or other behavior one seeks to modify. Having earlier explained to the target youngster the nature of time-out, as well as when and why it will be used, the teacher initiates the procedure in a more or less automatic manner—that is, in a manner that minimizes social reinforcement. Concretely, this means placing the youngster in time-out without a lengthy explanation but with a brief, matter-of-fact description of the precipitating behaviors. This process is best conducted without anger and, when possible, without physically removing the youngster from the classroom or other setting in which ART is being conducted. To minimize reinforcement of aggression during this process, it is also best if the distance between training room and time-out area is small: The shorter the distance and the briefer the transportation time, the less opportunity exists for inadvertent social reinforcement by the trainer. In addition to these considerations, the effectiveness of time-out is further enhanced by its consistent application, when appropriate, by the same trainer on other occasions as well as by other trainers. Immediacy, consistency, and various actions aimed at minimizing trainer reinforcement of inappropriate behavior augment the effectiveness of time-out.

The skilled contingency manager must deal with two questions during a youngster's period in time-out: What is the youngster doing? and How long should time out last? Monitoring helps the trainer make certain that the time-out experience is not in fact functioning as a pleasant, positively reinforcing one for a given youngster. For example, rather than serve as a removal from positive reinforcement, time-out may in reality be a removal from an aversive situation (negative reinforcement) if the trainer institutes it at a time when a youngster is in an unpleasant situation that or she would prefer to avoid or escape. If monitoring reveals that the youngster is singing or playing enjoyable games, the effectiveness of time-out is lessened. Unless the situation can be made essentially nonreinforcing, a different behavioral intervention may be required.

With regard to duration, most successful time-out implementations are from 5 to 20 minutes long, with some preference for the shorter durations in this range. When experimenting to find the optimal duration for any given youngster, it is best, as White, Nielson, and Johnson (1972) show, to begin with a short duration (e.g., 3 to 5 minutes) and to lengthen the time until an effective span is identified, rather than to shorten an initially lengthier span. This latter approach also presents the risk of introducing an event experienced as positive reinforcement by the youngster when the intention is quite the opposite.

We noted earlier in connection with extinction that withdrawal of positive reinforcement sometimes leads to an extinction burst, in which more intense or more frequent aggressiveness or other problem behaviors appear before they begin to subside. This same pattern is evident with withdrawal from positive reinforcement—that is, time-out. The first few times a youngster is placed in time-out, what might be termed a *time-out burst* of heightened aggression or other problem behavior may occur. These outbursts usually subside, especially if the trainer adds to the duration of the time-out span the same number of minutes that the outburst lasts.

Whether the release from time-out is on schedule or is delayed for the reason just specified, it should be conducted in a matter-of-fact manner, and the youngster quickly returned to regular ART activities. Lengthy trainer explanations or moralizing at this point are tactically erroneous provisions of positive reinforcement that communicate to the youngster that acting out in the classroom brings a short period of removal from reinforcement and then a (probably lengthier) period of undivided trainer attention.

Response cost

Response cost involves the removal of previously acquired reinforcers contingent upon and in order to reduce future instances of the occurrence of inappropriate behaviors. These reinforcers may be earned, as when the use of response-cost procedures is a component of a token-reinforcement system, or they may be provided, as is the case with a freestanding response-cost system. In either instance, reinforcers are removed (the cost) whenever previously targeted undesirable behaviors occur (the response).

Extinction and time-out sometimes prove insufficient for severely aggressive adolescents, even when combined with a trainer's praise or other reinforcement for appropriate behaviors. In a number of instances, response-cost procedures—especially when combined with positive reinforcement (via a token economy) for desirable prosocial behaviors—prove effective.

We will not detail here the rules for the effective implementation of a token-economy system because they overlap considerably with rules delineated earlier in this chapter for the provision of nontoken positive reinforcers. More detailed description of token-economy procedures can be found in Ayllon and Azrin (1968), Kazdin (1975), and Walker (1979). We will specify, however, those rules for removing token or nontoken reinforcement that constitute the response-cost procedure. Of primary consideration when using this procedure, as well as every other contingency management procedure, is for the trainer to think, plan, and act "behaviorally." When targeting inappropriate behaviors (whose occurrences cost tokens, points, privileges, or other commodities), the trainer must identify specific overt acts, not describe broad characterological or behavioral categories. Thus "is aggressive" (a characterological observation) and "acts withdrawn" (a broad behavioral observation) are too vague, but "swears, makes threats, raises voice, raises hands, pushes group mates, sits by self" are all useful specifications.

As is the case for the amount, level, or rate of positive reinforcement to be provided contingent upon desirable behaviors, the specific cost contingent upon undesirable behaviors must be determined—whether such cost is a finite number of tokens or points, a finite amount of schoolyard time, or another outcome. Cost setting is a crucial determinant of the success or failure of this approach. For example, Carr (1981) notes that

> the magnitude of response costs must be carefully controlled. If fines are too large, bankruptcy will ensue and the child will be unable to purchase any back-up reinforcers. Further, if the child develops too large a deficit, he may adapt an attitude of "what do I have to lose?" and engage in considerable misbehavior. On the other hand, if the fines are too small, the child will be able to negate his loss easily by performing any of a variety of appropriate behaviors. (p. 52)

Yet other aspects of response-cost implementation make demands on the trainer's skills as a creative economist. The relationship of points or other reinforcers to earn to those that can be lost; the relationship of cost to the severity of inappropriate behavior; and a host of similar marketing, pricing, and, ultimately, motivational considerations come into play. This is especially true if the trainer is not only the implementer of the response-cost system, but also its originator, planner, and monitor. Once the trainer has decided the specific token, point, or privilege value of the appropriate and inappropriate behaviors relevant to the effective management of the ART group, it is necessary to communicate these values to the participating trainees.

ART group members must know in advance what earnings and losses are contingent upon what desirable and undesirable behaviors; they must also have ongoing knowledge of their own earning status. Walker (1995) has developed a simple, easily used delivery/feedback system that gives each youngster ongoing cumulative information indicating (a) when response cost or earnings are applied; (b) to which specific behaviors response cost or earnings are applied; and (c) how many points are lost or earned as a result.

Finally, as is true for the other major procedures for the removal of positive reinforcement (extinction and time-out), response-cost procedures require the trainer to be (a) *consistent* in the application of procedures across students and across time for each student; (b) *immediate* in delivering contingent costs after the inappropriate behavior occurs; and (c) *impartial* in ensuring that the instance of inappropriate behavior leads to an *inevitable* instance of response cost, with an absolute minimum of exceptions.

Punishment and Negative Reinforcement

The two contingency management approaches in this section, punishment and negative reinforcement, involve the presentation and removal of aversive stimuli, respectively. In our view, these procedures are generally less recommendable than procedures for presenting and removing positive reinforcement. Our disinclination to recommend and use these procedures is explained in the following discussion.

Punishment

Punishment is the presentation of an aversive stimulus contingent upon the performance of a given behavior and usually intended to decrease the likelihood of future occurrences of that behavior. Two of the major forms that punishment takes in U.S. classrooms and delinquency centers are verbal punishment (i.e., reprimands) and corporal punishment (i.e., paddling, spanking, slapping). As noted in chapter 1, the effectiveness of these and other forms of punishment in altering inappropriate behaviors such as aggression has been shown to be a function of several factors: likelihood, consistency, immediacy, duration, severity, possibility for escape or avoidance, availability of alternative routes to goal, level of instigation to aggression, level of reward for aggression, and characteristics of the prohibiting agents. Punishment is more likely to lead to behavior-change consequences the more certain its application, the more consistently and rapidly it is applied, the longer and more intense its quality, the less the likelihood that it can be avoided, the more available are alternative means to goal satisfaction, the lower the level of instigation to or reward for aggression, and the more potent as a contingency manager the prohibiting agent.

Clearly, several factors determine the effect of an aversive stimulus on a youngster's behavior. But let us assume an instance in which these determinants combine to yield a substantial impact. What, ideally, can we hope the effect of punishment on aggression or other undesirable behavior will be? A reprimand or a paddling does not teach new behaviors. If the youngster is deficient in the ability to ask rather than take, request rather than command, and negotiate rather than strike out, all the trainer's scolding, scowling, and spanking will not teach the youngster desirable alternative behaviors.

Most investigators report the main effect of punishment to be a temporary suppression of inappropriate behaviors. We appreciate the potential value of temporary suppression to trainers who seek an environment in which training time exceeds discipline time; however, it is common for trainers to punish the same youngsters over and over again for the same inappropriate behaviors. Therefore, if used at all, punishment must be combined with efforts to instruct the youngster in those behaviors in which he or she is deficient. When the youngster possesses appropriate behaviors but is not displaying them, trainer use of punishment is optimally combined with any of the other procedures described earlier for the systematic presentation of positive reinforcement. In short, the application of punishment techniques must always be combined with a procedure for strengthening appropriate alternative behaviors, whether these behaviors are absent, weak, or merely unused.

In part because of this temporary effect, but also for several even more consequential reasons, a number of contingency management researchers have assumed an antipunishment stance, seeing little place for punishment in the behavior modification effort. This view corresponds to punishment research that demonstrates such undesirable side effects of punishment as withdrawal from social contact, counteraggression toward the punisher, modeling of punishing behavior, disruption of social relationships, failure of effects to generalize, selective avoidance (refraining from inappropriate behaviors only when under surveillance), and stigmatizing labeling effects (Azrin & Holz, 1966; Bandura, 1973; Sobsey, 1990).

An alternative, propunishment view does exist. It is less widespread and more controversial, but it too makes its case based upon empirical evidence. These investigators hold that there are numerous favorable effects of punishment: rapid and dependable reduction of inappropriate behaviors; the consequent opening up of new sources of positive reinforcement; the possibility of complete suppression of inappropriate behaviors; increased social and emotional, imitation, and discrimination learning; and other potential positive outcomes (Axelrod & Apsche, 1982; Newsom, Favell, & Rincover, 1982; Van Houten, 1982; Walker, 1995).

The evidence is clearly not all in. Data are incomplete on which punishments to use with which youngsters under which circumstances. At present, decisions regarding the use in ART of aversive stimuli to alter inappropriate behaviors must derive from partial data and each trainer's carefully considered ethical beliefs regarding the relative costs and benefits of employing punishment procedures. Our own weighing of relevant data and ethical considerations leads to our stance favoring ART's selective use of verbal punishment techniques, such as reprimands. We reject under all circumstances the use of physical punishment techniques.

Negative reinforcement

Negative reinforcement is the final contingency management procedure we will consider, and our consideration of it will be brief. As defined earlier, negative reinforcement is the removal of aversive stimuli contingent upon the occurrence of desirable behaviors. Negative reinforcement is seldom used as a behavior modification approach in classroom or delinquency facility contexts. The exception to this rule is the manner in which youngsters are contingently released from time-out (an aversive environment), depending upon such desirable behaviors as quietness and calmness. Such release serves as negative reinforcement for these behaviors. Unfortunately, negative reinforcement often appears in classroom and other contexts to less constructive effect. Consider a teacher-student interaction in which the student behaves disruptively (shouts, swears, fights), the teacher responds with anger and physical punishment toward the youngster, and the punishment brings about a temporary suppression of the youngster's disruptiveness. The decrease in the student's disruptiveness may be viewed as a decrease in aversive stimulation experienced by the teacher, which functions to negatively reinforce the immediately preceding teacher behavior (in this case, corporal punishment). The net effect of this sequence is to increase the likelihood of the teacher's use of corporal punishment. Analogous sequences may occur and function to increase the likelihood of other ineffective or inappropriate teacher behaviors.

Other Behavior Modification Procedures

In addition to the various procedures previously examined for the presentation or removal of positive reinforcement or aversive stimuli, two other behavior modification procedures are available for ART use. These approaches—overcorrection and contingency contracting—do not rely upon the management of contingencies.

Overcorrection

Overcorrection is a behavior modification approach developed by Foxx and Azrin (1973) for those circumstances when extinction, time-out, and response cost either fail or cannot be used and when few alternative appropriate behaviors are available to reinforce. Overcorrection is a two-part procedure, having both restitutional and positive practice components. The restitutional aspect requires the target individual to return the behavioral setting (e.g., the classroom, the center's cafeteria, the institution's gymnasium) to its status prior to disruption or better. Thus, objects broken by an angry youngster must be repaired, the unit mates or classmates struck in anger apologized to, the papers scattered across the room picked up. Further, the positive practice component of overcorrection requires that the disruptive youngster then, in the specific examples just cited, be made to repair objects broken by others, apologize to peers who witnessed the unit mates or classmates being struck, or clean up the rest of the room (including areas not disturbed by the target youngster). It is clear that the restitution and positive practice requirements may serve both a punitive and an instructional function.

Contingency contracting

A contingency contract is a written agreement between a trainer and trainee. It is a document each signs that specifies, in detailed behavioral terms, desirable trainee behaviors and their positive consequences, as well as undesirable trainee behaviors and their undesirable consequences. As Homme et al. (1969) have specified in their description of this proce-dure, such contracts will more reliably lead to desirable trainee behaviors when the contract payoff is immediate; approximations to the desirable behavior are rewarded; the contract rewards accomplishment rather than obedience; accomplishment precedes reward; and the contract is fair, clear, honest, positive, and systematically implemented.

Capturing Teachable Moments

We have examined in detail two strategies for the successful management of trainee resistance in ART groups. The first involves using diagnosis of the cause of misbehavior to develop plans to address the problems—for example, problems due to complexity are managed with simplification, those due to threat with threat-reduction steps, and so forth. The second approach is modification of trainees' problematic behaviors via the pro-vision and withdrawal of reinforcement contingent upon the presence or absence of appropriate or inappropriate behaviors. The third strategy employs Skillstreaming to manage ART.

The problematic behaviors that are the concern of this chapter—minimal participation, disruptiveness, digression, bullying, bizarre behavior, and so forth—can each be viewed as a behavioral excess to be reduced by one or more of the means already examined. Each such behavior, however, can also be construed as a behavioral deficiency (e.g., too much monopolizing is too little listening to others, too much bullying is too little empathy directed toward others, etc.). Thus, an additional means for reducing problem behaviors is to replace them with desirable behaviors. The Skillstreaming curriculum is made up of just such alternatives. These skills may be taught as previously scheduled, as part of regular sessions, or at opportune times (teachable moments) that help trainees reduce resistance and open up to learning yet other skills.

The following dialogue illustrates what is meant by capturing a teachable moment. The situation is as follows: The trainers are conducting the session-opening homework report segment of their Skillstreaming meeting. The skill role-played the previous session, on which homework is to be reported, is Expressing Affection. In her previous role-playing of this skill, one group member, Jane, rehearsed with another member skill steps involving approaching a male student in another class to invite him to an upcoming party.

Trainer: Jane, how did your homework work out? Did you go to Lee and ask him to go to that Saturday party with you?

Jane: No, I didn't. I didn't say anything to Lee, and I want you to know that I'm really pissed off today.

Trainer: Oh, what's going on?

Jane: You said this group was a confidential group, that one of our rules is whatever happens in the group stays in the group. Somebody told Lee that I think he's cute. It really makes me mad as hell and embarrassed as hell. I don't know who told him, but right after the meeting last week I saw Jennifer go over to Lee and say something. I think she told him, and I'm going to smack her in the face right now. (*Stands up and begins moving toward Jennifer.*)

It is the trainer's responsibility at this point to do two things. The first is to make clear that Jane will not be permitted to physically harm Jennifer and to take immediate, proper steps to make sure such containment occurs. We have described elsewhere a training program for teachers and other school personnel in which skills for the safe and rapid management of such confrontations may be learned (Goldstein et al., 1995).

The trainer's second responsibility, to be implemented once safety is assured, is to capture the opportunity presented by the confrontation and turn it into a teaching experience. The trainee, Jane, is in the process of resolving an anger-arousing experience by attacking Jennifer, whom she believes is its source. The trainer can seize the chance provided here to teach Jane an alternative, more prosocially skilled way of handling the same situation. As a bonus, the situation also presents the opportunity to accomplish the same prosocial skill training goal for Jennifer, the one Jane wants to attack.

> Trainer: Jane, we are not going to permit you to hit Jennifer, but I know you're really angry. I think there are better ways to express how you feel. Do you remember about three sessions back we learned the skill Standing Up for Your Rights? As I recall, you did a pretty good job role-playing it, but your homework on it with your father was a bit of a problem. Remember? I'd like you to practice the skill right now with Jennifer. Here's the skill card on it. Rather than hit her, let her know what you think and feel by acting out these steps.
>
> Jennifer, you can see that Jane is really angry with you. She's going to say something to you about her suspicion that you spoke to Lee about what happened in here. You might get angry back at her, I don't know, but I want you to respond to her with a skill we haven't learned yet. It's called Dealing with an Accusation. Here is the skill card for it. Got it? Jane, you use this skill; Jennifer, you use the other one. Let's try it.

ART's skill curriculum is more readily learned by youngsters in need of such training if their motivation for attendance and participation is high and their resistance to such involvement is low. In the present chapter we have examined a number of procedures for enhancing the former and reducing the latter. Which particular means of increasing motivation and resolving resistance are optimal for any given ART group varies as a function of trainer, trainee, and setting characteristics. We urge trainers to experiment in this regard. The pool of methods we have described captures, we believe, the best in available group management technology. Their trial use in various combinations and sequences will enable trainers to determine which means, used in which sequence, are most effective.

CHAPTER SEVEN

Enhancing Generalization of Performance

As the behavior modification and social skills movements mature and relevant evidence regarding their effectiveness accumulates, it becomes clear that, whereas the acquisition of new behaviors is a reliable finding across both training methods and populations, generalization is another matter. Both generalization to new settings (transfer) and over time (maintenance) are reported to occur in only a minority of training outcomes. In this chapter, we examine the alternative approaches that have been taken to enhance generalization. We also propose that embedding and delivering Aggression Replacement Training within an even more comprehensive psychoeducational curriculum—namely, the Prepare Curriculum (Goldstein, 1988)—has the potential to maximize both transfer and maintenance of acquired skills.

APPROACHES TO ENHANCE GENERALIZATION

Interventions as Inoculations

Many traditional interventions reflect a core belief in personality change as both target and outcome in treatment. Such interventions express a strong tendency to ignore environmental influences on behavior, viewing successful intervention as a sort of psychological inoculation. Positive changes purported to take place within the individual's personality structure are believed to help the client deal effectively with problematic events wherever and whenever they occur. That is, transfer and maintenance are viewed as automatically occurring processes. With reference to the prevailing psychoanalytic view on this matter, Ford and Urban (1963) note:

> If the patient's behavior toward the therapist is modified, the changes are expected to transfer automatically to other situations. The conflicts involved in the neurosis all become directed

toward the therapist during the "transference neurosis." They are not situation-specific. They are responses looking for an object to happen to. Thus, if they are changed while they are occurring in relation to the therapist, they will be permanently changed, and can no longer attach themselves to any object in their old form. No special procedures are necessary to facilitate the transfer from the therapist to other situations if the therapist has successfully resolved the transference pattern of behavior. (p. 173)

Such purported automatic maintenance and transfer, variously explained, are also characteristic of the therapeutic positions of Adler (1924), Horney (1939), Rank (1945), Rogers (1951), and Sullivan (1953). In each instance, the view put forth is that, when the therapeutic process results in positive intrapsychic changes in the patient, the patient is able to apply these changes where and when needed in the real-life environment. As Ford and Urban (1963) comment further, Rogers, like Freud,

assumes that changes in behaviors outside of the therapy interview will follow automatically upon changes in the self-evaluative thoughts and associated emotions during the therapy hour. Changes in the self-evaluative thoughts and their emotional concomitants result in reduced anxiety, improved discrimination among situational events and responses, more accurate symbolization of them, and greater confidence in one's own decisions. These provide the conditions from which more appropriate instrumental and interpersonal responses will naturally grow. (p. 435)

This intervention-as-inoculation perspective was widespread among approaches to psychological change throughout the 1950s. No call was made for the development of purposeful means for the enhancement of transfer and maintenance because these outcomes were held to occur inexorably as a consequence of within-treatment gains.

Train and Hope

Psychotherapy research as a viable enterprise began in the 1950s and grew in both quantity and scope during the 1960s and 1970s. Much of the outcome research conducted during this time included systematic follow-up probes, which sought to ascertain whether gains evident at the termination of formal intervention had generalized across settings and/or time. Stokes and Baer (1977) describe this phase as one in which transfer and maintenance were hoped for and noted but not pursued. They comment as follows:

> Studies that are examples of Train and Hope across time are those in which there was a change from the intervention procedures, either to a less intensive but procedurally different program, or to no program or no specifically defined program. Data or anecdotal observations were reported concerning the maintenance of the original behavior change over the specified time intervening between the termination of the formal program and the post-checks. (p. 351)

The overwhelming result of these many investigations was that, much more often than not, transfer and maintenance of intervention gains did not occur. Treatment and training did not often serve as an inoculation, gains did not persist automatically, transfer and maintenance did not necessarily follow from the initial training and the hoped-for generalization of its effects (Goldstein & Kanfer, 1979; Keeley, Shemberg, & Carbonell, 1976). As a result, observers concluded that transfer and maintenance must be actively sought. In fact, the failure of the inoculation model, as revealed by the evidence accumulated during the train-and-hope phase, led to a third phase of concern with generalization—the energetic development, evaluation, and use of a number of procedures explicitly designed to enhance transfer and maintenance of intervention gains.

Development of Transfer and Maintenance Enhancers

The early call from us and others for the development of transfer and maintenance enhancers also made explicit the belief that the enhancement that might result would have its roots in the empirical literature on learning and its transfer:

> A different assumption regarding response maintenance and transfer of therapeutic gains has in recent years begun to emerge in the psychotherapy research literature, especially that devoted to the outcome of behavior modification interventions. This assumption also rests on the belief that maintenance and transfer of therapeutic gain are not common events but, instead of positing that they should occur via an automatic process whose instigation lies within the procedures of the therapy itself, the position taken is that new maintenance-enhancing and transfer-enhancing techniques must be developed and purposefully and

systematically incorporated into the ongoing treatment process. Thus, not satisfied that "behaviors usually extinguish when a program is withdrawn" (Kazdin, 1975, p. 213), or that "removal of the contingencies usually results in a decline of performance to or near baseline levels" (Kazdin, 1975, p. 215), a number of therapy practitioners and researchers are actively seeking to identify, evaluate, and incorporate into ongoing treatment a series of procedures explicitly designed to enhance the level of transfer which ensues. As we have stated elsewhere, the starting point in this search for effective gain maintenance and transfer-enhancers is clear: We need specific knowledge of the conditions under which learning or other changes that take place in therapy will be carried over into extra-therapy situations. . . . We cannot assume that a behavior acquired in the therapy situation, however well learned, will carry over into other situations. Unquestionably the phenomena of therapy are orderly and lawful; they follow definite rules. We must, then, understand the rules that determine what responses will be generalized, or transferred, to other situations and what responses will not. As a first approximation to the rules obtaining in psychotherapy, we suggest the knowledge gained from study of transfer of other habits. (Goldstein, Heller, & Sechrest, 1966, p. 244)

TRANSFER-ENHANCING PROCEDURES

The effort to develop effective and reliable means for maximizing transfer and maintenance, though clearly still in progress, shows considerable initial success. A variety of useful techniques have been developed, evaluated, and incorporated into practice. These procedures, which collectively constitute the current technology of transfer and maintenance enhancement, are listed in Table 7.1 and are examined in detail in the rest of this section.

Provision of General Principles

Transfer of training is facilitated by providing the trainee with the general mediating principles that govern satisfactory performance on both the original and the transfer tasks. The trainee is given the rules, strategies, or organizing principles that lead to successful performance. This general finding—that understanding the principles that underlie successful performance enhances transfer to new tasks and contexts—is reported

Table 7.1

TRANSFER- AND MAINTENANCE-ENHANCING PROCEDURES

Transfer
1. Provision of general principles (general case programming)
2. Overlearning (maximizing response availability)
3. Stimulus variability (training sufficient exemplars, training loosely)
4. Identical elements (programming common stimuli)
5. Mediated generalization (self-recording, self-reinforcement, self-punishment, self-instruction)

Maintenance
1. Thinning reinforcement (increased intermittency, unpredictability)
2. Delaying reinforcement
3. Fading prompts
4. Providing booster sessions
5. Preparing for nonreinforcement in the natural environment
   a. Self-reinforcement
   b. Relapse and failure management skills
   c. Graduated homework assignments
6. Programming for reinforcement in the natural environment
7. Using natural reinforcers
   a. Real-life settings
   b. Easily reinforced behaviors
   c. Reinforcement recruitment
   d. Reinforcement recognition

in a number of domains of psychological research, including studies of labeling, rules, advance organizers, learning sets, and deutero-learning. It is a robust finding indeed, with empirical support in both laboratory and psychoeducational settings. For example, no matter how competently the ART trainer seeks to create in the role-play setting the "feel" of the real-life setting in which the trainee will use the skill, and no matter how well the co-actor in the given role-play matches the actual qualities and likely response of the real target figure, there are always differences that matter between role-play and real world. Even when the trainee role-plays the skill or step a number of times, the demands of his or her actual real-world situation depart at least in some respects from the demands as portrayed in the role-play. And the real parent, real peer, real teacher, and real probation officer are likely to respond to the trainee's use of the skill or step (even if correct) somewhat differently than does his or her role-play partner. When the trainee has a good grasp of the principles underlying the role-play and real situations he or she is addressing (their demands, expected behaviors, norms, purposes, rules, and the principles underlying the skill or step—why *these* steps, in *this* order, toward *which* ends), a successful training to real-life transfer of performance becomes more likely. Correctly discerning the general principles associated with different skill-relevant settings is enhanced by the trainee's participation in a process we term Situational Perception Training, described in detail later in this chapter.

Overlearning

Transfer of training is enhanced by procedures that maximize over-learning or response availability: The likelihood that a response will be available is very clearly a function of its prior use. We repeat over and over foreign language phrases we are learning, we insist that our child spend an hour each day in piano practice, or we devote considerable time in practice making a golf swing smooth and "automatic." These are simply expressions of the response-availability notion—that is, the more we practice responses (especially *correct* ones), the easier it is to use them in other contexts or at later times. We need not rely solely on everyday experiences to find support for this conclusion. It is well established empirically that, other things being equal, the response made most fre-quently in the past is more likely to be made on subsequent occasions. However, it is not sheer practice of attempts at effective behaviors that is most beneficial to transfer, but practice of *successful* attempts. Over-learning involves extending learning over more trials than is necessary to produce initial changes in the individual's behavior. In all too many instances of training, one or two successes at a given task are taken as evidence to move on to the next task or the next level of the original task. This is a training error if the goal is to maximize transfer. To maximize transfer through overlearning, the guiding rule is not "practice makes perfect" (implying that one simply practices until one gets it right and then moves on), but "practice of perfect" (implying numerous trials of correct responses after the initial success).

Youths who receive feedback from co-trainees and the trainer to the effect that their just completed role-play is a good one (all steps followed and well portrayed) may object to the trainer's request that they role-play a second or third time. While we are sympathetic to concerns about the consequences boredom may have for the group's behavior management, the value of skill overlearning must nonetheless be considered. Frequently, to assuage trainees' objections, we point to the value of grossly repetitive pregame practice (warm-ups, shoot-arounds, batting practice) for professional athletic performance. Such practice makes core skills near automatic and frees up the player's attention for strategy or other planning efforts. It is common and appropriate for a Skillstreaming group to spend two, three, or even more sessions role-playing a single skill. Similarly, in the Anger Control Training sequence, each step is repeated several times as the weeks progress. Given that real-life people and events may work *against* trainees' use of prosocial behaviors and anger control techniques, the need for overlearning becomes all the more apparent.

Stimulus Variability

In the previous section, we addressed transfer enhancement by means of practice and repetition—that is, by the sheer number of correct responses. Transfer is also enhanced by the variability or range of situations to which the individual responds. Training even on two situations is better than training on one. As we noted several years ago in response to research on stimulus variability, "The implication is clear that in order to maximize positive transfer, training should provide for some sampling of the population of stimuli to which the response must ultimately be given" (Goldstein et al., 1966, p. 220). As Kazdin (1975) comments:

> One way to program response maintenance and transfer of training is to develop the target behavior in a variety of situations and in the presence of several individuals. If the response is associated with a range of settings, individuals, and other cues, it is less likely to be lost when the situations change. (p. 21)

Epps, Thompson, and Lane (1985) discuss stimulus variability for transfer enhancement purposes as it operates in school contexts under the rubrics "Train sufficient examples" and "Train loosely." They observe that generalization of new skills or behaviors is also facilitated by training students under a wide variety of conditions. Manipulating the numbers of trainers, settings, and response classes involved in the intervention promotes generalization by exposing students to a variety of situations. Thus, if for purposes of overlearning trainees are asked to role-play a given Skillstreaming skill correctly three times, each attempt should involve a different co-actor, a different constructed setting, and especially a different need for the same skill.

Identical Elements

In perhaps the earliest experimental work dealing with transfer enhancement, Thorndike and Woodworth (1901) concluded that, when there is a facilitative effect of one habit on another, it is to the extent that and because the habits share identical elements. Ellis (1965) and Osgood (1953) have more recently emphasized the importance for transfer of similarity between characteristics of the training and application tasks. As Osgood notes, "The greater the similarity between practice and test stimuli, the greater the amount of positive transfer" (p. 213). This conclusion rests on a particularly solid base of experimental support.

In the context of ART, the principle of identical elements is implemented by procedures that function to increase the "real-lifeness" of the stimuli (places, people, events, etc.) to which the trainer helps the trainee learn to respond with effective, satisfying behaviors. Two broad strategies exist for attaining such high levels of correspondence between in-group and extra-group stimuli. The first concerns the actual physical location in which ART takes place. Typically, we remain in the school or institution and by use of props and imagination recreate the physical feel of the real-world context in which the trainee plans to use the skill or step. Whenever possible, however, the ART group leaves the formal training setting and meets in the actual locations in which the problem behaviors occur. "Fight in the schoolyard? Let's have our session there." "Argument with the director's secretary? Let's move the group to her office." "Stare-downs in the hallway? Today's group will meet out there."

In addition to implementing identical elements by using in vivo locations for the ART sessions, the principle of transfer enhancement is well served when the co-trainees in the group are the same people the youngster interacts with on a regular basis outside of the group. It is especially valuable to employ this strategy when the others involved are people with whom the trainee is not getting along with well and with whom more prosocially skilled, controlled interactions are desirable. If a trainer wishes to compose two ART groups of six adolescents each, and two of the youngsters fight a lot, the natural response would be, for the sake of behavior management and expediency, to place one youth in one group, the second youth in the other. Not so in ART. Fight outside? Put them in the same group and even hope that they fight during a group session.

These two youths are real-world figures for one another. They employ poor quality prosocial (and high quality antisocial) behaviors in their chronic behavior of not getting along outside the group. What a fine opportunity their participation in the same group presents to teach them positive alternative means for dealing with their real-life difficulties.

Thus, in starting a single ART group, it is best to select all members from one class, rather than one or a few each from more than one class. Live together, play together, go to class together, fight together—get trained together. For the same rationale as for identical elements, when implementing ART in residential, agency, or institutional settings, our training groups are most often constructed to parallel the facility's unit, crew, cottage, or ward structure.

Mediated Generalization

The one commonality, which by definition is present in both training and application settings, is the individual trainee. Mediated generalization—mediated by the trainee, not by others—is an approach to transfer enhancement that relies on instructing the trainee in a series of context-bridging self-regulation competencies (Kanfer & Karoly, 1972; Nielans & Israel, 1981). Operationally, it consists of instructing the trainee in self-recording, self-reinforcement, self-punishment, and self-instruction. Epps et al. (1985), working in a special education setting, structured these generalization-mediating steps as follows.

Self-Recording

1. The teacher sets up the data collection system—that is, selects a target behavior, defines it in measurable terms, and decides on an appropriate recording technique.

2. The teacher tries out the data collection system.

3. The teacher teaches the trainee how to use the data collection system.

4. The teacher reinforces the trainee for taking accurate data.

Self-Reinforcement

1. The teacher determines how many points a trainee has earned, and the trainee simply records these.

2. The teacher tells the trainee to decide how many points should be awarded for appropriate behavior.

3. The trainee practices self-reinforcement under teacher supervision.

4. The trainee employs self-reinforcement without teacher supervision.

Self-Punishment

Self-punishment, operationalized in this example by response cost (taking away points), is taught in a manner directly parallel to that just described for self-reinforcement, in which the teacher employs the technique of fading.

Self-Instruction

1. The teacher models the appropriate behavior while talking himself or herself through the task aloud so that the trainee can hear.

2. The trainee performs the task with overt instructions from the teacher.

3. The trainee performs the task with overt self-instructions.

4. The trainee performs the task with covert self-instructions.

In recent years, as the cognitive behavior modification therapies, especially those relying heavily on self-instructional processes, have grown in popularity, the use of self-mediated approaches to generalization have grown correspondingly.

MAINTENANCE-ENHANCING PROCEDURES

The persistence, durability, or maintenance of behaviors developed by diverse skills training approaches is primarily a matter of the manipulation of reinforcement during the original training and in the youngster's natural environment. Several means exist by which maintenance-enhancing manipulation of reinforcement may proceed. We will examine the following matters first: thinning reinforcement, delaying reinforcement, fading prompts, providing booster sessions, and preparing for nonreinforcement in the natural environment. We will then examine two similar concerns as they occur beyond the ART group setting: programming for reinforcement in the natural environment and using natural reinforcers.

Thinning Reinforcement

A rich, continuous reinforcement schedule is optimal for the establishment of new behaviors. Maintenance of such behaviors is enhanced if the reinforcement schedule is gradually thinned. Thinning of reinforcement proceeds best by moving from a continuous (every trial) schedule, to an intermittent schedule, to a level of sparse and infrequent reinforcement characteristic of the natural environment. In fact, the maintenance-enhancing goal of such a thinning process is to make the trainer's reinforcement schedule indistinguishable from that typically found in real-world contexts.

Delaying Reinforcement

Resistance to extinction is also enhanced by delaying reinforcement. As Epps et al. (1985) note:

> During the early stages of an intervention, reinforcement should be immediate and continuously presented contingent on the desired response. . . . After the behavior becomes firmly established in the student's repertoire, it is important to introduce a delay in presenting the reinforcement. Delayed reinforcement is a closer approximation to reinforcement conditions in the natural environment. (p. 21)

Delay of reinforcement is implemented, according to Sulzer-Azaroff and Mayer (1977), by (a) increasing the size or complexity of the response required before reinforcement is provided; (b) adding a time delay between the response and the delivery of reinforcement; and (c) in token systems, increasing the time interval between the receipt of tokens and the opportunity to spend them and/or requiring more tokens in exchange for a given reinforcer.

Fading Prompts

Maintenance is enhanced by the gradual removal of suggestions, reminders, prompts, or other similar coaching or instruction. Fading of prompts is a means of moving away from artificial control (the trainer's) to more natural (self-) control of desirable behaviors. As with all the enhancement techniques examined here, fading of prompts must be carefully planned and systematically implemented.

Providing Booster Sessions

Notwithstanding the importance of fading prompts, it is necessary periodically to reinstate instruction in the specifics of given appropriate behaviors in order for the trainee to continue those behaviors in the natural environment. Booster sessions between trainer and trainee, either on a preplanned schedule or as needed, often prove valuable in this regard (Feindler & Ecton, 1986; Karoly & Steffen, 1980).

Preparing for Nonreinforcement in the Natural Environment

Trainer and trainee may take several steps to maximize the likelihood that reinforcement for appropriate behaviors will occur in the natural environment. Nevertheless, on a number of occasions, reinforcement is not forthcoming. Thus, it is important for maintenance purposes that the trainee be prepared for this eventuality. As described in our earlier examination of mediated generalization, self-reinforcement is one means of responding when desirable behaviors are performed correctly but are unrewarded by external sources.

Research on relapse prevention and failure management in the area of addiction treatment suggests another way to maintain newly learned prosocial behaviors. Appropriate, prosocially directed self-instructional talk and rearrangement of environmental cues toward prosocial patterns (where one goes, with whom one associates, what one does) can help in this regard. Mastery of such Skillstreaming skills as Responding to Failure, Dealing with Contradictory Messages, Using Self-Control, and Avoiding Trouble with Others, singly or in combination, may also serve the purpose of relapse and failure management.

A third way in which the ART trainee is prepared for nonreinforcement in the natural environment is by using graduated homework assignments. In Skillstreaming, it becomes clear at times as the homework is discussed that the real-life figure is too difficult a target—too harsh, too unresponsive, or simply too unlikely to provide reinforcement for competent skill use. When faced with this circumstance, with the newly learned skill still fragile and the potential homework environment unfriendly, we have recast the homework assignment toward two or three more benevolent and potentially responsive target figures. When the trainee finally does use the skill correctly with the original target figure and receives no contingent reinforcement, his or her previously reinforced trials help minimize the likelihood that the behavior will be extinguished.

Programming for Reinforcement in the Natural Environment

The maintenance-enhancing techniques examined thus far are targeted toward the trainee—his or her reinforcement schedule, instruction, booster sessions, and preparation for nonreinforcing consequences. But maintenance of appropriate behaviors is also enhanced by efforts directed toward others, especially those in the trainee's natural environment who function as the main providers of the trainee's reinforcement.

This larger interpersonal world of which the trainee is a part consists of a variety of people—parents, siblings, peers, teachers, neighbors, classmates, and others. By their responsiveness or unresponsiveness to the trainee's newly learned skill behaviors, they control the destiny of these behaviors to a large extent. By contrast with the earlier inoculation view, we maintain that all of us—including ART trainees—react to what important people in our lives think or feel about our behavior. What they reward, we are more likely to continue doing. What they are indifferent or even hostile to tends to fall into disuse.

During the past several years, we and others have suggested means for increasing the likelihood that school, agency, and institutional staff, as well as parents and peers, will respond to trainees' displays of newly learned skills with active approval, encouragement, or other social rewards. Specific procedures for offering such crucial support are described in detail in Appendix D, "The Transfer Coach." We strongly recommend that ART program planners reproduce this appendix along with the Skillstreaming skills from Appendix A, distribute these to all school, agency, or institutional staff, and enthusiastically encourage their use.

Parents are our second primary targets for procedures designed to enhance the likelihood that prosocial skills, once learned, are maintained. We have regularly employed the Skillstreaming School-Home Note (Figure 7.1) to increase the likelihood that trainees' parents will reward skill performance. Each time a new skill is introduced in the Skillstreaming group, the trainees' parents are sent this note to inform them about the purpose and value of the skill, its steps, and any homework assigned (often involving the parents as homework targets). The form also asks parents to (a) reward competent skill use, (b) reciprocate (another type of reward) if it is a skill (like Negotiating) requiring reciprocation, and (c) give suggestions to the trainers to make the training and homework aspects of Skillstreaming more effective. We also use the Parent/Staff Skill Rating Form (see Figure 7.2) to help build a skill-maintaining collaboration between group trainers and trainees' parents, teachers, and other significant adults.

As described in detail in chapter 8, one major evaluation of ART, in which the focus was on maintaining trainee skill performance, involved

Figure 7.1

SCHOOL–HOME NOTE

Student: _____ Date: _____

DESCRIPTION OF LESSON

Skill name: _____

Skill steps:

Skill purpose, use, value: _____

_____

DESCRIPTION OF SKILL HOMEWORK

_____

_____

REQUEST TO PARENTS

1. Provide skill homework recognition and reward.

2. Provide skill homework reciprocation.

3. Return this School-Home Note with your comments (on the back) about:

   • Quality of homework done

   • Rewards that work/don't work at home

   • Suggestions or questions regarding this skill, other skills needed, additional homework assignments, other ways to promote school-home collaboration, and so on

4. Please sign and return this form to _____ by _____ .

Signature: _____ Date: _____

Figure 7.2

PARENT/STAFF SKILL RATING FORM

Date: _____

_____
(student's name)

is learning the skill of _____

The steps involved in this skill are:

1. Did he or she demonstrate this skill in your presence?
   ☐ yes ☐ no

2. How well would you rate his or her skill demonstration? *(check one)*
   ☐ poor ☐ below average ☐ average
   ☐ above average ☐ excellent

3. How sincere was he or she in performing the skill? *(check one)*
   ☐ not sincere ☐ somewhat sincere ☐ very sincere

   Comments: _____

   _____

   _____

4. Please sign and return this form to _____ by _____ .

   Signature: _____ Date: _____

the provision of ART sessions to parents as well (Goldstein et al., 1989). Parent training groups met independently of those held for their adolescent children three out of every four sessions, the fourth session being a joint meeting. In the same spirit of support for maintaining trainees' newly learned skills, we also conducted major ART training programs for trainees' peers. In one instance, the peers involved were fellow members of the trainees' juvenile gangs (Goldstein et al., 1994). In the second, the peers trained were fellow residents in a state facility for juvenile delinquents (Leeman, Gibbs, & Fuller, 1993). In both instances, research evaluations demonstrate that enhancing the ART skill levels of the significant people in trainees' lives enhances in turn the maintenance of trainee ART skill use. We consider these research outcomes quite important and reflective of a belief long held by many who work with troubled youths: Serious attempts to alter antisocial behaviors for the better must be directed toward the youths and toward significant people (e.g., parents, peers) in the youths' lives.

Using Natural Reinforcers

A final and especially valuable approach to maintenance enhancement is the use of reinforcers that exist in the trainee's real-world environment.

Galassi and Galassi (1984) comment:

> We need to target those behaviors for changes that are most likely to be seen as acceptable, desirable, and positive by others. Ayllon and Azrin (1968) refer to this as the "Relevance of Behavior Rule." "Teach only those behaviors that will continue to be reinforced after training." (p. 10)

Alberto and Troutman (1982) suggest a four-step process that facilitates effective use of natural reinforcers:

1. Observe which specific behaviors are regularly reinforced and how they are reinforced in the major settings that constitute the trainee's natural environment.

2. Instruct the trainee in a selected number of such naturally reinforced behaviors (e.g., certain social skills, grooming behaviors).

3. Teach the trainee how to recruit or request reinforcement (e.g., by tactfully asking peers or others for approval or recognition).

4. Teach the trainee how to recognize reinforcement when it is offered, because its presence in certain gestures or facial expressions may be quite subtle for many trainees.

To sum up, the call in the 1960s for a technology of transfer and maintenance enhancement has been vigorously answered. The technology examined in this section is substantial and still growing. Its full employment in the context of ART is strongly recommended.

EMBEDDING ART IN A BROADER CURRICULUM

It is our basic contention that generalization of acquired skills will be further promoted if the trainee is concurrently being taught an array of supportive psychological competencies. As we have noted elsewhere:

> Growing evidence suggests that generalization of gain will be more likely when the psychological treatment offered is both broad and multichannel. Bandwidth in this context refers to the breadth or number of client qualities targeted by the treatment; multichannelness refers to the range of different modes of client response targeted, respectively, by the different components of the treatment. Our approach to chronically aggressive adolescents, Aggression Replacement Training, consisting of separate but integrated weekly sessions of prosocial skills training (the behavior-targeted components), anger control training (the affect-targeted components), and moral reasoning (the values-targeted components), is [a beginning] example of such a broad band, multichannel treatment. Demonstrations of reductions in recidivism associated with this intervention are initial evidence of its generalization promoting efficacy. (Goldstein, 1994, p. 103)

In 1988, we expanded ART (itself an expansion of Skillstreaming) into a 10-course, prosocial competencies training program called the Prepare Curriculum (Goldstein, 1988). Although each Prepare course teaches competencies of value in their own right (empathy, cooperation, etc.), the courses also enhance generalization of social skills training, a central focus of ART.

Prepare Curriculum Courses 1, 2, and 3:
Skillstreaming, Anger Control Training, and Moral Reasoning Training

Since the early 1970s we have sought to teach an array of interpersonal, prosocial competencies to aggressive, withdrawn, immature, developmentally delayed, and other skill-deficient youths and children. The history, arrangement, procedures, and curricula for these skills have been described in earlier chapters. In the rest of this chapter, we describe the remaining Prepare Curriculum courses and, in each instance, specify the bases for their generalization-promoting potential. Because such potential has only recently come under scrutiny, the assertions that follow regarding the potentiating effects of each Prepare Curriculum course on the generalization of ART skills are stated in the form of hypotheses.

HYPOTHESIS I:

Skill generalization is promoted to the degree that the probability of competing responses is reduced.

Prepare Curriculum Course 4: Stress Management

It has been demonstrated by Arkowitz (1977) and by Curran (1977) that individuals may possess an array of skills in their repertoires but may not employ them in particularly challenging or difficult situations because of anxiety. A youth may have learned well the Skillstreaming skill Responding to Failure, but his embarrassment at receiving a failing grade in front of a teacher or at missing a foul shot in front of his friends may engender a level of anxiety that inhibits proper use of this skill. A young woman may possess the problem-solving competency to plan well for a job interview but may perform poorly in the interview itself because anxiety takes over. Such anxiety-inhibition as a source of prosocially incompetent and unsatisfying behavior is especially prevalent in the highly peer-conscious adolescent years.

A series of self-managed procedures exists for reducing stress-induced anxiety substantially. These procedures form the basis of the Prepare Curriculum course in Stress Management. Participating youngsters engage in systematic deep muscle relaxation (Benson, 1975; Jacobson, 1938), meditation techniques (Assagioli, 1973; Naranjo & Ornstein, 1971), environmental restructuring (Anderson, 1978), exercise (Walker, 1979), and related means for the management, control, and reduction of stress-induced anxiety.

HYPOTHESIS II:

Skill generalization is promoted to the degree that the trainee's level of motivation for skill use is increased.

Prepare Curriculum Course 5: Cooperation Training

Chronically aggressive and other skill-deficient youths have been shown to display a pattern of personality traits high in egocentricity and competitiveness and low in concern for others and cooperativeness (Slavin, 1980). We include a course in Cooperation Training not only because enhanced cooperation among individuals is a valuable social goal in itself, but also because cooperation is predicted to heighten motivation to employ other skills. An extended review of research on one set of approaches to Cooperation Training, namely cooperative learning, reveals outcomes of enhanced self-esteem, group cohesiveness, altruism, and cooperation itself, as well as reduced egocentricity. As long ago as 1929, Maller commented:

> The frequent staging of contests, the constant emphasis upon the making and breaking of records, and the glorification of the heroic individual achievement . . . in our present educational system lead toward the acquisition of competitiveness. The child is trained to look at the members of his group as constant competitors and urged to put forth a maximum effort to excel them. The lack of practice in group activities and community projects in which the child works with his fellows for a common goal precludes the formation of habits of cooperativeness. (p. 163)

It was many years before the educational establishment responded concretely to this Deweyan challenge, but when it did, it created a number of innovative, cooperation-enhancing methodologies. Each of these methods deserves consideration in the general educational context as well as in situations such as ART, which specifically involve uncooperative youths. Among these methods are Student Teams–Achievement Division (Slavin, 1980), Teams-Games-Tournaments (Slavin, 1980), Jigsaw Classrooms I (Aronson, Blaney, Stephan, Sikes, & Snapp, 1978), Jigsaw Classrooms II (Slavin, 1980), Group-Investigation (Sharon & Sharon, 1976), and Co-op Co-op (Kagan, 1985). Using shared materials, interdependent tasks, group rewards, and similar features, these methods (applied to any content area—mathematics, social studies, etc.) have consistently yielded the interpersonal, cooperation-enhancing, group, and individual benefits noted previously.

The Prepare Curriculum makes use of many of the features of the cooperative learning approaches noted here. In particular, we respond to the orientation towards physical action typical of many skill-deficient youths by relying heavily on cooperative sports and games. Cooperative athletic activities, though not yet popular in the United States, do exist elsewhere (Fluegelman, 1981; Orlick, 1978). Collective-score basketball, no-hitting football, cross-team rotational hockey, collective-fastest-time track meets, and other sports restructured to be what cooperative gaming creators term "all touch," "all play," "all positions," "all shoot," and so forth may seem strange to American youths, who have been weaned on highly competitive, individualistic sports. Such cooperative activities appear to be a valuable additional channel to enhance both cooperation and skill generalization.

HYPOTHESIS III:

Skill generalization is promoted to the degree that the
trainee concurrently acquires strategies for determining which
skills to employ (Course 6), and where, when, and with
whom to use them (Courses 7 and 8).

Prepare Curriculum Course 6: Problem-Solving Training

Adolescents and younger children may, as Ladd and Mize (1983) point out, be deficient in such problem-solving competencies as "(a) knowledge of appropriate goals for social interaction, (b) knowledge of appropriate strategies for reaching a social goal, and (c) knowledge of the contexts in which specific strategies may be appropriately applied" (p. 130). An analogous conclusion flows from the research program on interpersonal problem solving conducted by Spivack, Platt, and Shure (1976). At early and middle childhood, as well as in adolescence, chronically aggressive youngsters are less able than more typical youngsters to function effec- tively in most problem-solving subskills, such as identifying alternatives, considering consequences, determining causality, and engaging in means- ends thinking and perspective taking.

Several programs have been developed in an effort to remediate such problem-solving deficiencies with the types of youngsters of concern here (DeLange, Lanham, & Barton, 1981; Giebink, Stover, & Fahl, 1968; Sarason et al., 1972). Such programs represent a fine beginning, but problem-solving deficiencies in such youths are sub- stantial (Chandler, Greenspan, & Barenboim, 1974; Selman, 1980; Spivack et al., 1976), and substantial deficiencies require longer term, more comprehensive interventions. The Prepare Curriculum course provides just such an effort. In its pilot development, it is a comparatively longer term sequence of such graduated problem-solving skills as reflection, problem identification, information gathering, perspective taking, identification of alternatives, consideration of consequences, and decision making.

The potential value of problem-solving training for enhancement of skill generalization requires further examination. However, our evaluation of this sequence with an aggressive adolescent population has yielded significant gains in problem-solving skills thus defined, encouraging further development of this course (Grant, 1987). These results give substance to our earlier assertion that

> individuals can be provided systematic training in problem-solving skill both for purposes of building general competence in meeting life's challenges and as a specific means of supplying one more reliable, prosocial alternative to aggression. (Goldstein, 1981)

Prepare Curriculum Course 7: Situational Perception Training

Once armed with the interpersonal skills necessary to respond prosocially to others (Course 1) and the problem-solving strategies underlying skill selection and use (Course 6), the chronically skill-deficient youngster may still fail to behave prosocially because he or she misreads the context in which the behavior is to occur. A major thrust in psychology during the past several years has been the role of situation or setting as perceived by the individual in determining overt behavior. Morrison and Bellack (1981) comment, for example:

> Adequate social performance not only requires a repertoire of response skills, but knowledge about when and how these responses should be applied. Application of this knowledge, in turn, depends upon the ability to accurately "read" the social environment, determine the particular norms and conventions operating at the moment, and . . . understand the messages being sent . . . and intentions guiding the behavior of the interpersonal partner. (p. 70)

Dil (1972), Emery (1975), and Rothenberg (1970) have each shown that emotionally disturbed youngsters, as well as those "socially maladjusted" in other ways, are characteristically deficient in such social perceptiveness. Argyle (1981) observes:

It has been found that people who are socially inadequate are unable to read everyday situations and respond appropriately. They are unable to perform or interpret nonverbal signals, unaware of the rules of social behavior, mystified by ritualized routines and conventions of self-presentation and self-disclosure, and are hence like foreigners in their own land. (p. 37)

Argyle (1981) and Backman (1979) emphasize this same social-perceptual deficit in their work with aggressive individuals. Yet we believe that the ability to read social situations accurately can be taught, and we do so with this course. Its contents are responsive to the valuable leads provided in this context by Brown and Fraser (1979), who propose three salient dimensions of accurate social perceptiveness:

1. The setting of the interaction and its associated rules and norms

2. The purpose of the interaction and its goals, tasks, and topics

3. The relationship of the participants, their roles, responsibilities, expectations, and group memberships

Prepare Curriculum Course 8: Understanding and Using Group Processes

The acute responsiveness of preadolescents and adolescents to peer influences is a truism frequently cited in both lay and professional literature on child development. It is a conclusion resting on a solid research foundation (Baumrind, 1975; Field, 1981; Guralnick, 1981). As a result, the Prepare Curriculum includes a segment giving special emphasis to group—especially peer—processes. Its title includes both "understanding" and "using" because both clearly relate to this goal. Participating youths are helped to understand such group forces and phenomena as peer pressure, clique formation and dissolution, leaders and leadership, cohesiveness, imitation, reciprocity, in-group versus out-group relations, developmental phases, competition, within-group communication and its failure, and similar processes.

This course's instructional format relies heavily on group activities in which, experientially, participants learn means for resisting group pressure when they elect to do so, for seeking and enacting a group leadership role, for helping to build and enjoy the fruits of group cohesiveness, and so forth. Examples of specific activities of apparent value for such group-experiential learning include group simulations, structured experiences, and gaming (Pfeiffer & Jones, 1974; Thayer & Beeler, 1975).

HYPOTHESIS IV:

Skill generalization is promoted to the degree that the trainee concurrently acquires enhanced competence in assuming the perspective of the skill-use target person(s).

Prepare Curriculum Course 9: Empathy Training

Expression of empathic understanding simultaneously serves as an inhibitor of negative interactions and a facilitator of positive ones. Evidence clearly demonstrates that responding to another individual in an empathic manner and assuming temporarily [that person's] perspective decreases or inhibits one's potential for acting aggressively toward the other (Feshbach, 1982; Feshbach & Feshbach, 1969). Stated otherwise, empathy and aggression are incompatible interpersonal responses, hence learning to be more skilled in the former serves as an aid to diminishing the latter.

The notion of empathy as a facilitator of positive interpersonal relations stands on an even broader base of research evidence. Our recent review of hundreds of investigations inquiring into the interpersonal consequences of empathic responding reveal such responding to be a consistently potent promoter of interpersonal attraction, dyadic openness, conflict resolution, and individual growth (Goldstein & Michaels, 1985). It is a most potent facilitator indeed.

This same review effort leads us to define empathy as a multistage process of perception of emotional cues, affective reverberation of the emotions perceived, their cognitive labeling, and communication. The Prepare Curriculum course is the multistage training program by which these four components are taught.

HYPOTHESIS V:

Skill generalization is promoted to the degree that the trainee learns to construct and employ skill sequences and combinations and is rewarded for such behaviors in his or her real-life environment.

Prepare Curriculum Course 10: Recruiting Supportive Models

Aggressive youths typically are regularly exposed to highly aggressive models in their interpersonal worlds. Parents, siblings, and peers are frequently chronically aggressive individuals themselves (Loeber & Dishion, 1983; Robins, West, & Herjanic, 1975). Simultaneously, there tend to be relatively few countervailing prosocial models to be observed and imitated. When such models are available, however, they can make a tremendous difference in the daily lives and development of such youths. In support of this assertion we turn to community examples of prosocial modeling— Big Brothers, Big Sisters, the Police Athletic League, Boy Scouts, and the like—as well as to laboratory research consistently showing that rewarded prosocial behaviors (e.g., sharing, altruism, cooperation) are often imitated (Bryan & Test, 1967; Canale, 1977; Evers & Schwartz, 1973). We also point to more direct evidence. For example, Werner and Smith (1982), in their impressive longitudinal study of aggressive and nonaggressive youths, *Vulnerable but Invincible,* clearly demonstrate that many youngsters growing up in a community characterized by high crime, high unemployment, high secondary school dropout rates, and high numbers of aggressive models are able to prevail and develop into effective, prosocially oriented individuals if they experience exposure to at least one significant prosocial model—be it parent, relative, teacher, coach, neighbor, or peer.

Because such models are often scarce in the real-world environments of aggressive youths, efforts must be put forth to help them find and create attachments to others who function prosocially themselves and who also can sustain direct support for the youths' own prosocial efforts. The Prepare Curriculum course for teaching skills to identify, encourage, attract, elicit, and at times perhaps even create such prosocial models relies on the teaching procedures of Skillstreaming as well as specific sequences of Skillstreaming skills.

CHAPTER EIGHT

Application Models and Evaluations of Program Effectiveness

This chapter describes a wide range of Aggression Replacement Training program applications and settings and summarizes efficacy evaluations of ART conducted to date. The programs described in this chapter's first section show how creative practitioners in diverse educational and correctional settings are able to respond to their own contextual needs and to innovate to meet these needs—thus helping ART to grow and develop. The second section, devoted to ART program evaluations, describes investigations conducted by our own research group as well as those undertaken by independent investigators. We present the findings of these investigations for what they reveal about the impact of ART—its apparent strengths and weaknesses—and as examples of the scrutiny we feel all school violence and juvenile delinquency interventions should receive.

APPLICATION MODELS

An Alternative School: Positive Alternative Learning Program

Alternative schools have arisen to meet the needs of the 3% of approximately 50 million U.S. schoolchildren who are chronically disruptive and aggressive and in response to the ineffectiveness of out-of-school suspension as a means of dealing with these problems (Goldstein & Conoley, 1997). Many alternative schools are, in function and form, no more than "soft jails" in which students spend boring and unproductive days learning little to advance their own competency or ability to return to mainstream schools. Other alternative settings are truly schools in the best sense, with high expectations for educational and behavioral performance. These settings may be viewed as "hyper-schools." Such is the case at the Positive Alternative Learning (PAL) Program at the Ferguson-Florissant School District in St. Louis.

In an innovative manner, this district first uses ART in its regular classrooms as a classwide guidance activity in which the school counselor and classroom teachers present modeling displays of selected Skillstreaming skills or anger control steps. The second regular school use involves "capturing teachable moments." As aggressive or other disruptive behaviors occur during the school day, teachers use ART methods to teach desirable alternatives.

The PAL Program incorporates a 10-week ART sequence for elementary and middle school youngsters. Some youths are assigned to the program preventively, in response to a series of low-level disruptive acts and before major crises occur. Others are sent rehabilitatively, following disciplinary hearings for major infractions.

No intervention—whether it be educational, therapeutic, or other—succeeds if it is offered in a context in which its participants feel unsafe, where members are out of control and adult leaders fail to provide a safe and protective atmosphere. Therefore, to be effective, an ART program must rest on the foundation of a well-run behavior management system. As the following excerpt from the PAL program manual shows, the PAL behavior management system consists of expectations, rules, and levels (Positive Alternative Learning Program, 1996).

Expectations

PAL students are expected to:

1. Wait at the door for a staff person to escort them to their classrooms after the bus drops them off.

2. Put hats, jackets, and coveralls in lockers when they enter their classrooms.

3. Bring all necessary materials (notebooks, pencils, paper, etc.) to class and report to class on time.

4. Stay in their seats unless directed otherwise by a teacher.

5. Be on task and complete assignments.

6. Have no food, drinks, gum, or anything else in their mouths.

7. Sit straight in their chairs with their feet on the floor and their heads up, and not sit on tables or desks.

8. Raise their hands and wait to be called on.

9. Use respectful language.

10. Keep radios, tape players, video games, headphones, telephones, games, and toys out of the school.

11. Keep any gang-related dress or behavior out of the school— keep their pants up to their waists, avoid dressing in gang colors, and use no hand signs, gang writing, or gang language.

Rules

Rule number 1: Physical danger

Students are not allowed to do anything potentially harmful to themselves or others.

- *Rationale:* School is a safe place for all, and PAL students are encouraged to practice safety for everyone in all environments.

- *No:* Hitting, kicking, stabbing, pulling chairs, having a weapon (anything that can be used or misused to harm another person— knives, guns, chains, locks, etc.), hostile gesturing, or physical threats.

- *Instead:* Students keep their hands to themselves, walk instead of run, and sit with their feet on the floor.

Rule number 2: Verbal abuse

Students are not to say anything that insults, hurts, or threatens another person.

- *Rationale:* Staff and students' purpose is to help and encourage one another, and everyone must feel respected and comfortable. Proper verbal expression helps prevent misunderstandings, quarrels, and fights.

- *No:* Name calling, cussing, sarcasm, shouting, getting in someone's face, verbal threats, or coercion.

- *Instead:* Students are expected to call people by their names, use a normal volume and tone when speaking, listen, and wait for their turn to speak.

Rule number 3: Social appropriateness

Students are to act in a manner that is appropriate for public behavior and to show good manners.

- *Rationale:* In order to be successful at their home schools, students must know how to behave in a manner that is socially appropriate.

- *No:* Nose-picking, kissing or sexual touching, passing gas, or burping.

- *Instead:* Students are to sit in their seats, keep their hands to themselves, use a tissue when needed, and say please, thank-you, and excuse me.

Rule number 4: Disruptions

Disruptions that prevent the teacher from teaching or one's classmates from learning are not permitted.

- *Rationale:* Students are in school to learn. While in the PAL Program, they are acquiring skills to enable them to return to their home schools and meet with success.

- *No:* Calling out answers, interrupting a lesson when entering or leaving, being off task, or making inappropriate comments.

- *Instead:* Students raise their hands and wait to be called on before speaking, enter and leave the room quietly, and stay on the subject.

Rule number 5: Not getting along/arguing

Arguing with teachers or other students is not permitted.

- *Rationale:* Working to understand others' views and to become more tolerant of those who disagree is an important goal.

- *No:* Continuing to voice an opinion after others have expressed their ideas and understand one another.

- *Instead:* When all have expressed their ideas and understand one another, students are instructed to drop the subject or do something else. They shake hands and agree to disagree.

Levels

The PAL level system involves three levels of student responsibilities and privileges. The probationary level is designed to orient students to the system. Movement from one level to the next is governed by several factors. Each student has a daily point card, which is carried from class to class. Accumulation of points, passing grades, and demonstration of progress in using the [Skillstreaming] skills are required to progress from one level to the next. Each successive level places greater responsibility on the student and allows greater movement, freedom, and choices within the school.

Level I: Responsibilities

Level I students are expected to:

1. Learn the program, building, and classroom rules and expectations, and pass a test on them.

2. Follow the daily schedule and routines.

3. Remain under staff supervision at all times.

4. Respond respectfully to staff requests.

5. Sit in assigned seats at lunch in the cafeteria with others.

6. Take care of the cafeteria and clean up after lunch.

7. Begin to resolve their problems/conflicts with peers and staff appropriately.

8. Begin to practice the prosocial skills they learn in group sessions.

9. Begin to interact with their peers in a productive manner.

10. Begin to identify and take responsibility for their own problems in individual or group sessions.

Level I: Privileges

Level I students have no privileges. They remain under supervision at all times and are escorted to the restroom before and after lunch. They eat lunch in assigned seats and are not allowed to socialize—students study for the rules test after they finish eating.

Level II: Responsibilities

Level II students are expected to:

1. Follow the program, building, and classroom rules and expectations.

2. Follow the daily schedule and routines.

3. Respond respectfully to staff requests.

4. Eat lunch in the cafeteria with others.

5. Take care of the cafeteria and clean up after lunch.

6. Resolve their problems/conflicts with peers and staff appropriately.

7. Practice the prosocial skills they learn in group sessions.

8. Generally interact with their peers in a productive manner.

9. Generally identify and take responsibility for their own problems in individual or group sessions.

Level II: Privileges

Level II students are allowed to:

1. Eat with their friends and socialize during the lunch period.

2. Play games during the lunch period.

3. Go on class field trips.

4. Have free time at the end of the day on Fridays.

5. Apply to work in the day care center after 2 weeks on Level II if they have excellent attendance, all work is completed satisfactorily and on time, point requirements are maintained, and teachers give their recommendation.

Level III: Responsibilities

Level III students are expected to:

1. Follow and model the program, building, and classroom rules and expectations.

2. Control their behavior and respond appropriately with minimal staff direction.

3. Eat lunch in the lounge with others.

4. Take care of the lounge and clean up after lunch.

5. Usually resolve their problems/conflicts with peers and staff appropriately.

6. Usually interact with their peers and the staff in a positive, productive manner.

7. Demonstrate the ability to identify their own problems and assist others in group counseling.

Level III: Privileges

Level III students are allowed to:

1. Eat lunch in the student lounge.

2. Play games, listen to music, and watch TV at lunch in the student lounge.

3. Go on field trips with priority given on limited-seating trips.

4. Have free time at the end of the day on Fridays.

5. Work in the day care center.

Advancing to a Higher Level

Every time students move up a level, they gain new privileges, but they also take on greater responsibilities. In order to move from one level to the next, students must meet several criteria. For moving from probation at Level I to Level II, students are required to:

1. Accumulate 320 points.

2. Complete 3 days in a row with at least 70 points.

3. Pass a test on the program rules.

4. Pass the staff review committee.

To move up to Level III, students are required to:

1. Accumulate 650 points at Level II.

2. Complete 5 days in a row with at least 70 points.

3. Receive positive recommendations from four staff members who observe them practicing the prosocial skills learned in class.

4. Have passing grades in all classes.

5. Pass the staff review committee.

Systems Involvement

A final and noteworthy feature of the PAL Program is its major outreach to the interpersonal systems of its target youths. Stated simply, after a student learns a new behavior, a new perception, a new way of coping or responding in an ART series, he or she goes out to interact with key people who respond to these new ways of being. If these real-world figures respond with indifference or even hostility to the youngster's efforts, the new behaviors and perceptions rapidly disappear. If, on the other hand, they respond with interest, praise, or approval, the behavioral changes have a much better chance to endure. The transfer coach (see Appendix D) provides this sustaining function. At PAL the real-world figures are the school's staff, PAL peers, and the youngsters' parents. The program makes an energetic and sustained effort to reach out to such figures, makes clear in concrete terms precisely how they can contribute positively to the behavior-change process, and monitors whether such a contribution is in fact being made. With regard to parents of PAL students, for example, PAL holds weekly parent empowerment meetings. At the beginning of each youth's stay at PAL, his or her parents are required as a condition of the youth's acceptance into the program to attend parent meetings for 8 weeks. Each parent meeting contains major elements of ART programming. If a parent fails to attend, a PAL staff member goes to the home the next morning and conducts an on-site skill lesson. If the parent continues to miss meetings, the youth is suspended from the program. Since the program's inception, only a few students have been dropped for parental nonattendance. While such a step may appear to some to be revictimizing the student, we agree that, given the crucial nature of parental support, such attendance is necessary.

A Community Agency: Brownsville Community Neighborhood Action Center

The Adolescent Vocational Exploration Program, the Juvenile Justice Prevention Program, the Youth Training and Employment Program, counseling, advocacy, and family intervention are but a few of the program offerings available at Brownsville Community Neighborhood Action Center in Brooklyn, New York. This energetic, community-oriented agency is one of the two sites at which the ART Gang Intervention Project was conducted, as described later in this chapter. Located in a low-income section of Brooklyn, the agency is in a neighborhood that has more than its share of poverty-related problems: substandard housing, a declining population, disproportionate single-parent households, substance abuse, early school dropout, and juvenile crime. Worth noting are this program's innovations and qualities valuable to others working with similarly aggressive and disadvantaged youths.

Reaching out and offering program participation to youths with strong gang affiliations presents two difficulties: how to engage them in the first place and how to maintain their attendance over time. A second agency participating in the same ART evaluation project, Youth D.A.R.E.S of Coney Island, establishes and maintains trainee attendance with the threat of parole revocation for failure to appear. By contrast, the Brownsville center offers a strong and consistent expectation for success. Beginning with their first trainee contact, program staff verbally and behaviorally deliver the message that "you can succeed, stay out of jail, get your equivalency diploma, find and keep a job, and get along better with your family." Staff commitment to trainee success has been shown in the research literature, as well as in this particular program, to motivate, encourage, and set a standard that many youths emulate. In brief, the message of this agency's ART program is "expect the best of your trainees; it helps them to achieve it."

A second noteworthy feature of the Brownsville effort is its systems focus. Central to our beliefs and experiences is the assertion that efforts to change aggressive behavior are more likely to succeed when they are directed not only toward perpetrators but also toward significant people in the perpetrators' lives (e.g., family, peers). These people have the power to reward or punish participants for their new, nonaggressive behaviors. We provide a firm research base for this assertion in our later discussion of the Gang Intervention Project. Klein (1995) and others claim that working with a gang as a unit gives the gang added credibility and cohesiveness by affording the gang recognition as a unified group. While caution is warranted, we feel the potential for systems change (i.e., in the responses of fellow gang members) overrides the concern for increased gang unification.

The Brownsville program also demonstrates how to select, train, monitor, and supervise ART trainers effectively and how to ensure program integrity—that is, the degree to which the actual implementation corresponds to the ART program plan. After reading the first edition of the ART text (Goldstein & Glick, 1987), all staff members undergo a series of intensive, experiential workshops, followed by supervised mock and then actual conduct of ART groups. These workshops and groups provide project directors with the opportunity, based on demonstrated role-play and leadership abilities, to select the most competent ART program trainers. In addition, these experiences also help determine which one of the three components of ART each selected trainer is most willing and able to lead.

From the Brownsville program, we have learned that program integrity can be maintained even when great distances separate program managers and trainers. As program managers for a number of sites, including Brownsville, we follow several procedures. First, trainers keep weekly session notes detailing events, successes, failures, and other pertinent information about their ART groups. These notes are then mailed to us, the project managers. Second, we discuss these notes with the trainers in twice-weekly telephone conversations. Third, we travel once each month to the facility for an on-site supervisory session. At Brownsville, given the high level of trainer expertise, much of this face-to-face time is spent in praising trainers. In addition, when necessary, we point out and correct any intervention delivery "errors" (i.e., trainer behaviors that depart from established ART procedures).

A School District: Erie, Pennsylvania

The school district in Erie, Pennsylvania, has implemented ART at 3 high schools, 3 middle schools, and 17 elementary schools. As of this writing, approximately 5,000 students have participated. Programs that serve as vehicles for ART delivery include the school district's Collaborative Intensive Community Treatment Program, Alternative Education Program, Student Assistance Program, After-School Student Support Program, Delinquency Prevention Program, and Program for After School Suspension and Saturday Detention. In none of these programs is ART offered alone. Each program consists of ART plus some combination of parent workshops, home visits, peer mediation, mental health counseling, tutoring, and field trips.

Many innovative approaches are used in this multiprogram, districtwide ART implementation—extensive and sustained staff training; the use of diverse staff as ART trainers (e.g., school-based probation officers); the requirement that trainees carry behavior management cards that display the "skill of the week" and on which staff provide social reinforcement points; weekly progress sheets sent home to parents, who are asked to rate the frequency and level of skill performance; and other creative procedures. The school district's most significant achievement, however, is its ability to stimulate and sustain staff involvement in ART delivery at numerous program sites over a long period of time. How do they do it? In brief, trainers are motivated by active participation in program development and amendment and by a process of consensus building and ongoing opportunity for trainer feedback. While program strategy (ART and others) and organizing philosophy are set largely at the district supervisory level, commitment to participatory management is communicated to, and carried out by, trainer staff at the program's tactical level. Program staff contribute substantially and on a continuing basis to decisions about their own program's content, intensity, staffing, structure, and more. Clearly, the sense of joint ownership is a major factor in developing and maintaining high levels of districtwide staff motivation.

A Limited Security Delinquency Facility: Taberg Residential Center

Taberg is a New York State Office of Children and Families facility for adolescent boys ages 14 to 18 who have committed assaults, robberies, or similar felonies. The Center's operating manual (Taberg Residential Center, 1994) further describes its residents:

> The adolescents admitted to Taberg Residential Center share in all of the characteristics attributed to the typical adolescent. Yet unlike the typical adolescent, Taberg residents have been unsuccessful in their transition period between childhood and adulthood. They have often been the victims of a "deprivation syndrome" in which they have not received the appropriate direction, nurturing, encouragement or guidance from significant adults. Thus, they have been unable to develop the pro-social attitudes and values necessary to be successful individuals. Many Taberg residents have been exposed to extremely poor role models, the victims of severe emotional deprivation during their early childhood years. Taberg residents typically are deficient in both academic skills as well as their interpersonal relationship skills. Essentially they are impulsive, lacking planning skills, decision making skills, problem solving skills, and negotiating skills, as well as the ability to

appropriately control and deal with their anger. The result has frequently been their involvement in delinquent activities, verbal and physical aggression, and the acceptance of an anti-social value system.

Taberg Residential Center residents admitted to Taberg can, with the proper interventions from staff, give back to the facility community as well as society upon release. Taberg Residential Center staff provide residents a habilitation program that is structured, with controlled program standards and behavioral expectations. Residents experience programs within the institution with opportunities that allow them to practice what they have learned.

The centerpiece of the overall Taberg program is ART, and it is competently administered by the center's staff. Yet trainees' learning and performance of ART's prosocial lessons are greatly influenced by (and also influence in return) the attitudes of the significant people to whom the youths relate day after day—in this particular instance, the Taberg staff. The operating manual notes in this regard:

> It is imperative that Taberg staff be impeccable role models. Residents need staff whom they can emulate; who convey a genuine concern and caring, with unconditional positive regard and empathic understanding. As positive role models we must be ever cognizant of our own interpersonal interactions with both residents and colleagues and exhibit an ability to appropriately handle conflict, decision making, problem solving, and planning. In order to demonstrate a genuine concern for youth, staff must be warm and friendly, yet firm in holding residents accountable to expectations for their growth and development. We will need a staff capable to achieve a delicate balance between establishing close, personal relationships with youth and yet perform roles as adult authority figures. Staff always have to demonstrate and model respectful behavior, toward residents and colleagues.

> As staff engage in the serious profession of being change agents their interactions and interventions with one another are as crucial to the habilitative process as our interventions and interactions with residents. To be successful in our mission, staff must work cooperatively and supportively with one another as members of a treatment team. Inherent to this team spirit are characteristics which all staff need to possess:

1. Involvement: An ability to develop and demonstrate a commitment to the group with which one works as well as a commitment to the Taberg Program.

2. Initiative: Willingness to accept responsibility; contribute more than may be required even when it may seem risky or beyond one's role or function.

3. Understanding of Self: The ability to possess a knowledge of one's own feelings, values, beliefs, abilities, limitations and needs.

4. Understanding Others: A willingness to explore and listen to what others (co-workers) feel, believe, think and need.

5. Openness: An ability to say what is on one's mind—is able and willing to confront peers constructively to enhance job performance; is clear about where he/she stands.

6. Listening Ability: Is willing and able to listen carefully to what others say and mean; listens for necessary information and instructions; asks questions to assist in better understanding what he/she has heard.

7. Uses Feedback: Is able and willing to accept constructive criticism from others in a positive manner; avoids being defensive and personalizing feedback; learns from . . . experiences and is able to make changes which will improve job performance.

8. Ability to Communicate: Shares and receives information/data with co-workers.

9. Participates in Decision Making: Is willing to take the time and energy to share in the decision-making process.

10. Perseverance: Does not abandon youth or staff with whom he/she is working (is able to work under stress without giving up).

11. Self Development: Takes the initiative to continually
     expand . . . knowledge and experience in order to reach
     the highest level of his/her professional development.

In ongoing interactions with Taberg youths, these desirable staff
characteristics find concrete expression in a behavior management system
resting on Hersey's (1984) Situational Leadership Model. At the heart of
this management system lies the notion that staff interventions with youths
("parenting styles") are based on the maturity level of each youngster:

> The assumption is made that the residents admitted to Taberg
> lack the skills (abilities) and willingness to act in a prosocial
> manner. They have made poor decisions and have acted irre-
> sponsibly in the community. Staff will continually be involved in
> both *directive behavior* (i.e., involves one-way communication—
> the staff simply tells the resident what, where, when and how to
> do something), as well as *supportive behavior* (i.e., involves two-
> way communication—the staff listens to the resident, provides
> support, encouragement and positive feedback). The profession-
> al staff person is adept at knowing when it is appropriate to be
> directive and when it is appropriate to be supportive, based on
> the situation and the maturity level of the resident involved.
> Initially staff will interact in a highly directive and in a low sup-
> portive manner (especially with a new admission) with residents
> who are unwilling or unable (reluctant beginner) to act in a re-
> sponsible manner. As the resident matures and demonstrates . . .
> ability and willingness to accept and fulfill . . . responsibilities,
> staff will gradually move towards providing the resident with low
> directive and high supportive behavior. This process moves
> through four stages of a resident's development that require staff
> to use four different parenting styles as the situation dictates. The
> following are the four parenting styles used by staff based on the
> situation and maturity level of the resident:
>
> • Directing Style: This style is called directing because it is charac-
>   terized by one-way communication. The adult defines the role
>   of the resident and tells [the resident] what, when and where
>   to do various tasks. The residents are resistive to program
>   (reluctant beginner) and lack the appropriate prosocial skills
>   and willingness to act in a responsible manner. (low maturity)

- Coaching Style: Most of the direction is still provided by the adult but allows the resident two-way communication to ask questions. The staff provides support and encouragement to get the resident to buy into decisions that the adult feels have been made. The resident at this stage is willing to learn (enthusiastic learner) and is accepting of placement. (low to moderate maturity)

- Participating Style: The staff and resident now share in decision making through two-way communication. The resident has the ability and knowledge to share ideas about how the problem can be solved and agrees with the adult what needs to be done. (moderate to high maturity)

- Delegating Style: The staff may still define the problem or what needs to be done, yet the resident is now permitted to function in an independent manner by deciding on the when, where and how of doing the task. The resident has both the ability and motivation to work alone successfully (competent and committed performer). (high maturity)

The behavior change goals of ART, at Taberg and elsewhere, are never addressed in a vacuum. The staff, by their personal characteristics and formal behavior management styles, provide the context for all that transpires, including ART. This staff or system context impedes or facilitates prosocial progress. At Taberg, it clearly serves the latter process.

A Residential School District: Children's Village

Founded in 1851 as the New York Juvenile Asylum, Children's Village of Dobbs Ferry, New York, today is a residential campus agency providing schooling and mental health services for 300 resident boys—almost all of whom come to this facility with histories of abuse and neglect, current emotional patterns of disturbed functioning, and often serious behavioral and learning problems. The many programs provided in its cottage residences and its three elementary, middle, and high schools are diverse and often ground breaking. Included in its offerings are independent living and work ethics training; individual and group counseling; Project WAY (Work Appreciation for Youth), to help focus youths on future school and work planning and preparation; Project IMPACT (Interventions to Maintain Parents and Children Together), designed to reconstruct disordered parent-child relationships; other programs for residents' parents, including parent skills training, family therapy, and consultation services; and a wide variety of tailored and innovative arrangements in the campus's three schools. These innovations include small class size, individual tutoring, Dream Street (a micro-community program), recreational activities, conflict management training, and more.

Much of the programming at Children's Village is intended to enhance daily living and prepare residents for a better future. Because interpersonal, social, planning, and anger management skills hold great potential for facilitating resident progress toward such goals, Children's Village in 1996 added a major ART component to its program offerings. Beginning at the elementary level, moving to secondary levels, and then to the cottage residences, a substantial facility-wide effort took root and grew. In the course of developing and implementing ART, a number of useful adaptations and innovations were initiated.

Staff training for competency in ART group leadership at Children's Village is operationalized as an apprenticeship program in which novice trainers participate in a series of orienting workshops followed by practice group experiences ("trainees" are staff playing the roles of residents). These experiences are followed by the supervised running of actual ART groups, and finally by the unsupervised running of groups.

Because youths participating at this facility often display high levels of disturbance and low levels of attention, group behavior management and motivational challenges are substantial. One creative staff member was able to minimize such interference by employing useful ancillary materials. As she observed in her session notes:

> In our setting, in which students have many cognitive deficien-
> cies and developmental delays, supplementing the group with
> visual aids, related (brief) videos, and story books has proven to
> be very effective. First, most children benefit from a multisenso-
> ry approach. If the group gets too verbal, they easily tune out and
> act up. These supplemental materials reduce boredom and repe-
> tition. . . . They also serve to increase students' motivation and
> overall understanding of the topic. (B. Kutcher, personal com-
> munication, July 17, 1997)

As has been noted throughout the model program descriptions so far, the challenge of intervention work—whether ART or another effort—is generalization. Does the training extend beyond the training room to other settings, and does it endure over time? At Children's

Village, a major effort is made to extend the outcomes of the ART meetings to both the campus residence settings and to the residents' families. Using both formal and informal means of communication, the school, cottage, and family regularly communicate and collaborate in the skill acquisition and skill performance efforts. Such generalization is not easily accomplished, but the effort at Children's Village to do so is broad and energetic, and stands as a model to be emulated.

A Residential Family Treatment Center: The Oasis

Swedish law permits children to be removed from the home and placed in foster care when home/family conditions are deemed a threat to the children's welfare. The Oasis, in Aneby, Sweden, offers an alternative to foster care. The children, and often the entire family, are invited to move to The Oasis for an extended period of evaluation and intervention, typically lasting several months. Such full-time, full-family availability offers a unique opportunity for implementation of family systems–oriented ART, a strategy particularly well supported by several of the ART efficacy evaluations described later in this chapter.

Thus, at The Oasis, ART groups may consist of children only, but frequently they are made up of families. In one instance, for example, an ART group consisted of a mother and her eight children. Skillstreaming skills taught were pulled simultaneously from the adolescent, elementary, and preschool Skillstreaming curricula (Goldstein & McGinnis, 1997; McGinnis & Goldstein, 1990, 1997), a tactic made possible by the fact that all three curricula are comprised of similar skills altered to fit different levels of literacy.

In addition to a systems orientation, the program at The Oasis possesses two other operational qualities that promote the generalization of learned skills. One is careful training of all staff in the ART rationale and procedures. Though only a portion of the staff become group trainers for Skillstreaming, Anger Control Training, or Moral Reasoning Training sessions, all staff have daily interactions with residents and their families. Consistent with our notion that all staff serve as transfer coaches, supervisory, social work, teaching, psychology, office, maintenance, and housekeeping personnel are all trained and expected to reward competent skill use when they see it and to coach such competency when skills should be used but are not.

Like many treatment organizations, The Oasis holds regular staff supervisory meetings. These are, however, far more than typical case conferences. In addition to discussion of client-related concerns, considerable time and energy are devoted to examining staff behavior (and, in a sense, counseling staff). In other words, The Oasis is keenly aware that in an organization espousing the remedial value of modeling, staff behavior toward clients and one another is a potent force. Often clients learn not so much from what staff say, but from what they do. These staff meetings are one more significant ingredient in the successful learning and generalization of ART programs at The Oasis.

One final noteworthy feature of operation at The Oasis is the promotion of generalization through energetic outreach, during the family's stay, to other people in the family system who may have important influences on the family's adjustment after discharge from the program. Grandparents, other relatives, friends, and staff from the agencies that made the initial referral to The Oasis are contacted and invited to lend their support to what is functionally a team effort to enhance generalization.

There is, we believe, much to learn from this model ART program. For all interventions, including ART, generalization of client change is paramount. The in-facility and outreach systems of The Oasis, its training of all staff as transfer coaches, and its regular focus on the impact of its staff as models combine to yield an example of what creativity and commitment can achieve in effecting lasting change for clients.

EVALUATIONS OF EFFECTIVENESS

Annsville Youth Center

Our first evaluation of ART was conducted at a New York State Division for Youth facility in central New York State (Goldstein & Glick, 1987). Sixty youths at Annsville were included, most of them incarcerated at this limited-security institution for such crimes as burglary, unarmed robbery, and various drug offenses. Twenty-four youngsters received the 10-week ART program described in chapter 2 (see Table 2.1). As noted earlier, this program required them to attend three sessions per week, one each of Skillstreaming, Anger Control Training, and Moral Reasoning Training. An additional 24 youths were assigned to a no-ART, brief instruction control group. This group controlled for the possibility that any apparent ART-derived gains in skill performance were due not to ART per se, but to the youngsters' enhanced motivation to display skills they already possessed but simply were not using. A third group, the no-treatment control group, consisted of 12 youths not participating in either ART or the brief instruction control group.

The overall goal of this evaluation was to examine the effectiveness of ART for the purposes of:

1. Skill acquisition: Do the youngsters learn the 10 Skillstreaming skills in the ART curriculum?

2. Minimal skill transfer: Can the youngsters perform the skills in response to new situations similar in format to those in which they were trained?

3. Extended skill transfer: Can the youngsters perform the skills in response to new situations dissimilar in format and more "real-lifelike" than those in which they were trained?

4. Anger control enhancement: Do the youngsters actually demonstrate fewer altercations or other acting-out behaviors as reflected in weekly behavior incident reports, completed for all participating youths by the center's staff?

5. Impulse reduction: Are the youngsters rated as less impulsive and more reflective and self-controlled in their interpersonal behaviors?

Analyses of study data revealed, first, that youths undergoing ART, compared with youths in both control groups, significantly acquired and transferred (minimal and extended) 4 of the 10 Skillstreaming skills: Making a Complaint, Getting Ready for a Difficult Conversation, Dealing with Someone Else's Anger, and Dealing with Group Pressure. Similarly significant ART versus control group comparisons emerged on both the number and intensity of in-facility acting-out behaviors (as measured by the behavior incident reports) as well as on staff-rated impulsiveness.

Following completion of the project's posttesting, in Week 11 new ART groups were formed for the 36 youths in the two control groups. As before, these sessions were held three times per week for 10 weeks and duplicated the first-phase ART sessions in all other major respects (curriculum, group size, materials, etc.). Our goal in this second phase was an own-control test of the efficacy of ART, with particular attention to discerning possible reductions in acting-out behaviors by comparing, for these 36 youths, their behavior incident reports during Weeks 11 through 20 (while in ART) with their behavior incident reports from the period when they had served as control group members (Weeks 1 through 10). Both of the statistical comparisons (number and severity) conducted to test for replication effects yielded positive results.

Real-world figures such as family and peers frequently express indifference or even hostility toward trainees' use of newly learned prosocial skills. As a result, incarcerated delinquents experience considerable difficulty in effecting the transfer of skills from the more protective and benign training environment to the community environment. Family and peers frequently serve as reinforcers of antisocial behaviors, ignoring or even punishing constructive alternative actions. Our hope was that ART would serve as a sufficiently powerful intervention to effect at least moderate carryover of in-facility ART gains.

In order to test for such possible transfer effects, we constructed a global rating measurement of community functioning. During the 1-year period following initiation of ART at Annsville, 54 youths were released from this facility. Seventeen had received ART; 37 had not. We contacted the Division for Youth team members (analogous to parole officers) around New York State to whom the 54 released youths regularly reported and, without informing the workers as to whether the youths had or had not received ART, asked the workers to complete global rating measurements for each of the Annsville youths. In four of the six areas—namely, home and family, peer, legal, and overall—ART youths were rated significantly higher with regard to in-community functioning than were youths who had not received ART. In the areas of school and work, no significant differences emerged.

MacCormick Youth Center

Our second evaluation of the efficacy of ART was conducted at MacCormick Youth Center, a New York State Division for Youth maximum security facility for male juvenile delinquents between the ages of 13 and 21 (Goldstein & Glick, 1987). In essence, this second evaluation project sought to replicate the exact procedures and findings of the Annsville project and to include youths incarcerated for substantially more serious felonies. Fifty-one youths were in residence at MacCormick at the time of the evaluation. Crimes committed by these youths included murder, manslaughter, rape, sodomy, attempted murder, assault, and robbery. In all its procedural and experimental particulars, the MacCormick evaluation project replicated the effort at Annsville. It employed the same preparatory activities, materials, curriculum, testing, staff training, resident training, supervision, and data analysis procedures.

On 5 of the 10 Skillstreaming skills, significant acquisition and/or transfer results emerged. These findings essentially replicate the Annsville

Skillstreaming results. In contrast to the Annsville results, however, the MacCormick data also yielded a significant result on the Sociomoral Reflection Measure (Gibbs, Basinger, & Fuller, 1992). At MacCormick, but not at Annsville, youths participating in Moral Reasoning Training sessions grew significantly in moral reasoning stages over the 10-week intervention period.

Regarding overt, in-facility behavior, youths receiving ART, compared with those who did not, increased significantly over their base rate levels in their use of constructive, prosocial behaviors (e.g., offering or accepting criticism appropriately, employing self-control when provoked) and decreased significantly in their rated levels of impulsiveness. In contrast to the Annsville findings, MacCormick youths who received ART did not differ from controls in either the number or intensity of acting-out behaviors. Annsville, internally, is not a locked facility. Its 60 youths live in one dormitory, in contrast to the locked, single-room arrangement at MacCormick. MacCormick's staff is twice the size of Annsville's, and the facility operates under a considerably tighter system of sanctions and controls than does Annsville. Because of these operational differences, the opportunity for acting-out behaviors is lower across all conditions at MacCormick as compared with Annsville. A "floor effect" therefore seemed to be operating at MacCormick that made a decrease in acting-out at MacCormick less likely to be a direct result of ART participation than at Annsville. At Annsville, such behaviors were contextually more possible at base rate, and they could (and did) decrease over the intervention period. At MacCormick, all youths started with low base rates and, likely for these same contextual reasons (e.g., sanctions, controls, rich staffing, etc.), they remained low. Subjects' use of prosocial behaviors, to which no floor or ceiling influences were relevant, did increase differentially as a function of the ART intervention.

A Community-Based Evaluation

The findings of our first two investigations revealed ART to be a multimodal, habilitation intervention of considerable potency with incarcerated juvenile delinquents: It enhanced prosocial skill competency and overt prosocial behavior and reduced levels of impulsiveness. And, in one of the two samples studied, decreases (where possible) in the frequency and intensity of acting-out behaviors and enhancement of participants' levels of moral reasoning were verified.

Furthermore, some evidence provided independently revealed ART to lead to valuable changes in community functioning. In light of the general movement away from residential-based and toward community-based programming for delinquent youths, this possibility for community change led to our third evaluation of the efficacy of ART. This evaluation sought to discern the value of ART when provided to 84 youths on a postrelease basis, while youths were living in the community (Goldstein et al., 1989). We were aware of the potent contribution to effective community functioning that parents and others make in the lives of delinquent youths. This belief led to our attempt to discern the effects of offering ART not only to the youths, but also to their parents and other family members.

This community-based project was essentially a three-way comparison of ART provided directly to youths plus ART provided to the youths' parents or other family members (Condition 1), versus ART for youths only (Condition 2), versus a no-ART control group (Condition 3). For the most part, participating youths were assigned to project conditions on a random basis, with departures from randomization becoming necessary on occasion as a function of the five-city, multisite, time-extended nature of the project. Largely as a result of how long the New York State Division for Youth had after-care responsibility for youths discharged from their facilities, the ART program offered to project participants was designed to last 3 months, with sessions meeting twice per week, for a total of approximately 24 sessions. Each session, 1½ to 2 hours long, was spent in (a) brief discussion of current life events and difficulties; (b) Skillstreaming (training of a skill relevant to the life events/difficulties discussed); and, on an alternating basis, (c) Anger Control Training or Moral Reasoning Training. Once weekly, an ART session was held for the parents and other family members of a sample of participating youths. Those parents selected to participate, but who did not appear, were provided ART in modified form via a weekly home visit or telephone call.

Since the different ART groups comprising the project's two treatment conditions chose which of the 50 Skillstreaming skills they wished to learn, different groups learned different (if overlapping) skills. We did not, therefore, examine in our statistical analyses participant change on individual skills. Instead, analyses focused on total skill change for the youths participating in ART (Conditions 1 and 2) versus each other and non-ART control group youths (Condition 3). Results indicated that, although results for the two ART conditions did not differ significantly, participants in each of these conditions increased significantly in their overall interpersonal skill competence when compared to Condition 3 (no-ART) youths. A similarly significant outcome emerged (both ART groups versus no-ART group) for decrease in self-reported anger levels in response to mild (e.g., minor nuisance, unfair treatment) but not severe (e.g., betrayal of trust, control/coercion, physical abuse) anger-provoking situations.

A particularly important evaluation criterion in delinquency intervention work is recidivism. The majority of previously incarcerated youths who recidivate do so within the first 6 months following their release (Maltz, 1984). Thus, the recidivism criterion employed in this project, rearrest, was tracked during the first 3 months, in which youths received ART, and during the 3 subsequent no-ART months. Condition 3 youths, of course, received no ART during the entire tracking period. Analyses examining the frequency of rearrest by condition showed a significant effect for ART participation. Both Condition 1 and Condition 2 youths were rearrested significantly less than were youths not receiving ART. A substantial decrease in rearrest occurred when the youths' families (i.e., parents and siblings) participated simultaneously in their own ART groups. Table 8.1 represents the actual frequency and percentages of rearrests by condition.

From this study it appears that teaching family members interpersonal skills and anger control techniques reciprocal to those the delinquent youths are learning may well provide the youths with a more responsive and prosocially reinforcing real-world environment—an environment in which prosocial instead of antisocial behaviors are supported, encouraged, and reinforced.

Table 8.1

FREQUENCY OF REARREST BY CONDITION IN THE COMMUNITY-BASED EVALUATION

Condition	Total N	Rearrested N	Percent Rearrested
Youth ART plus parent/sibling ART	13	2	15
Youth ART only	20	6	30
No-ART control	32	14	43

The Gang Intervention Project

Our research group's fourth ART evaluation (Goldstein, Glick, Carthan, & Blancero, 1994), in which trainees were all gang members, also grew from a systems-oriented spirit. If our community-based effort captured that part of the delinquent youths' interpersonal world made up of family members and turned it, at least in part, toward a prosocially reinforcing direction, could the same be done with delinquent gang youths and their peer groups (i.e., other gang members)? Could we use ART not only to teach youths to behave more prosocially but also to increase the likelihood that their prosocial efforts in real life would be met by acceptance, support, and even praise from fellow gang members?

This project was conducted in two Brooklyn, New York, youth care agencies, the Brownsville Community Neighborhood Action Center and Youth D.A.R.E.S. of Coney Island. Each agency conducted three 4-month sequences of ART. Within each sequence, trainees were all members of the same gang. We constituted a control group for each sequence whose members were also from the same gang but from a gang different than the one to which the ART trainees belonged. Thus, across both agencies, twelve different gangs participated in the program—six receiving ART, six as no-ART controls. All the youths, ART and controls, received the same educational, vocational, and recreational services offered by the two participating agencies.

Repeated measures analysis of variables crossing project conditions (ART versus control) with time of measurement (pre- versus poststudy) revealed a significant interaction effect favoring ART participants for each of the seven Skillstreaming categories—Beginning Social Skills, Advanced Social Skills, Skills for Dealing with Feelings, Skill Alternatives to Aggression, Skills for Dealing with Stress, and Planning Skills—as well as on a total skills score.

None of the ANOVA comparisons of ART scores with control group scores for the study's measure of anger control yielded significant differences. Of the five community domains, only work adjustment yielded a significant difference. This result accords well with (and no doubt largely reflects) the real-world employment pattern for project participants. For example, in the months immediately following their ART sequence, the majority of the participating Lo-Lives left their gang and took jobs in retail businesses. At an analogous point in time, following their own ART participation, a substantial minority of the participating Baby Wolfpack members obtained employment in the construction trades.

Arrest data were available for the youths participating in our first two ART gang intervention sequences and their respective control groups. Five of the 38 ART participants (13%) and 14 of the 27 control group members (52%) were rearrested during the 8-month tracking period (Chi square = 6.08, p < .01). Our primary rationale for working with intact gangs in this project was the opportunity afforded by such a strategy to capture a major portion of the youth's environment and turn it in a prosocial direction. The question was, once trainees learned given prosocial behaviors, would the transfer and maintenance of these skills be facilitated or discouraged by the people with whom the youths regularly interacted in the real-world environment? Our favorable outcome verified by rearrest rates implies the possibility that a more harmonious and prosocially promotive post-ART peer environment was created. While it is important for future research to examine this possibility more directly, it is of considerable interest to note that similar rearrest outcomes were obtained in our earlier attempt to create a prosocially reinforcing post-ART environment for delinquent youths by employing this intervention with them and their families. For these youths (ART for self and family), rearrest rates on follow-up were 15%; for no-ART control group youths, the comparable figure was 43%. Both of these outcomes from the community-based project closely parallel the outcomes found here (13% and 52%, respectively) for the presence or absence of support from a rather different type of "family"—fellow gang members.

Other Efficacy Evaluations

Our studies of the effectiveness of ART have yielded several promising findings, both proximal to the ART procedures (i.e., skill acquisition, anger control, enhanced moral reasoning) and distal to ART procedures but central to the program's ultimate purposes (i.e., reduced rearrests, enhanced community functioning). But what of the independent findings of other investigators?

Coleman, Pfeiffer, and Oakland (1991) evaluated the effectiveness of a 10-week ART program for behaviorally disordered adolescents in a Texas residential treatment center. Study results indicated improvement in participant skill knowledge but not in overt skill behaviors. Coleman et al. comment:

> The current study thus provides additional support for the contention that although cognitive gains can be demonstrated, the link to actual behavior is tenuous, especially with disturbed populations. (p. 17)

As our own previous discussion suggests, however, we believe that the likelihood for overt behavioral expression (performance) of newly acquired skills is less a function of the degree of trainee emotional disturbance than it is a matter of trainee motivation to perform and staff or other significant persons' perceived receptivity to and likely reward for such overt behaviors.

Coleman et al. continue:

> Of the ten social skills that were taught, three accounted for the improvement in social skills knowledge: keeping out of fights, dealing with group pressure, and expressing a complaint. The fact that Goldstein and Glick (1987) also found these same skills to be improved in two separate studies suggests that these skills may be the most responsive to intervention. One plausible explanation is that these three skills may be construed as contributing to self-preservation, especially within the context of residential or institutional living. (p. 15)

Curulla (1990) evaluated (a) a 14-week ART program versus (b) ART without the moral education component versus (c) a no-ART control condition. Trainees were 67 young adult offenders participating in a community intervention setting in Seattle. Curulla reports:

> Tendency toward recidivism and actual recidivism were compared among the three groups. Tendency towards recidivism as measured by the Weekly Activity Record was significantly reduced in the dilemma group. . . . The nondilemma . . . and control . . . groups showed no significant reduction. The dilemma group also had the lowest frequency of subsequent offense. . . . However, the differences in actual recidivism among the three groups did not reach statistical significance due to the low incidence of recorded changes during the six-month followup. (pp. 1–2)

Unlike Coleman et al.'s (1991) result, in Curulla's study—as in our own—overt acting-out behaviors were significantly reduced via ART participation. However, unlike our own results, post-ART recidivism was not.

In a second effort to examine the impact of ART component procedures singly and in combination, Kennedy (1989) assessed the efficacy of Skillstreaming and Anger Control Training with a sample of 37 adult incarcerated offenders, all of whom had a history of serious anger control difficulties. Outcome comparisons were made of the two procedures used in combination versus either Skillstreaming alone or Anger Control Training alone. Kennedy states:

The results of this study demonstrated that anger control training and structured learning therapy [Skillstreaming] are both effective treatment modalities for incarcerated adult male offenders with severe anger and aggressive behavioral problems. Subjects in all four active treatment conditions displayed the following changes. They self-reported less anger to a variety of provocations common to the prison setting. They self-reported decreases in the frequency, intensity, and duration of anger, more appropriate modalities of expression, and fewer consequences of anger reactions. Objective behavioral ratings of their verbal responses to laboratory role-played provocations indicated their responses were more appropriate, as were their self-reported reactions to these provocations. In addition, subjects demonstrated more prosocial attitudes following completion of the program. The overall findings from the followup measures provide strong support for the extended maintenance of treatment benefits. Subjects continued to demonstrate lower levels of anger arousal on cognitive indices of anger. (p. 3)

Jones (1990) compared ART to moral education and a no-treatment control using a sample of aggressive male students in a Brisbane, Australia, high school. Her results were consistent and positive:

Compared to the two control conditions, students completing the ART program: showed a significant decrease in aggressive incidences, a significant increase in coping incidences, and acquired more social skills. Students in condition 1 [also] improved on . . . self-control and impulsivity. . . . ART appears to be an effective intervention for aggressive youth within a high school setting. (p. 1)

A further investigation, also affirming the efficacy of ART, takes this intervention in a new direction. Gibbs and his coworkers in the Ohio Department of Youth Services have for some years employed and evaluated a Positive Peer Culture approach in their work with delinquent youths. This technique, described as an "adult-guided but youth-run group approach," places major responsibility upon the youth group itself for the management of the living environment as well as for changes in their own behaviors. Believing that youths are sufficiently motivated to conduct much of their own governance and direction but that they too frequently lack the skills and anger control to do so, Gibbs and his group combined the Positive Peer Culture approach with ART to yield a motivational, skills-oriented intervention they call EQUIP (Gibbs, Potter, & Goldstein, 1995). Leeman et al. (1993) note: "In EQUIP, moral discussion, anger management, or social skills sessions are designated as 'equipment meetings,' i.e., meetings wherein the group gains 'equipment' for helping group members" (pp. 5–6). These investigators conducted an efficacy evaluation of EQUIP at a medium-security institution for juvenile felony offenders, the Buckeye Youth Center in Columbus, Ohio. Three conditions were constituted—EQUIP, a motivational control group, and a no-treatment group. Outcome results were significant and supportive of the EQUIP intervention on both proximal and distal criteria. The investigators comment that "institutional conduct improvements were highly significant for the EQUIP relative to the control groups in terms of self-reported misconduct, staff-filed incident reports, and unexcused absences from school" (p. 18).

The investigators also found that, whereas the recidivism rate of EQUIP subjects was low (15%) at both 6 and 12 months following release, the control group rates worsened from 6 through 12 months (25 to 35% for the motivational control, 30 to 40% for the simple passage-of-time control). This pattern suggests that the treatment result was maintained as a stable effect.

Table 8.2 shows the results of the Leeman et al. (1993) investigation, as well as the findings of the community-based project (Goldstein et al., 1989) and the Gang Intervention Project (Goldstein, Glick et al., 1994). In all three studies, each of which yielded significant differences between the treatment versus control conditions, ART was offered both to the delinquent youths and to the other people (parents, fellow gang members, or fellow unit members) serving as arbitrators, reinforcers, or punishers of the youths' behavior. As change agents of all types have noted for decades, the client's system is as crucial a treatment target as is the client. As was the case for our community-based and gang ART evaluations, this investigation strongly confirms this assertion.

Two additional efficacy evaluations, both quasi-experimental in design, complete our survey of efforts to examine the impact of ART on the functioning of chronically aggressive youths. The first, the Collaborative Intensive Community Treatment Program, was conducted by Perseus House, a multisite community-based agency in Erie, Pennsylvania (M. Amendola, personal communication, November 17, 1997). ART lasted 13 weeks, for 7 days each week, and was presented to both youths and

Table 8.2

REARREST OUTCOMES FOR DELINQUENT
YOUTHS PLUS SIGNIFICANT OTHERS

	Months Following	Percent Recidivism	
		ART+	*No-ART control*
Youth plus family (community-based evaluation)[1]	4	15	43
Youth plus peers (Gang Intervention Project)[2]	8	13	52
Youth plus peers (Positive Peer Culture)[3]	12	15	40

[1] Goldstein and Glick (1987), Goldstein et al. (1989)
[2] Goldstein, Glick et al. (1994)
[3] Leeman et al. (1993)

their parents. Participating youths, all referred by juvenile court, were assigned to the program on either a deferred placement basis (diversion to the program instead of incarceration) or on a community reintegration basis (following a period of incarceration). Youth ART sessions were conducted daily. Parent sessions were held on Saturdays and Sundays. Compared to pre-ART status, gain scores revealed significant increases in participant (both youth and parent) Skillstreaming skill scores, youth school attendance and achievement scores (in math but not in reading), and staff ratings of youth overall psychological and social functioning (American Psychiatric Association, 1997).

The final evaluation was conducted by the Michigan Department of Social Services at five sites collectively constituting their Maxey Training School (S. White, personal communication, August 5, 1997). Participants, 44 youths sentenced to Maxey by juvenile court, underwent a 10-week ART program. Again, pre- and post-ART comparisons revealed significant growth in Skillstreaming skill competency. In all but one of the participating sites, there was also a significant decrease in within-institution acting-out behaviors.

The efficacy evaluations described in this chapter combine to suggest that ART is an effective intervention. With considerable reliability it appears to promote skills acquisition and performance, improve anger control, decrease the frequency of acting-out behaviors, and increase the frequency of constructive, prosocial behaviors. Beyond institutional walls, its effects persist, less fully perhaps than when the youth is in the controlled institutional environment, but persist nonetheless. These effects are especially pronounced when significant others in the youth's real-world environment are simultaneous recipients of ART. In general, the ART program's potency appears more than adequate to warrant continued program implementation and evaluation with chronically aggressive youngsters.

AFTERWORD

Summary and Future Directions

In chapter 1, we proposed that effective interventions for aggressive youth would, in their design and use, reflect four strategies. They would be complex, prescriptive, situational, and learning oriented. The journey this book represents through the history, procedures, applications, and evaluations of Aggression Replacement Training has reflected these strategic imperatives. ART's simultaneous targeting of behavioral, emotional, and values channels responds to the similarly situated, complex roots of the aggressive behaviors the program seeks to change. Its origin as a response to the paucity of appropriate interventions for youths from low-income environments gives early and full expression to the program's prescriptive intent. Reflecting the situational strategy, we and others have demonstrated across a series of studies that ART outcomes are substantially enhanced when aggressive youths and the significant family or peer figures in their lives are involved (see chapter 8). Such persons frequently control the destiny of trainees' newly learned positive behaviors; thus, "capturing" and employing such figures toward outcome advantage are crucial intervention goals. Finally, in its roots, procedures, and goals, ART is a teaching-learning intervention. Its group leaders are trainers, its targets are trainees, its methods are psychoeducational, and its successes are measured in terms of learning.

It is common in the use over time of most educational, mental health, or delinquency interventions for testing of program limits—or range of effective application—to take place. The intervention is applied first to one type of individual, then progressively to a variety of others for whom it also might be effective. If judgments of effectiveness and ineffectiveness are made in an objective, unbiased manner, the intervention's limits can be established.

We have begun testing ART's range of application and hope others will continue to do so. Further directions for limit testing might include assessment of ART's effectiveness with trainees both younger (lower elementary, preschool) and older (adult abusers, prison inmates) than the program's typical adolescent targets. ART programs have been run for young children and adults, but evaluations of program effectiveness with these groups are as yet forthcoming.

A second and most important direction for further tests of ART's range of application responds to the strong systems-oriented emphasis we have incorporated into our own tests of program limits. Our initial studies of the benefits of family and peer involvement in ART are but a beginning. We hope we have shown that such involvement is critical to the intervention's success. Much, much more needs to be discovered about the influence of such generalization-promoters. Specifically, we need to establish means to identify and involve them in the ART effort as well as methods to assess other aspects of their immensely significant role.

Finally, a majority of ART applications in school settings, though not in delinquency facilities, have been "pull-out" programs. That is, schools identify their "troublemakers" and assign them to ART in resource rooms, in-school suspension settings, or other similar contexts. While program use in this way is appropriate and effective, we hope others will build upon the already beginning attempts to employ and evaluate ART's use on a classwide, schoolwide, and even districtwide basis. We hope evaluations of such widespread applications will prove to be particularly rewarding tests of ART's limits. ART applied to all youth avoids the stigmatization possible with pull-out programs and has marked preventive potential. Let us teach youth what they need to know in order to manage difficult experiences before they begin to respond with chronic aggression.

APPENDIX A

Skillstreaming Skills for Adolescents

GROUP I: BEGINNING SOCIAL SKILLS

1. Listening   213
2. Starting a Conversation   214
3. Having a Conversation   215
4. Asking a Question   216
5. Saying Thank You   217
6. Introducing Yourself   218
7. Introducing Other People   219
8. Giving a Compliment   220

GROUP II: ADVANCED SOCIAL SKILLS

9. Asking for Help   221
10. Joining In   222
11. Giving Instructions   223
12. Following Instructions   224
13. Apologizing   225
14. Convincing Others   226

GROUP III: SKILLS FOR DEALING WITH FEELINGS

15. Knowing Your Feelings   227
16. Expressing Your Feelings   228
17. Understanding the Feelings of Others   229
18. Dealing with Someone Else's Anger   230
19. Expressing Affection   231
20. Dealing with Fear   232
21. Rewarding Yourself   233

GROUP IV: SKILL ALTERNATIVES TO AGGRESSION

22. Asking Permission   234
23. Sharing Something   235
24. Helping Others   236
25. Negotiating   237
26. Using Self-Control   238
27. Standing Up for Your Rights   239
28. Responding to Teasing   240
29. Avoiding Trouble with Others   241
30. Keeping Out of Fights   242

GROUP V: SKILLS FOR DEALING WITH STRESS

31. Making a Complaint   243
32. Answering a Complaint   244
33. Being a Good Sport   245
34. Dealing with Embarrassment   246
35. Dealing with Being Left Out   247
36. Standing Up for a Friend   248
37. Responding to Persuasion   249
38. Responding to Failure   250
39. Dealing with Contradictory Messages   251
40. Dealing with an Accusation   252
41. Getting Ready for a Difficult Conversation   253
42. Dealing with Group Pressure   254

GROUP VI: PLANNING SKILLS

43. Deciding on Something to Do   255
44. Deciding What Caused a Problem   256
45. Setting a Goal   257
46. Deciding on Your Abilities   258
47. Gathering Information   259
48. Arranging Problems by Importance   260
49. Making a Decision   261
50. Concentrating on a Task   262

GROUP I: BEGINNING SOCIAL SKILLS

Skill 1: Listening

STEPS	TRAINER NOTES
1. Look at the person who is talking.	Face the person; establish eye contact.
2. Think about what is being said.	Show this by nodding your head, saying "mm-hmm."
3. Wait your turn to talk.	Don't fidget; don't shuffle your feet.
4. Say what you want to say.	Ask questions; express feelings; express your ideas.

SUGGESTED CONTENT FOR MODELING DISPLAYS

School or neighborhood: Teacher explains classroom assignment to main actor.

Home: Mother feels sad, and main actor listens.

Peer group: Friend describes interesting movie to main actor.

COMMENTS

All of the beginning social skills are basic to the functioning of the group. In starting a Skillstreaming group, it is useful for trainees to have a reasonable grasp of these skills before proceeding to other skills.

Like Step 2, above, many of the behavioral steps that make up the skills described in this chapter are *thinking* steps. That is, in actual, real-world use of many skills, certain steps are private and occur only in the thinking of the skill user. When modeling or role-playing such thinking steps in Skillstreaming, however, it is crucial that the enactment be aloud. Such public display of thinking steps is a significant aid to rapid and lasting learning.

Skill 2: Starting a Conversation

STEPS	TRAINER NOTES
1. Greet the other person.	Say "hi"; shake hands; choose the right time and place.
2. Make small talk.	Talk about sports, the weather, school events, and so forth.
3. Decide if the other person is listening.	Check if the other person is listening: looking at you, nodding, saying "mm-hmm."
4. Bring up the main topic.	

SUGGESTED CONTENT FOR MODELING DISPLAYS

School or neighborhood: Main actor starts conversation with secretary in school office.

Home: Main actor discusses allowance and/or privileges with parent.

Peer group: Main actor suggests weekend plans to a friend.

COMMENTS

We have found that this is frequently one of the best skills to teach in the first Skillstreaming session with a new group of trainees.

GROUP I: BEGINNING SOCIAL SKILLS

Skill 3: Having a Conversation

STEPS	TRAINER NOTES
1. Say what you want to say.	
2. Ask the other person what he/she thinks.	
3. Listen to what the other person says.	Review steps for Skill 1 (Listening).
4. Say what you think.	Respond to the other person; add new information; ask questions.
5. Make a closing remark.	Discuss types of closing remarks. Steps 1–4 can be repeated many times before Step 5 is done.

SUGGESTED CONTENT FOR MODELING DISPLAYS

School or neighborhood: Main actor talks with coach about upcoming game.

Home: Main actor talks with brother or sister about school experiences.

Peer group: Main actor discusses vacation plans with friend.

COMMENTS

This skill starts where Skill 2 (Starting a Conversation) leaves off. After separate practice of each skill, trainers may want to give trainees practice in using these skills successively.

Skill 4: Asking a Question

STEPS

TRAINER NOTES

1. Decide what you'd like to know more about.

Ask about something you don't understand, something you didn't hear, or something confusing.

2. Decide whom to ask.

Think about who has the best information on a topic; consider asking several people.

3. Think about different ways to ask your question and pick one way.

Think about wording; raise your hand; ask nonchallengingly.

4. Pick the right time and place to ask your question.

Wait for a pause; wait for privacy.

5. Ask your question.

SUGGESTED CONTENT FOR MODELING DISPLAYS

School or neighborhood: Main actor asks teacher to explain something he/she finds unclear.

Home: Main actor asks mother to explain new curfew decision.

Peer group: Main actor asks classmate about missed schoolwork.

COMMENTS

Trainers are advised to model only single, answerable questions. In role-plays, trainees should be instructed to do likewise.

GROUP I: BEGINNING SOCIAL SKILLS

Skill 5: Saying Thank You

STEPS	TRAINER NOTES
1. Decide if the other person said or did something that you want to thank him/her for.	It may be a compliment, favor, or gift.
2. Choose a good time and place to thank the other person.	This is a quiet time, a private place, or other time and place where you are sure you will have the other person's attention.
3. Thank the other person in a friendly way.	Express thanks with words, a gift, a letter, or a return favor.
4. Tell the other person why you are thanking him/her.	

SUGGESTED CONTENT FOR MODELING DISPLAYS

School or neighborhood: Main actor thanks teacher for help on a project.

Home: Main actor thanks mother for fixing shirt.

Peer group: Main actor thanks friend for advice.

GROUP I: BEGINNING SOCIAL SKILLS

Skill 6: Introducing Yourself

STEPS	TRAINER NOTES
1. Choose the right time and place to introduce yourself.	
2. Greet the other person and tell your name.	Shake hands, if appropriate.
3. Ask the other person his/her name if you need to.	
4. Tell or ask the other person something to help start your conversation.	Tell something about yourself; comment on something you both have in common; ask a question.

SUGGESTED CONTENT FOR MODELING DISPLAYS

School or neighborhood: Main actor introduces self to a new neighbor.

Home: Main actor introduces self to friend of parents.

Peer group: Main actor introduces self to several classmates at start of school year.

COMMENTS

This skill and Skill 7 (Introducing Other People) are extremely important in a youngster's efforts to establish social contacts. They are not intended as lessons in "etiquette." Trainers should be attuned to choosing language appropriate to the particular interpersonal situation.

Skill 7: Introducing Other People

STEPS

TRAINER NOTES

1. Name the first person and tell him/her the name of the second person.

Speak clearly and loudly enough so that the names are heard by both people.

2. Name the second person and tell him/her the name of the first person.

3. Say something that helps the two people get to know each other.

Mention something they have in common; invite them to talk or do something with you; say how you know each of them.

SUGGESTED CONTENT FOR MODELING DISPLAYS

School or neighborhood: Main actor introduces parent to guidance counselor or teacher.

Home: Main actor introduces new friend to parent.

Peer group: Main actor introduces new neighbor to friends.

Skill 8: Giving a Compliment

STEPS	TRAINER NOTES
1. Decide what you want to compliment about the other person.	It may be the person's appearance, behavior, or another accomplishment.
2. Decide how to give the compliment.	Consider the wording and ways to keep the other person and yourself from feeling embarrassed.
3. Choose the right time and place to say it.	It may be a private place or a time when the other person is unoccupied.
4. Give the compliment.	Be friendly and sincere.

SUGGESTED CONTENT FOR MODELING DISPLAYS

School or neighborhood: Main actor compliments neighbor on new car.

Home: Main actor compliments parent on good dinner.

Peer group: Main actor compliments friend for avoiding fight.

GROUP II: ADVANCED SOCIAL SKILLS

Skill 9: Asking for Help

STEPS	TRAINER NOTES
1. Decide what the problem is.	Be specific: Who and what are contributing to the problem; what is its effect on you?
2. Decide if you want help for the problem.	Figure out if you can solve the problem alone.
3. Think about different people who might help you and pick one.	Consider all possible helpers and choose the best one.
4. Tell the person about the problem and ask that person to help you.	If the person wants to help you but is unable to do so at the moment, ask the person when a good time would be.

SUGGESTED CONTENT FOR MODELING DISPLAYS

School or neighborhood: Main actor asks teacher for help with difficult homework problem.

Home: Main actor asks parent for help with personal problem.

Peer group: Main actor asks friend for advice with dating.

COMMENTS

The definition of *problem*, as used in this skill, is anything one needs help with, varying from problems with other people to school and other informational problems.

GROUP II: ADVANCED SOCIAL SKILLS

Skill 10: Joining In

STEPS	TRAINER NOTES
1. Decide if you want to join in an activity others are doing.	Check the advantages and disadvantages. Be sure you want to participate in and not disrupt what others are doing.
2. Decide the best way to join in.	You might ask, apply, start a conversation, or introduce yourself.
3. Choose the best time to join in.	Good times are usually during a break in the activity or before the activity gets started.
4. Join in the activity.	

SUGGESTED CONTENT FOR MODELING DISPLAYS

School or neighborhood: Main actor signs up for neighborhood sports team.

Home: Main actor joins family in recreational activity.

Peer group: Main actor joins peers in ongoing game, recreational activity, or conversation.

GROUP II: ADVANCED SOCIAL SKILLS

Skill 11: Giving Instructions

STEPS	TRAINER NOTES
1. Decide what needs to be done.	It might be a chore or a favor.
2. Think about the different people who could do it and choose one.	
3. Ask that person to do what you want done.	Tell the person how to do it when the task is complex.
4. Ask the other person if he/she understands what to do.	
5. Change or repeat your instructions if you need to.	This step is optional.

SUGGESTED CONTENT FOR MODELING DISPLAYS

School or neighborhood: Main actor divides chores for decorating gym for school party.

Home: Main actor tells younger brother how to refuse drugs if offered to him.

Peer group: Main actor instructs friends on how to care for pet.

COMMENTS

This skill often refers to the enlistment of others to carry out a task and thus requires youngsters to think about division of responsibility.

Skill 12: Following Instructions

STEPS	TRAINER NOTES
1. Listen carefully while you are being told what to do.	Take notes if necessary; nod your head; say "mm-hmm."
2. Ask questions about anything you don't understand.	The goal is making instructions more specific, more clear.
3. Decide if you want to follow the instructions and let the other person know your decision.	Think about the positive and negative consequences of following the instructions.
4. Repeat the instructions to yourself.	Do this in your own words.
5. Do what you have been asked to do.	

SUGGESTED CONTENT FOR MODELING DISPLAYS

School or neighborhood: Main actor follows classroom instructions given by teacher.

Home: Main actor follows parent's instructions on operating home appliance.

Peer group: Main actor follows friend's instructions on fixing bicycle.

COMMENTS

This skill concerns complying with the requests of another person. If the task seems unreasonable, it may be an instance in which another skill is needed (e.g., Negotiating, Making a Complaint).

GROUP II: ADVANCED SOCIAL SKILLS

Skill 13: Apologizing

STEPS	TRAINER NOTES
1. Decide if it would be best for you to apologize for something you did.	You might apologize for breaking something, making an error, interrupting someone, or hurting someone's feelings.
2. Think of the different ways you could apologize.	Say something; do something; write something.
3. Choose the best time and place to apologize.	Do it privately and as quickly as possible after creating the problem.
4. Make your apology.	This might include an offer to make up for what happened.

SUGGESTED CONTENT FOR MODELING DISPLAYS

School or neighborhood: Main actor apologizes to neighbor for broken window.

Home: Main actor apologizes to younger sister for picking on her.

Peer group: Main actor apologizes to friend for betraying a confidence.

GROUP II: ADVANCED SOCIAL SKILLS

Skill 14: Convincing Others

STEPS	TRAINER NOTES
1. Decide if you want to convince someone about something.	It might be doing something your way, going someplace, interpreting events, or evaluating ideas.
2. Tell the other person your idea.	Focus on both content of ideas and feelings about point of view.
3. Ask the other person what he/she thinks about it.	This requires use of Listening (Skill 1).
4. Tell why you think your idea is a good one.	Try your best to be fair; "get into the other person's shoes."
5. Ask the other person to think about what you said before making up his/her mind.	Check on the other person's decision at a later point in time.

SUGGESTED CONTENT FOR MODELING DISPLAYS

School or neighborhood: Main actor convinces storekeeper that he/she deserves job.

Home: Main actor convinces parent that he/she is responsible enough to stay out late.

Peer group: Main actor convinces friend to include new person in game.

COMMENTS

In persuading someone of something, a person needs to understand both sides of the argument. Use of this skill assumes that if the other person is asked about his/her position and there is no difference of opinion, the role-play should end at Step 3.

Skill 15: Knowing Your Feelings

STEPS	TRAINER NOTES
1. Tune in to what is going on in your body that helps you know what you are feeling.	Some cues are blushing, butterflies in your stomach, tight muscles, and so on.
2. Decide what happened to make you feel that way.	Focus on outside events such as a fight, a surprise, and so forth.
3. Decide what you could call the feeling.	Possibilities are anger, fear, embarrassment, joy, happiness, sadness, disappointment, frustration, excitement, anxiety, and so on. (Trainer should create a list of feelings and encourage trainees to contribute additional suggestions.)

SUGGESTED CONTENT FOR MODELING DISPLAYS

School or neighborhood: Main actor feels embarrassed when peers call him/her "chickenshit" after refusal to use drugs.

Home: Main actor is angry when unjustly accused at home.

Peer group: Main actor is happy when friend pays compliment.

COMMENTS

This has been included as a separate skill for adolescents to learn prior to practicing the expression of feelings to another person. Frequently, feelings can be confused with one another, resulting in rather vague, but strong, emotions. Once the feeling can be labeled accurately, the trainee can go on to the next skill, which involves prosocial modes of expressing the feeling.

Step 1, involving "tuning in" to body feelings, is often a new experience for many people. Spend as much time as needed in discussing, giving examples, and practicing this step before going on to subsequent steps.

GROUP III: SKILLS FOR DEALING WITH FEELINGS

Skill 16: Expressing Your Feelings

STEPS	**TRAINER NOTES**
1. Tune in to what is going on in your body.	
2. Decide what happened to make you feel that way.	
3. Decide what you are feeling.	Possibilities are happy, sad, in a bad mood, nervous, worried, scared, embarrassed, disappointed, frustrated, and so forth. (Trainer and trainees should develop a list of feelings.)
4. Think about the different ways to express your feeling and pick one.	Consider prosocial alternatives such as talking about a feeling, doing a physical activity, telling the object of the feeling about the feeling, walking away from emotional situations, or delaying action. Consider how, when, where, and to whom the feeling could be expressed.
5. Express your feeling.	

SUGGESTED CONTENT FOR MODELING DISPLAYS

School or neighborhood: Main actor tells teacher about feeling nervous before test.

Home: Main actor tells parent about feeling embarrassed when treated like a child.

Peer group: Main actor hugs friend when learning of friend's success.

GROUP III: SKILLS FOR DEALING WITH FEELINGS

Skill 17: Understanding the Feelings of Others

STEPS	TRAINER NOTES
1. Watch the other person.	Notice tone of voice, posture, and facial expression.
2. Listen to what the other person is saying.	Try to understand the content.
3. Figure out what the person might be feeling.	He/she may be angry, sad, anxious, and so on.
4. Think about ways to show you understand what he/she is feeling.	You might tell him/her, touch him/her, or leave the person alone.
5. Decide on the best way and do it.	

SUGGESTED CONTENT FOR MODELING DISPLAYS

School or neighborhood: Main actor brings gift to neighbor whose spouse has been ill.

Home: Main actor recognizes parent is preoccupied with financial concerns and decides to leave parent alone.

Peer group: Main actor lets friend know he/she understands friend's discomfort on meeting new people.

COMMENTS

This skill is well known by the term *empathy*. Although difficult to teach, it is most important that many trainees add it to their repertoire of skills. Also, see chapter 7 for a description of the Prepare Curriculum course on empathy training, which is an elaboration of this skill.

Skill 18: Dealing with Someone Else's Anger

STEPS

TRAINER NOTES

1. Listen to the person who is angry.

Don't interrupt; stay calm.

2. Try to understand what the angry person is saying and feeling.

Ask questions to get explanations of what you don't understand; restate them to yourself.

3. Decide if you can say or do something to deal with the situation.

Think about ways of dealing with the problem. This may include just listening, being empathic, doing something to correct the problem, ignoring it, or being assertive.

4. If you can, deal with the other person's anger.

SUGGESTED CONTENT FOR MODELING DISPLAYS

School or neighborhood: Main actor responds to teacher who is angry about disruptive behavior in class by agreeing to cooperate and pay attention.

Home: Main actor responds to parent who is angry about messy house by agreeing to do a fair share of work.

Peer group: Main actor responds to admired older sibling's anger when main actor refuses to go drinking.

COMMENTS

This skill refers to anger directed at the trainee. As such, it usually requires some action on the part of the trainee to deal with the situation. Trainers should have the trainee make use of the steps for Skill 1 (Listening) when enacting the first step of this skill.

GROUP III: SKILLS FOR DEALING WITH FEELINGS

Skill 19: Expressing Affection

STEPS	TRAINER NOTES
1. Decide if you have good feelings about the other person.	
2. Decide if the other person would like to know about your feelings.	Consider the possible consequences (e.g., happiness, misinterpretation, embarrassment, encouragement of friendship).
3. Choose the best way to express your feelings.	Do something, say something, give gift, send card, telephone, offer invitation.
4. Choose the best time and place to express your feelings.	Minimize distractions and possible interruptions.
5. Express your feelings in a friendly way.	

SUGGESTED CONTENT FOR MODELING DISPLAYS

School or neighborhood: Main actor expresses positive feelings toward guidance counselor after sharing personal problem.

Home: Main actor brings small gift to parent as token of affection.

Peer group: Main actor expresses friendly feelings toward new acquaintance.

COMMENTS

Although trainees initially will associate this skill with romantic relationships, they will soon grasp the notion that affection and caring can be expressed toward a wide variety of persons.

Skill 20: Dealing with Fear

STEPS

1. Decide if you are feeling afraid.

2. Think about what you might be afraid of.

3. Figure out if the fear is realistic.

4. Take steps to reduce your fear.

TRAINER NOTES

Use Skill 15 (Knowing Your Feelings).

Think about alternative possibilities and choose the most likely one.

Is the feared object really a threat? You may need to check this out with another person or may need more information.

You might talk with someone, leave the scene, or gradually approach the frightening situation.

SUGGESTED CONTENT FOR MODELING DISPLAYS

School or neighborhood: Main actor is fearful of repercussions after breaking neighbor's window and discusses feeling with parent.

Home: Main actor is afraid of being home alone and arranges to have friend visit.

Peer group: After being teased by older neighborhood youth, main actor is fearful of being beaten up and takes steps to avoid confrontation.

COMMENTS

Group discussion can be quite useful in examining how realistic particular fears are. Trainers should be sensitive to the fact that trainees may be reluctant to reveal their fears to peers. Modeling of frightening situations may help them overcome this reluctance.

GROUP III: SKILLS FOR DEALING WITH FEELINGS

Skill 21: Rewarding Yourself

STEPS	TRAINER NOTES
1. Decide if you have done something that deserves a reward.	It might be something you have succeeded at or some area of progress.
2. Decide what you could say to reward yourself.	Use praise, approval, or encouragement.
3. Decide what you could do to reward yourself.	You might buy something, go someplace, or increase or decrease an activity.
4. Reward yourself.	Say and do it.

SUGGESTED CONTENT FOR MODELING DISPLAYS

School or neighborhood: Main actor rewards self after studying hard and doing well on exam by going to movie after school.

Home: Main actor rewards self with positive self-statement after avoiding fight with older sibling.

Peer group: Main actor rewards self by buying soda after convincing peers to join neighborhood club.

COMMENTS

Be sure trainees apply the following rules, all of which increase the effectiveness of self-reward:

- Reward yourself as soon as possible after successful performance.

- Reward yourself only after successful performance, not before.

- The better your performance, the better your self-reward.

GROUP IV: SKILL ALTERNATIVES TO AGGRESSION

Skill 22: Asking Permission

STEPS	TRAINER NOTES
1. Decide what you would like to do for which you need permission.	Ask if you want to borrow something or request a special privilege.
2. Decide whom you have to ask for permission.	Ask the owner, manager, or teacher.
3. Decide how to ask for permission.	Ask out loud; ask privately; ask in writing.
4. Pick the right time and place.	
5. Ask for permission.	

SUGGESTED CONTENT FOR MODELING DISPLAYS

School or neighborhood: Main actor asks shop teacher for permission to use new power tool.

Home: Main actor asks parent for permission to stay out past curfew.

Peer group: Main actor asks friend for permission to borrow sporting equipment.

COMMENTS

Prior to practicing this skill, it is frequently useful to discuss situations that require permission. Some youngsters tend to ask permission for things that could be done independently (without permission), whereas others neglect to ask permission in situations that require doing so.

GROUP IV: SKILL ALTERNATIVES TO AGGRESSION

Skill 23: Sharing Something

STEPS	TRAINER NOTES
1. Decide if you might like to share some of what you have.	Divide the item between yourself and the other person or allow the other to use the item.
2. Think about how the other person might feel about your sharing.	He/she might feel pleased, indifferent, suspicious, or insulted.
3. Offer to share in a direct and friendly way.	Make the offer sincere, allowing the other to decline if he/she wishes.

SUGGESTED CONTENT FOR MODELING DISPLAYS

School or neighborhood: Main actor offers to share books with classmate who has forgotten own book.

Home: Main actor offers to share candy with sibling.

Peer group: Main actor invites friend to try his new bicycle.

GROUP IV: SKILL ALTERNATIVES TO AGGRESSION

Skill 24: Helping Others

STEPS	**TRAINER NOTES**
1. Decide if the other person might need and want your help.	Think about the needs of the other person; observe.
2. Think of the ways you could be helpful.	
3. Ask the other person if he/she needs and wants your help.	Make the offer sincere, allowing the other to decline if he/she wishes.
4. Help the other person.	

SUGGESTED CONTENT FOR MODELING DISPLAYS

School or neighborhood: Main actor offers to help teacher arrange chairs in classroom.

Home: Main actor offers to help prepare dinner.

Peer group: Main actor offers to bring class assignments home for sick friend.

GROUP IV: SKILL ALTERNATIVES TO AGGRESSION

Skill 25: Negotiating

STEPS	TRAINER NOTES
1. Decide if you and the other person are having a difference of opinion.	Are you getting tense or arguing?
2. Tell the other person what you think about the problem.	State your own position and your perception of the other's position.
3. Ask the other person what he/she thinks about the problem.	
4. Listen openly to his/her answer.	
5. Think about why the other person might feel this way.	
6. Suggest a compromise.	Be sure the proposed compromise takes into account the opinions and feelings of both persons.

SUGGESTED CONTENT FOR MODELING DISPLAYS

School or neighborhood: Main actor negotiates with neighbor a fee for after-school chores.

Home: Main actor negotiates with parent about curfew or chores.

Peer group: Main actor negotiates with friend about recreational activity in which to participate.

COMMENTS

Negotiating is a skill that presupposes mastery of Understanding the Feelings of Others (Skill 17). We suggest that Skill 17 be reviewed prior to teaching Negotiating. Negotiating is also similar in some respects to Skill 14 (Convincing Others). Negotiating, however, introduces the concept of compromise, a concept that is often worth discussing before role-playing this skill.

GROUP IV: SKILL ALTERNATIVES TO AGGRESSION

Skill 26: Using Self-Control

STEPS

TRAINER NOTES

1. Tune in to what is going on in your body that helps you know you are about to lose control of yourself.

Are you getting tense, angry, hot, fidgety?

2. Decide what happened to make you feel this way.

Consider both outside events and "internal" events (thoughts).

3. Think about ways in which you might control yourself.

Slow down; count to 10; breathe deeply; assert yourself; leave; do something else.

4. Choose the best way to control yourself and do it.

SUGGESTED CONTENT FOR MODELING DISPLAYS

School or neighborhood: Main actor keeps from yelling at teacher when teacher criticizes harshly.

Home: Main actor controls self when parent forbids desired activity.

Peer group: Main actor controls self when friend takes something without asking permission.

COMMENTS

It is often helpful to discuss various ways of controlling oneself before role-playing the skill. The list of self-control techniques can be written on the chalkboard or easel pad and used to generate alternative tactics youngsters can use in a variety of situations.

GROUP IV: SKILL ALTERNATIVES TO AGGRESSION

Skill 27: Standing Up for Your Rights

STEPS	TRAINER NOTES
1. Pay attention to what is going on in your body that helps you know that you are dissatisfied and would like to stand up for yourself.	Some cues are tight muscles, butterflies in your stomach, and so forth.
2. Decide what happened to make you feel dissatisfied.	Are you being taken advantage of, ignored, mistreated, or teased?
3. Think about ways in which you might stand up for yourself and choose one.	Seek help; say what is on your mind; get a majority opinion; choose the right time and place.
4. Stand up for yourself in a direct and reasonable way.	

SUGGESTED CONTENT FOR MODELING DISPLAYS

School or neighborhood: Main actor approaches teacher after being disciplined unfairly.

Home: Main actor talks with parent about need for more privacy.

Peer group: Main actor talks with peer after not being chosen for the club (team).

COMMENTS

Also known as *assertiveness*, this skill is particularly important for withdrawn or shy trainees, as well as for trainees whose typical responses are inappropriately aggressive.

GROUP IV: SKILL ALTERNATIVES TO AGGRESSION

Skill 28: Responding to Teasing

STEPS	TRAINER NOTES
1. Decide if you are being teased.	Are others making jokes or whispering?
2. Think about ways to deal with the teasing.	Gracefully accept it; make a joke of it; ignore it.
3. Choose the best way and do it.	When possible, avoid alternatives that foster aggression, malicious counterteasing, and withdrawal.

SUGGESTED CONTENT FOR MODELING DISPLAYS

School or neighborhood: Main actor ignores classmate's comments when volunteering to help teacher after class.

Home: Main actor tells sibling to stop teasing about new haircut.

Peer group: Main actor deals with peer's teasing about a girlfriend or boyfriend by making a joke of it.

GROUP IV: SKILL ALTERNATIVES TO AGGRESSION

Skill 29: Avoiding Trouble with Others

STEPS	TRAINER NOTES
1. Decide if you are in a situation that might get you into trouble.	Examine immediate and long-range consequences.
2. Decide if you want to get out of the situation.	Consider risks versus gains.
3. Tell the other people what you decided and why.	
4. Suggest other things you might do.	Consider prosocial alternatives.
5. Do what you think is best for you.	

SUGGESTED CONTENT FOR MODELING DISPLAYS

School or neighborhood: Main actor tells classmates he/she will not cut class with them.

Home: Main actor refuses to take family car without permission.

Peer group: Main actor decides not to join peers in petty shoplifting.

COMMENTS

In Step 3, the reasons for decisions may vary according to the trainee's level of moral reasoning (e.g., fear of punishment, social conformity, concern for others).

GROUP IV: SKILL ALTERNATIVES TO AGGRESSION

Skill 30: Keeping Out of Fights

STEPS

1. Stop and think about why you want to fight.

2. Decide what you want to happen in the long run.

3. Think about other ways to handle the situation besides fighting.

4. Decide on the best way to handle the situation and do it.

TRAINER NOTES

What is the long-range outcome?

You might negotiate, stand up for your rights, ask for help, or pacify the person.

SUGGESTED CONTENT FOR MODELING DISPLAYS

School or neighborhood: Main actor tells classmate that he/she wants to talk out their differences instead of being pressured to fight.

Home: Main actor resolves potential fight with older sibling by asking parent to intervene.

Peer group: Main actor goes for help when he/she sees peers fighting on school steps.

COMMENTS

Prior to teaching this skill, it is often useful to review Skill 26 (Using Self-Control).

GROUP V: SKILLS FOR DEALING WITH STRESS

Skill 31: Making a Complaint

STEPS

1. Decide what your complaint is.

2. Decide whom to complain to.

3. Tell that person your complaint.

4. Tell that person what you would like done about the problem.

5. Ask how he/she feels about what you've said.

TRAINER NOTES

What is the problem?

Who can resolve it?

Consider alternative ways to complain (e.g., politely, assertively, privately).

Offer a helpful suggestion about resolving the problem.

SUGGESTED CONTENT FOR MODELING DISPLAYS

School or neighborhood: Main actor complains to guidance counselor about being assigned to class that is too difficult.

Home: Main actor complains to sibling about unfair division of chores.

Peer group: Main actor complains to friend about spreading a rumor.

GROUP V: SKILLS FOR DEALING WITH STRESS

Skill 32: Answering a Complaint

STEPS

TRAINER NOTES

1. Listen to the complaint.

Listen openly.

2. Ask the person to explain anything you don't understand.

3. Tell the person that you understand the complaint.

Rephrase; acknowledge the content and feeling.

4. State your ideas about the complaint, accepting the blame if appropriate.

5. Suggest what each of you could do about the complaint.

You might compromise, defend your position, or apologize.

SUGGESTED CONTENT FOR MODELING DISPLAYS

School or neighborhood: Main actor responds to neighbor's complaint about noisy party.

Home: Main actor responds to parent's complaint about selection of friends.

Peer group: Main actor responds to friend's complaint about returning sporting equipment in poor condition.

GROUP V: SKILLS FOR DEALING WITH STRESS

Skill 33: Being a Good Sport

STEPS	TRAINER NOTES
1. Think about how you did and how the other person did in the game you played.	
2. Think of a true compliment you could give the other person about his/her game.	Say "Good try," "Congratulations," or "Getting better."
3. Think about his/her reactions to what you might say.	The reaction might be pleasure, anger, or embarrassment.
4. Choose the compliment you think is best and say it.	

SUGGESTED CONTENT FOR MODELING DISPLAYS

School or neighborhood: Main actor talks to classmate who has made starting team.

Home: Main actor wins Monopoly game with younger sibling.

Peer group: New acquaintance does well in pickup game.

GROUP V: SKILLS FOR DEALING WITH STRESS

Skill 34: Dealing with Embarrassment

STEPS	TRAINER NOTES
1. Decide if you are feeling embarrassed.	
2. Decide what happened to make you feel embarrassed.	
3. Decide on what will help you feel less embarrassed and do it.	Correct the cause; minimize it; ignore it; distract others; use humor; reassure yourself.

SUGGESTED CONTENT FOR MODELING DISPLAYS

School or neighborhood: Main actor deals with embarrassment the day after refusing pressure from peers to use drugs.

Home: Mother catches main actor necking with boyfriend or girlfriend.

Peer group: Main actor is embarrassed by being overheard when discussing private matter.

COMMENTS

Prior to teaching this skill, it is often useful to review Skill 15 (Knowing Your Feelings).

GROUP V: SKILLS FOR DEALING WITH STRESS

Skill 35: Dealing with Being Left Out

STEPS	TRAINER NOTES
1. Decide if you are being left out.	Are you being ignored or rejected?
2. Think about why the other people might be leaving you out of something.	
3. Decide how you could deal with the problem.	You might wait, leave, tell the other people how their behavior affects you, or ask to be included.
4. Choose the best way and do it.	

SUGGESTED CONTENT FOR MODELING DISPLAYS

School or neighborhood: Main actor tells teacher about disappointment after not being picked for committee.

Home: Main actor asks sibling to include him/her in planned activity with other friends.

Peer group: Main actor is left out of plans for party.

GROUP V: SKILLS FOR DEALING WITH STRESS

Skill 36: Standing Up for a Friend

STEPS	TRAINER NOTES
1. Decide if your friend has not been treated fairly by others.	Has your friend been criticized, teased, or taken advantage of?
2. Decide if your friend wants you to stand up for him/her.	
3. Decide how to stand up for your friend.	You might assert his/her rights, explain, or apologize.
4. Stand up for your friend.	

SUGGESTED CONTENT FOR MODELING DISPLAYS

School or neighborhood: Main actor explains to teacher that friend has been accused unjustly.

Home: Main actor defends friend's reputation when parent is critical.

Peer group: Main actor defends friend when peers are teasing.

GROUP V: SKILLS FOR DEALING WITH STRESS

Skill 37: Responding to Persuasion

STEPS	TRAINER NOTES
1. Listen to the other person's ideas on the topic.	Listen openly; try to see the topic from the other person's viewpoint.
2. Decide what you think about the topic.	Distinguish your own ideas from the ideas of others.
3. Compare what he/she said with what you think.	Agree; disagree; modify; postpone a decision.
4. Decide which idea you like better and tell the other person about it.	

SUGGESTED CONTENT FOR MODELING DISPLAYS

School or neighborhood: Main actor deals with high-pressure sales pitch.

Home: Main actor deals with parental pressure to dress in a particular way for a party or a job interview.

Peer group: Main actor deals with friend's persuasive argument to try drugs.

GROUP V: SKILLS FOR DEALING WITH STRESS

Skill 38: Responding to Failure

STEPS	**TRAINER NOTES**
1. Decide if you have failed at something.	The failure may be interpersonal, academic, or athletic.
2. Think about why you failed.	It could be due to skill, motivation, or luck. Include personal reasons and circumstances.
3. Think about what you could do to keep from failing another time.	Evaluate what is under your control to change: If a skill problem, practice; if motivation, increase effort; if circumstances, think of ways to change them.
4. Decide if you want to try again.	
5. Try again using your new idea.	

SUGGESTED CONTENT FOR MODELING DISPLAYS

School or neighborhood: Main actor deals with failing grade on exam.

Home: Main actor fails at attempt to help younger sibling with a project.

Peer group: Main actor deals with being turned down for date.

GROUP V: SKILLS FOR DEALING WITH STRESS

Skill 39: Dealing with Contradictory Messages

STEPS	TRAINER NOTES
1. Decide if someone is telling you two opposite things at the same time.	This could be in words, in non-verbal behavior, or in saying one thing and doing another.
2. Think of ways to tell the other person that you don't understand what he/she means.	Confront the person; ask.
3. Choose the best way to tell the person and do it.	

SUGGESTED CONTENT FOR MODELING DISPLAYS

School or neighborhood: Main actor deals with teacher who verbalizes approval but scowls at same time.

Home: Main actor confronts parent who verbalizes trust but refuses to grant privileges.

Peer group: Main actor deals with friend who makes general invitation but never really includes main actor in plans.

COMMENTS

In teaching this skill, it is important to encourage youngsters to observe closely the behaviors of others around them. See if they can think about a person who says yes but at the same time shakes his or her head to mean no. See if they can think about a person who says, "Take your time" but at the same time makes them hurry up. That is, be sure to include situations in which the person is told two conflicting things, as well as those involving a person saying one thing and doing the opposite. In Step 1, this deciphering of the message is essential; otherwise, the trainee will be unable to proceed to Steps 2 and 3.

GROUP V: SKILLS FOR DEALING WITH STRESS

Skill 40: Dealing with an Accusation

STEPS	**TRAINER NOTES**
1. Think about what the other person has accused you of.	Is the accusation accurate or inaccurate?
2. Think about why the person might have accused you.	Have you infringed on his/her rights or property? Has a rumor been started by someone else?
3. Think about ways to answer the person's accusation.	Deny it; explain your own behavior; correct the other person's perceptions; assert yourself; apologize; offer to make up for what happened.
4. Choose the best way and do it.	

SUGGESTED CONTENT FOR MODELING DISPLAYS

School or neighborhood: Main actor is accused of breaking neighbor's window.

Home: Parent accuses main actor of hurting sibling's feelings.

Peer group: Friend accuses main actor of lying.

Skill 41: Getting Ready for a Difficult Conversation

STEPS	TRAINER NOTES
1. Think about how you will feel during the conversation.	You might be tense, anxious, or impatient.
2. Think about how the other person will feel.	He/she may feel anxious, bored, or angry.
3. Think about different ways you could say what you want to say.	
4. Think about what the other person might say back to you.	
5. Think about any other things that might happen during the conversation.	Repeat Steps 1–5 at least twice, using different approaches to the situation.
6. Choose the best approach you can think of and try it.	

SUGGESTED CONTENT FOR MODELING DISPLAYS

School or neighborhood: Main actor prepares to talk with teacher about dropping subject.

Home: Main actor prepares to tell parent about school failure.

Peer group: Main actor prepares to ask for first date.

COMMENTS

In preparing for difficult or stressful conversations, it is useful for youngsters to see that the way they approach the situation can influence the final outcome. This skill involves rehearsing a variety of approaches and then reflecting upon which approach produces the best results. Feedback from group members on the effectiveness of each approach can be particularly useful in this regard.

GROUP V: SKILLS FOR DEALING WITH STRESS

Skill 42: Dealing with Group Pressure

STEPS	TRAINER NOTES
1. Think about what the group wants you to do and why.	Listen to other people; decide what the real meaning is; try to understand what is being said.
2. Decide what you want to do.	Yield; resist; delay; negotiate.
3. Decide how to tell the group what you want to do.	Give reasons; talk to one person only; delay; assert yourself.
4. Tell the group what you have decided.	

SUGGESTED CONTENT FOR MODELING DISPLAYS

School or neighborhood: Main actor deals with group pressure to vandalize neighborhood.

Home: Main actor deals with family pressure to break up friendship.

Peer group: Main actor deals with pressure to fight.

GROUP VI: PLANNING SKILLS

Skill 43: Deciding on Something to Do

STEPS	**TRAINER NOTES**
1. Decide whether you are feeling bored or dissatisfied with what you are doing.	Are you not concentrating, getting fidgety, disrupting others who are involved in an activity?
2. Think of things you have enjoyed doing in the past.	
3. Decide which one you might be able to do now.	Focus on prosocial alternatives; include others if appropriate.
4. Start the activity.	

SUGGESTED CONTENT FOR MODELING DISPLAYS

School or neighborhood: Main actor chooses after-school activity in which to participate.

Home: Main actor thinks up activity that will earn him/her money.

Peer group: Main actor suggests that friends play basketball instead of hanging around.

Skill 44: Deciding What Caused a Problem

STEPS	TRAINER NOTES
1. Define what the problem is.	
2. Think about possible causes of the problem.	Was it yourself, others, or events; intentional, accidental, or both?
3. Decide which are the most likely causes of the problem.	
4. Check out what really caused the problem.	Ask others; observe the situation again.

SUGGESTED CONTENT FOR MODELING DISPLAYS

School or neighborhood: Main actor evaluates reasons for teacher's abruptness.

Home: Main actor evaluates likely causes of parents having an argument.

Peer group: Main actor evaluates why he/she feels nervous with particular friend.

COMMENT

This skill is intended to help youngsters determine the degree to which they are responsible for a particular problem and the degree to which the causes of the problem are outside of their control.

GROUP VI: PLANNING SKILLS

Skill 45: Setting a Goal

STEPS	TRAINER NOTES
1. Figure out what goal you want to reach.	
2. Find out all the information you can about how to reach your goal.	Talk with friends; read; observe others; ask authorities.
3. Think about the steps you will need to take to reach your goal.	Consider your abilities, materials, help from others, and skills needed.
4. Take the first step toward your goal.	

SUGGESTED CONTENT FOR MODELING DISPLAYS

School or neighborhood: Main actor decides to find a job.

Home: Main actor decides to improve appearance.

Peer group: Main actor decides to have a party.

GROUP VI: PLANNING SKILLS

Skill 46: Deciding on Your Abilities

STEPS	TRAINER NOTES
1. Decide which abilities you might want to use.	Take the setting, circumstances, and goal into account.
2. Think about how you have done in the past when you have tried to use these abilities.	
3. Get other people's opinions about your abilities.	Ask others; take tests; check records.
4. Think about what you found out and decide how well you use these abilities.	Consider the evidence from both Steps 2 and 3.

SUGGESTED CONTENT FOR MODELING DISPLAYS

School or neighborhood: Main actor decides type of school curriculum.

Home: Main actor evaluates ability to repair broken bicycle.

Peer group: Main actor decides whether to try out for team (school play).

COMMENTS

This skill is intended to help youngsters evaluate their capabilities realistically in view of available evidence. This skill is often tied to Skill 45 (Setting a Goal).

Skill 47: Gathering Information

STEPS	TRAINER NOTES
1. Decide what information you need.	
2. Decide how you can get the information.	You can get information from people, books, and so on.
3. Do things to get the information.	Ask questions; make telephone calls; look in books.

SUGGESTED CONTENT FOR MODELING DISPLAYS

School or neighborhood: Main actor gathers information on available jobs.

Home: Main actor gathers information on where to shop for particular item.

Peer group: Main actor finds out what kinds of things date likes to do.

COMMENTS

This skill often precedes Skill 49 (Making a Decision). Although each constitutes a separate skill, when taken together they often comprise an effective approach to problem solving.

Skill 48: Arranging Problems by Importance

STEPS	TRAINER NOTES
1. Think about the problems that are bothering you.	Make a list; be inclusive.
2. List these problems from most to least important.	
3. Do what you can to hold off on your less important problems.	Delegate them; postpone them; avoid them.
4. Go to work on your most important problems.	Plan first steps in dealing with the most important problem; rehearse these steps in your imagination.

SUGGESTED CONTENT FOR MODELING DISPLAYS

School or neighborhood: Main actor is worried about large number of school assignments.

Home: Parent tells main actor to take care of several chores before going out.

Peer group: Main actor has difficulty balancing school responsibilities, chores, and time with friends.

COMMENTS

This skill is intended to help the youngster who feels overwhelmed by a number of difficulties. The youngster is taught how to evaluate the relative urgency of the various problems and to deal with each according to the priority of its importance.

Skill 49: Making a Decision

STEPS	TRAINER NOTES
1. Think about the problem that requires you to make a decision.	
2. Think about possible decisions you could make.	Generate a number of possible alternatives; avoid premature closure.
3. Gather accurate information about these possible decisions.	Ask others; read; observe.
4. Reconsider your possible decisions using the information you have gathered.	
5. Make the best decision.	

SUGGESTED CONTENT FOR MODELING DISPLAYS

School or neighborhood: Main actor decides what job to apply for.

Home: Main actor decides how to spend money he/she has earned.

Peer group: Main actor decides whether to participate with friends in a weekend activity.

COMMENTS

This skill follows Skill 47 (Gathering Information) to constitute the general skill of problem solving.

GROUP VI: PLANNING SKILLS

Skill 50: Concentrating on a Task

STEPS	TRAINER NOTES
1. Decide what your task is.	
2. Decide on a time to work on this task.	Consider when and how long to work.
3. Gather the materials you need.	
4. Decide on a place to work.	Consider where: Minimize noise level, people present, possible interruptions.
5. Decide if you are ready to concentrate.	

SUGGESTED CONTENT FOR MODELING DISPLAYS

School or neighborhood: Main actor prepares to research and write a report.

Home: Main actor prepares to repair bicycle (appliance).

Peer group: Main actor gathers materials necessary for trip with friends.

COMMENTS

This skill helps youngsters overcome problems with distractions by focusing on relevant planning prior to undertaking a task. Planning, in this sense, involves scheduling and arranging materials and work environment.

Skillstreaming Checklists and Grouping Chart

Teacher/Staff Skillstreaming Checklist   265

Parent Skillstreaming Checklist   275

Student Skillstreaming Checklist   284

Skillstreaming Grouping Chart   288

TEACHER/STAFF SKILLSTREAMING CHECKLIST

Student: _____ Class/age: _____

Teacher/staff: _____ Date: _____

Instructions: Listed below you will find a number of skills that young-sters are more or less proficient in using. This checklist will help you evaluate how well each youngster uses the various skills. For each youngster, rate his or her use of each skill, based on your observations of the youngster's behavior in various situations.

Circle 1 if the youngster *almost never* uses the skill.

Circle 2 if the youngster *seldom* uses the skill.

Circle 3 if the youngster *sometimes* uses the skill.

Circle 4 if the youngster *often* uses the skill.

Circle 5 if the youngster *almost always* uses the skill.

Please rate the youngster on all skills listed. If you know of a situation in which the youngster has particular difficulty in using the skill well, please note it briefly in the space marked "Problem situation."

	ALMOST NEVER	SELDOM	SOMETIMES	OFTEN	ALMOST ALWAYS
1. **Listening:** Does the youngster pay attention to someone who is talking and make an effort to understand what is being said?	1	2	3	4	5
Problem situation:					
2. **Starting a Conversation:** Does the youngster talk to others about light topics and then lead into more serious topics?	1	2	3	4	5
Problem situation:					

ALMOST NEVER   SELDOM   SOMETIMES   OFTEN   ALMOST ALWAYS

3. **Having a Conversation:** Does the   1   2   3   4   5
youngster talk to others about things
of interest to both of them?

   Problem situation:

4. **Asking a Question:** Does the youngster   1   2   3   4   5
decide what information is needed and
ask the right person for that information?

   Problem situation:

5. **Saying Thank You:** Does the youngster   1   2   3   4   5
let others know that he/she is grateful
for favors, etc.?

   Problem situation:

6. **Introducing Yourself:** Does the youngster   1   2   3   4   5
become acquainted with new people on
his/her own initiative?

   Problem situation:

7. **Introducing Other People:** Does the   1   2   3   4   5
youngster help others become acquainted
with one another?

   Problem situation:

8. **Giving a Compliment:** Does the youngster   1   2   3   4   5
tell others that he/she likes something
about them or their activities?

   Problem situation:

ALMOST NEVER   SELDOM   SOMETIMES   OFTEN   ALMOST ALWAYS

9. **Asking for Help:** Does the youngster request assistance when he/she is having difficulty?   1 2 3 4 5

   Problem situation:

10. **Joining In:** Does the youngster decide on the best way to become part of an ongoing activity or group?   1 2 3 4 5

    Problem situation:

11. **Giving Instructions:** Does the youngster clearly explain to others how they are to do a specific task?   1 2 3 4 5

    Problem situation:

12. **Following Instructions:** Does the youngster pay attention to instructions, give his/her reactions, and carry the instructions out adequately?   1 2 3 4 5

    Problem situation:

13. **Apologizing:** Does the youngster tell others that he/she is sorry after doing something wrong?   1 2 3 4 5

    Problem situation:

14. **Convincing Others:** Does the youngster attempt to persuade others that his/her ideas are better and will be more useful than those of the other person?   1 2 3 4 5

    Problem situation:

ALMOST NEVER   SELDOM   SOMETIMES   OFTEN   ALMOST ALWAYS

15. **Knowing Your Feelings:** Does the   1   2   3   4   5
youngster try to recognize which
emotions he/she has at different times?

Problem situation:

16. **Expressing Your Feelings:** Does the   1   2   3   4   5
youngster let others know which
emotions he/she is feeling?

Problem situation:

17. **Understanding the Feelings of Others:**   1   2   3   4   5
Does the youngster try to figure out
what other people are feeling?

Problem situation:

18. **Dealing with Someone Else's Anger:**   1   2   3   4   5
Does the youngster try to understand
other people's angry feelings?

Problem situation:

19. **Expressing Affection:** Does the   1   2   3   4   5
youngster let others know that he/she
cares about them?

Problem situation:

20. **Dealing with Fear:** Does the youngster   1   2   3   4   5
figure out why he/she is afraid and do
something to reduce the fear?

Problem situation:

ALMOST NEVER SELDOM SOMETIMES OFTEN ALMOST ALWAYS

21. **Rewarding Yourself:** Does the youngster   1   2   3   4   5
say and do nice things for himself/herself
when the reward is deserved?

Problem situation:

22. **Asking Permission:** Does the youngster   1   2   3   4   5
figure out when permission is needed to
do something and then ask the right
person for permission?

Problem situation:

23. **Sharing Something:** Does the youngster   1   2   3   4   5
offer to share what he/she has with others
who might appreciate it?

Problem situation:

24. **Helping Others:** Does the youngster   1   2   3   4   5
give assistance to others who might
need or want help?

Problem situation:

25. **Negotiating:** Does the youngster arrive   1   2   3   4   5
at a plan that satisfies both him/her and
others who have taken different positions?

Problem situation:

26. **Using Self-Control:** Does the youngster   1   2   3   4   5
control his/her temper so that things do
not get out of hand?

Problem situation:

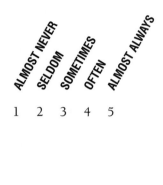

27. **Standing Up for Your Rights:** Does the   1   2   3   4   5
youngster assert his/her rights by letting
people know where he/she stands on
an issue?

Problem situation:

28. **Responding to Teasing:** Does the   1   2   3   4   5
youngster deal with being teased by
others in ways that allow him/her to
remain in control of himself/herself?

Problem situation:

29. **Avoiding Trouble with Others:** Does   1   2   3   4   5
the youngster stay out of situations that
might get him/her into trouble?

Problem situation:

30. **Keeping Out of Fights:** Does the   1   2   3   4   5
youngster figure out ways other than
fighting to handle difficult situations?

Problem situation:

31. **Making a Complaint:** Does the   1   2   3   4   5
youngster tell others when they are
responsible for creating a particular
problem for him/her and then attempt
to find a solution to the problem?

Problem situation:

ALMOST NEVER   SELDOM   SOMETIMES   OFTEN   ALMOST ALWAYS

32. **Answering a Complaint:** Does the   1   2   3   4   5
youngster try to arrive at a fair solution
to someone's justified complaint?

Problem situation:

33. **Being a Good Sport:** Does the youngster   1   2   3   4   5
express an honest compliment to others
about how they played a game?

Problem situation:

34. **Dealing with Embarrassment:** Does the   1   2   3   4   5
youngster do things that help him/her
feel less embarrassed or self-conscious?

Problem situation:

35. **Dealing with Being Left Out:** Does the   1   2   3   4   5
youngster decide whether he/she has
been left out of some activity and then do
things to feel better about the situation?

Problem situation:

36. **Standing Up for a Friend:** Does the   1   2   3   4   5
youngster let other people know when
a friend has not been treated fairly?

Problem situation:

37. **Responding to Persuasion:** Does the   1   2   3   4   5
youngster carefully consider the position
of another person, comparing it to his/her
own, before deciding what to do?

Problem situation:

38. **Responding to Failure:** Does the
    youngster figure out the reason for
    failing in a particular situation and
    what he/she can do about it in order
    to be more successful in the future?

    Problem situation:

39. **Dealing with Contradictory Messages:**
    Does the youngster recognize and deal with
    the confusion that results when others tell
    him/her one thing but say or do things that
    indicate that they mean something else?

    Problem situation:

40. **Dealing with an Accusation:** Does the
    youngster figure out what he/she has
    been accused of and why, then decide
    on the best way to deal with the person
    who made the accusation?

    Problem situation:

41. **Getting Ready for a Difficult Conversation:**
    Does the youngster plan on the best way
    to present his/her point of view prior to
    a stressful conversation?

    Problem situation:

42. **Dealing with Group Pressure:** Does the
    youngster decide what he/she wants to
    do when others want him/her to do
    something else?

    Problem situation:

ALMOST NEVER SELDOM SOMETIMES OFTEN ALMOST ALWAYS

43. **Deciding on Something to Do:** Does   1   2   3   4   5
    the youngster deal with feeling bored
    by starting an interesting activity?

    Problem situation:

44. **Deciding What Caused a Problem:**   1   2   3   4   5
    Does the youngster find out whether an
    event was caused by something that was
    within his/her control?

    Problem situation:

45. **Setting a Goal:** Does the youngster   1   2   3   4   5
    realistically decide on what he/she can
    accomplish prior to starting a task?

    Problem situation:

46. **Deciding on Your Abilities:** Does the   1   2   3   4   5
    youngster realistically figure out how
    well he/she might do at a particular task?

    Problem situation:

47. **Gathering Information:** Does the   1   2   3   4   5
    youngster decide what he/she needs to
    know and how to get that information?

    Problem situation:

48. **Arranging Problems by Importance:**   1   2   3   4   5
    Does the youngster decide realistically
    which of a number of problems is most
    important and should be dealt with first?

    Problem situation:

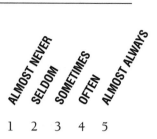

49. **Making a Decision:** Does the youngster   1   2   3   4   5
    consider possibilities and make choices
    that he/she feels will be best?

    Problem situation:

50. **Concentrating on a Task:** Does the   1   2   3   4   5
    youngster make those preparations that
    will help him/her get a job done?

    Problem situation:

PARENT SKILLSTREAMING CHECKLIST

Name: _____ Date: _____

Child's name: _____ Birth date: _____

Instructions: Based on your observations in various situations, rate your child's use of the following skills.

Circle 1 if your child *almost never* uses the skill.

Circle 2 if your child *seldom* uses the skill.

Circle 3 if your child *sometimes* uses the skill.

Circle 4 if your child *often* uses the skill.

Circle 5 if your child *almost always* uses the skill.

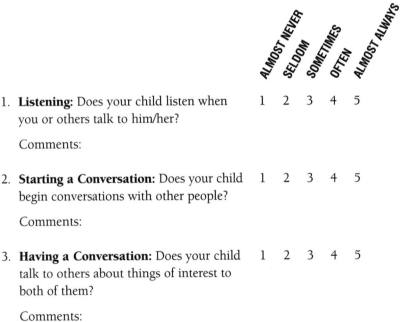

1. **Listening:** Does your child listen when you or others talk to him/her?
   1 2 3 4 5

   Comments:

2. **Starting a Conversation:** Does your child begin conversations with other people?
   1 2 3 4 5

   Comments:

3. **Having a Conversation:** Does your child talk to others about things of interest to both of them?
   1 2 3 4 5

   Comments:

		ALMOST NEVER	SELDOM	SOMETIMES	OFTEN	ALMOST ALWAYS

4. **Asking a Question:** Does your child know how and when to ask questions of another person?

                                 1   2   3   4   5

   Comments:

5. **Saying Thank You:** Does your child let others know that he/she is grateful for favors, etc.?

                                 1   2   3   4   5

   Comments:

6. **Introducing Yourself:** Does your child become acquainted with new people on his/her own?

                                 1   2   3   4   5

   Comments:

7. **Introducing Other People:** Does your child help others become acquainted with one another?

                                 1   2   3   4   5

   Comments:

8. **Giving a Compliment:** Does your child tell others that he/she likes something about them or something they have done?

                                 1   2   3   4   5

   Comments:

                                 1   2   3   4   5

9. **Asking for Help:** Does your child request assistance when he/she is having difficulty?

   Comments:

ALMOST NEVER   SELDOM   SOMETIMES   OFTEN   ALMOST ALWAYS

10. **Joining In:** Does your child take steps to become part of an ongoing activity or group?   1   2   3   4   5

Comments:

11. **Giving Instructions:** Does your child clearly explain to others how and why they should do something?   1   2   3   4   5

Comments:

12. **Following Instructions:** Does your child carry out instructions from others quickly and correctly?   1   2   3   4   5

Comments:

13. **Apologizing:** Does your child tell others he/she is sorry after doing something wrong?   1   2   3   4   5

Comments:

14. **Convincing Others:** Does your child attempt to persuade others that his/her ideas are better than theirs?   1   2   3   4   5

Comments:

15. **Knowing Your Feelings:** Does your child recognize which emotions he or she has at different times?   1   2   3   4   5

Comments:

ALMOST NEVER   SELDOM   SOMETIMES   OFTEN   ALMOST ALWAYS

16. **Expressing Your Feelings:** Does your   1   2   3   4   5
    child let others know which emotions
    he/she is feeling?

    Comments:

17. **Understanding the Feelings of Others:**   1   2   3   4   5
    Does your child understand what other
    people are feeling?

    Comments:

18. **Dealing with Someone Else's Anger:**   1   2   3   4   5
    Does your child try to understand
    someone else's anger without getting
    angry himself/herself?

    Comments:

19. **Expressing Affection:** Does your child let 1   2   3   4   5
    others know that he/she cares about them?

    Comments:

20. **Dealing with Fear:** Does your child   1   2   3   4   5
    figure out why he/she is afraid and do
    something to reduce the fear?

    Comments:

21. **Rewarding Yourself:** Does your child say   1   2   3   4   5
    and do nice things for himself/herself
    when it is deserved?

    Comments:

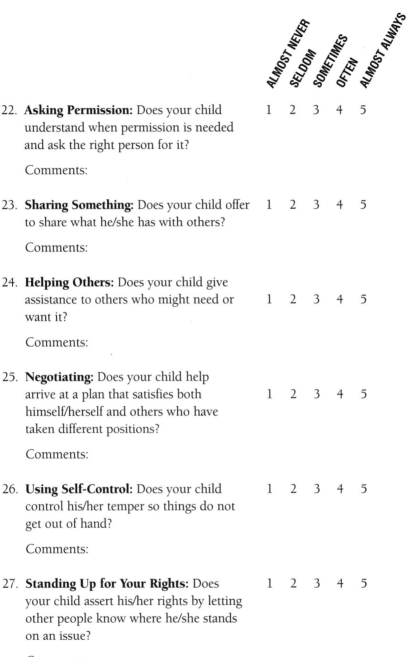

22. **Asking Permission:** Does your child understand when permission is needed and ask the right person for it?　1　2　3　4　5

    Comments:

23. **Sharing Something:** Does your child offer to share what he/she has with others?　1　2　3　4　5

    Comments:

24. **Helping Others:** Does your child give assistance to others who might need or want it?　1　2　3　4　5

    Comments:

25. **Negotiating:** Does your child help arrive at a plan that satisfies both himself/herself and others who have taken different positions?　1　2　3　4　5

    Comments:

26. **Using Self-Control:** Does your child control his/her temper so things do not get out of hand?　1　2　3　4　5

    Comments:

27. **Standing Up for Your Rights:** Does your child assert his/her rights by letting other people know where he/she stands on an issue?　1　2　3　4　5

    Comments:

ALMOST NEVER   SELDOM   SOMETIMES   OFTEN   ALMOST ALWAYS

28. **Responding to Teasing:** Does your child   1   2   3   4   5
deal in a constructive way with being
teased?

Comments:

29. **Avoiding Trouble with Others:** Does   1   2   3   4   5
your child stay out of situations that
might get him/her in trouble?

Comments:

30. **Keeping Out of Fights:** Does your child   1   2   3   4   5
figure out ways other than fighting to
handle difficult situations?

Comments:

31. **Making a Complaint:** Does your child   1   2   3   4   5
disagree with others in acceptable ways?

Comments:

32. **Answering a Complaint:** Does your   1   2   3   4   5
child try to arrive at a fair solution to
someone else's justified complaint?

Comments:

33. **Being a Good Sport:** Does your child   1   2   3   4   5
express an honest compliment to others
about how they played a game?

Comments:

34. **Dealing with Embarrassment:** Does your child do things that help him/her feel less embarrassed or self-conscious?

    Comments:

35. **Dealing with Being Left Out:** Does your child deal positively with being left out of some activity?

    Comments:

36. **Standing Up for a Friend:** Does your child let other people know when a friend has not been treated fairly?

    Comments:

37. **Responding to Persuasion:** Does your child think alternatives through before responding to persuasion from others?

    Comments:

38. **Responding to Failure:** Does your child figure out the reasons he/she failed at something and how to correct the failure?

    Comments:

39. **Dealing with Contradictory Messages:** Does your child recognize and deal with it when others say or do one thing but also indicate they mean something else?

    Comments:

	ALMOST NEVER	SELDOM	SOMETIMES	OFTEN	ALMOST ALWAYS

40. **Dealing with an Accusation:** Does your child figure out what he/she has been accused of, then use constructive ways of dealing with it?   1 2 3 4 5

   Comments:

41. **Getting Ready for a Difficult Conversation:** Does your child plan on the best way to present his/her own point of view before a stressful conversation?   1 2 3 4 5

   Comments:

42. **Dealing with Group Pressure:** Does your child decide what he/she wants to do when others are urging him/her to do something else?   1 2 3 4 5

   Comments:

43. **Deciding on Something to Do:** Does your child deal with feeling bored by starting an interesting activity?   1 2 3 4 5

   Comments:

44. **Deciding What Caused a Problem:** Does your child try to find out whether an event was caused by something under his/her control?   1 2 3 4 5

   Comments:

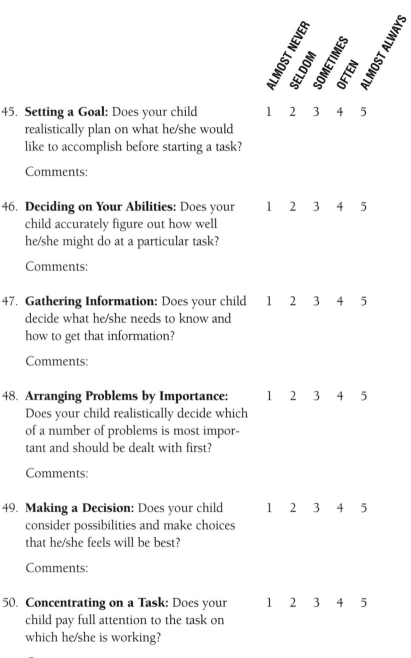

45. **Setting a Goal:** Does your child realistically plan on what he/she would like to accomplish before starting a task?   1   2   3   4   5

    Comments:

46. **Deciding on Your Abilities:** Does your child accurately figure out how well he/she might do at a particular task?   1   2   3   4   5

    Comments:

47. **Gathering Information:** Does your child decide what he/she needs to know and how to get that information?   1   2   3   4   5

    Comments:

48. **Arranging Problems by Importance:** Does your child realistically decide which of a number of problems is most important and should be dealt with first?   1   2   3   4   5

    Comments:

49. **Making a Decision:** Does your child consider possibilities and make choices that he/she feels will be best?   1   2   3   4   5

    Comments:

50. **Concentrating on a Task:** Does your child pay full attention to the task on which he/she is working?   1   2   3   4   5

    Comments:

STUDENT SKILLSTREAMING CHECKLIST

Name:_____ Date: _____

Instructions: Based on your observations in various situations, rate your use of the following skills.

Circle 1 if you *almost never* use the skill.

Circle 2 if you *seldom* use the skill.

Circle 3 if you *sometimes* use the skill.

Circle 4 if you *often* use the skill.

Circle 5 if you *almost always* use the skill.

	ALMOST NEVER	SELDOM	SOMETIMES	OFTEN	ALMOST ALWAYS
1. Do I listen to someone who is talking to me?	1	2	3	4	5
2. Do I start conversations with other people?	1	2	3	4	5
3. Do I talk with other people about things that interest both of us?	1	2	3	4	5
4. Do I ask questions when I need or want to know something?	1	2	3	4	5
5. Do I say thank you when someone does something for me?	1	2	3	4	5
6. Do I introduce myself to new people?	1	2	3	4	5
7. Do I introduce people who haven't met before to each other?	1	2	3	4	5
8. Do I tell other people when I like how they are or something they have done?	1	2	3	4	5
9. Do I ask for help when I am having difficulty doing something?	1	2	3	4	5

	ALMOST NEVER	SELDOM	SOMETIMES	OFTEN	ALMOST ALWAYS
10. Do I try to join in when others are doing something I'd like to be part of?	1	2	3	4	5
11. Do I clearly explain to others how and why they should do something?	1	2	3	4	5
12. Do I carry out instructions from other people quickly and correctly?	1	2	3	4	5
13. Do I apologize to others when I have done something wrong?	1	2	3	4	5
14. Do I try to convince others that my ideas are better than theirs?	1	2	3	4	5
15. Do I recognize the feelings I have at different times?	1	2	3	4	5
16. Do I let others know what I am feeling and do it in a good way?	1	2	3	4	5
17. Do I understand what other people are feeling?	1	2	3	4	5
18. Do I try to understand, and not get angry, when someone else is angry?	1	2	3	4	5
19. Do I let others know when I care about them?	1	2	3	4	5
20. Do I know what makes me afraid and do things so that I don't stay that way?	1	2	3	4	5
21. Do I say and do nice things for myself when I have earned it?	1	2	3	4	5
22. Do I understand when permission is needed to do something and ask the right person for it?	1	2	3	4	5
23. Do I offer to share what I have with others?	1	2	3	4	5

	ALMOST NEVER	SELDOM	SOMETIMES	OFTEN	ALMOST ALWAYS
24. Do I help others who might need or want help?	1	2	3	4	5
25. Do I try to make both of us satisfied with the result when someone and I disagree?	1	2	3	4	5
26. Do I control my temper when I feel upset?	1	2	3	4	5
27. Do I stand up for my rights to let other people know what I think or feel?	1	2	3	4	5
28. Do I stay in control when someone teases me?	1	2	3	4	5
29. Do I try to stay out of situations that might get me in trouble?	1	2	3	4	5
30. Do I figure out ways other than fighting to handle difficult situations?	1	2	3	4	5
31. Do I make complaints I have about others in a fair way?	1	2	3	4	5
32. Do I handle complaints made against me in a fair way?	1	2	3	4	5
33. Do I say nice things to others after a game about how they played?	1	2	3	4	5
34. Do I do things that help me feel less embarrassed when difficulties happen?	1	2	3	4	5
35. Do I deal positively with being left out of some activity?	1	2	3	4	5
36. Do I let people know when I feel a friend has not been treated fairly?	1	2	3	4	5
37. Do I think choices through before answering when someone is trying to convince me about something?	1	2	3	4	5

	ALMOST NEVER	SELDOM	SOMETIMES	OFTEN	ALMOST ALWAYS
38. Do I try to figure out the reasons it happened when I fail at something?	1	2	3	4	5
39. Do I deal with it well when someone says or does one thing but means something else?	1	2	3	4	5
40. Do I deal with it well when someone accuses me of doing something?	1	2	3	4	5
41. Do I plan ahead the best ways to handle it before I have a difficult conversation?	1	2	3	4	5
42. Do I decide what I want to do when others pressure me to do something else?	1	2	3	4	5
43. Do I think of good things to do and then do them when I feel bored?	1	2	3	4	5
44. Do I, when there is a problem, try to find out what caused it?	1	2	3	4	5
45. Do I think about what I would like to do before I start a new task?	1	2	3	4	5
46. Do I think about what I am really able to do before I start a new task?	1	2	3	4	5
47. Do I decide, before doing something, what I need to know and how to find out?	1	2	3	4	5
48. Do I decide which problem is most important and should be handled first?	1	2	3	4	5
49. Do I think about different possibilities and choose the one that is best?	1	2	3	4	5
50. Do I pay full attention to whatever I am working on?	1	2	3	4	5

SKILLSTREAMING GROUPING CHART

STUDENT NAMES

GROUP I
Beginning Social Skills

1. Listening									
2. Starting a Conversation									
3. Having a Conversation									
4. Asking a Question									
5. Saying Thank You									
6. Introducing Yourself									
7. Introducing Other People									
8. Giving a Compliment									

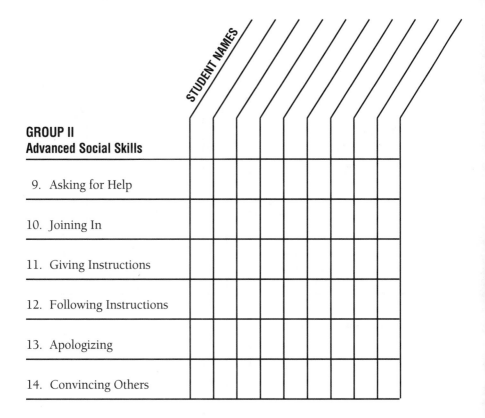

GROUP II
Advanced Social Skills

	STUDENT NAMES									
9. Asking for Help										
10. Joining In										
11. Giving Instructions										
12. Following Instructions										
13. Apologizing										
14. Convincing Others										

STUDENT NAMES

**GROUP III
Skills for Dealing
with Feelings**

15. Knowing Your Feelings

16. Expressing Your
    Feelings

17. Understanding the
    Feelings of Others

18. Dealing with Someone
    Else's Anger

19. Expressing Affection

20. Dealing with Fear

21. Rewarding Yourself

	STUDENT NAMES								
GROUP IV **Skill Alternatives** **to Aggression**									
22. Asking Permission									
23. Sharing Something									
24. Helping Others									
25. Negotiating									
26. Using Self-Control									
27. Standing Up for Your Rights									
28. Responding to Teasing									
29. Avoiding Trouble with Others									
30. Keeping Out of Fights									

	STUDENT NAMES									
GROUP V **Skills for Dealing** **with Stress**										
31. Making a Complaint										
32. Answering a Complaint										
33. Being a Good Sport										
34. Dealing with Embarrassment										
35. Dealing with Being Left Out										
36. Standing Up for a Friend										
37. Responding to Persuasion										
38. Responding to Failure										
39. Dealing with Contradictory Messages										
40. Dealing with an Accusation										
41. Getting Ready for a Difficult Conversation										
42. Dealing with Group Pressure										

	STUDENT NAMES									
GROUP VI **Planning Skills**										
43. Deciding on Something to Do										
44. Deciding What Caused a Problem										
45. Setting a Goal										
46. Deciding on Your Abilities										
47. Gathering Information										
48. Arranging Problems by Importance										
49. Making a Decision										
50. Concentrating on a Task										

Moral Reasoning Problem Situations

Jim's Problem Situation   297

Jerry's Problem Situation   300

Mark's Problem Situation   303

George's Problem Situation   307

Leon's Problem Situation   310

Sam's Problem Situation   312

Reggie's Problem Situation   314

Alonzo's Problem Situation   316

Juan's Problem Situation   319

Antonio's Problem Situation   322

Jim's Problem Situation

Jim and Derek are high school friends. Jim, whose birthday is coming up, has mentioned to Derek how great it would be to have a tape deck to listen to music while he goes about his job driving a van. Derek steals a tape deck from a car in the school parking lot and gives it to Jim for his birthday. Jim is appreciative, not realizing the present is stolen.

The next day Jim sees Scott, another friend. Jim knows Scott has a tape deck and is good at electronics. Jim mentions that he got a tape deck for a birthday present and asks Scott to come over to help install it. "Sure," Scott says with a sigh.

"You look down, Scott. What's wrong?" Jim asks.

"Oh, I was ripped off," Scott says.

"Oh, boy. What did they get?" Jim asks.

"My tape deck," Scott says. Scott starts describing the stolen tape deck.

Later, Jim starts thinking about how odd it is that Scott's tape deck was stolen just at the time Derek gave him one. Jim gets suspicious and calls Derek. Sure enough, Derek confesses that he stole it, and the car he stole it from turns out to be Scott's car!

It's time for Scott to arrive to help Jim install the tape deck. Scott will probably recognize the tape deck as his. Scott is at the door, ringing the doorbell.

What should Jim—the one who got the stolen birthday present from Derek—say or do?

1. Should Jim tell Scott that Derek took Scott's tape deck?

   should tell / shouldn't tell / can't decide *(circle one)*

2. How good a friend is Derek? Would Jim be able to trust Derek not to steal from him?

   yes, could trust / no, couldn't trust / can't decide *(circle one)*

3. Derek stole the tape deck for a good cause (Jim's birthday). Does that make it all right for Derek to steal the tape deck?

   yes, all right / no, not all right / can't decide *(circle one)*

4. What if Derek didn't steal the tape deck from Scott's car? What if instead Derek stole the tape deck from a stranger's car? Then would it be all right for Derek to steal the tape deck for Jim's birthday?

yes, all right / no, not all right / can't decide *(circle one)*

LEADER NOTES

Jim's Problem Situation focuses on the importance of trust in a friendship: How trustworthy is a friend who has a stealing problem? Should you tell on a friend who has stolen in order to give you a gift? Or is stealing all right if it's for a friend? Insofar as this problem situation addresses the value not only of affiliation but also of property, it serves as an excellent introduction to many of the problem situations that follow.

The majority positions tend to be that Jim should tell Scott that the tape deck is his (Question 1), that Jim would not be able to trust Derek not to steal from him (Question 2), and that it was not all right for Derek to steal the tape deck even though it was for Jim's birthday (Question 3) or even if the tape deck belonged to a stranger instead of another friend of Jim's (Question 4). The majority positions tend to be supported by fairly mature reasoning: Jim should tell Scott about the theft because otherwise Jim is letting Derek get away with hurting Scott, because it's the honest thing to do, because Jim would want to be told if he were Scott, and because it would be the way to keep Scott's trust and friendship. Stealing is wrong even if the victim is a stranger because it's against the law and because the stranger is still a person who should be respected instead of hurt. Jim should not consider Derek a good friend because Derek steals things and is untrustworthy: Derek will steal from Jim "the first time Derek thinks he can get away with it." Group members may also suggest that Jim should tell to avoid getting in trouble with Scott.

More pragmatic group members who advocate not telling Scott about the theft may point out that "you'll be out a birthday present" if you tell and that Derek will be angry if he finds out. These group members may also claim that you can trust a friend who steals not to steal from you (Question 2) and, by way of support, claim to have such friends. Because they may be adamant, don't count on achieving a unanimous group decision on Question 2.

The most controversial question, however, is whether Jim should tell on Derek (Question 1). Our groups have often been evenly divided on this question. Group members who favor telling emphasize that Derek took a risk and now has to face up to what he did; if Jim doesn't tell he becomes involved in Derek's stealing, and Derek learns nothing. Those who favor not telling emphasize that Derek is also a friend (after all, he stole because he wanted to do something nice for Jim), and you should never rat on a friend. They acknowledge the importance of disciplining Derek but caution against getting Scott involved—they will offer lurid descriptions, in fact, of what Scott would do to Derek. Don't expect to persuade the group to reach a unanimous decision on Question 1.

Occasionally, a group member will argue that it would have been all right for Derek to steal a tape deck for Jim's birthday if only the car hadn't belonged to one of Jim's friends. As noted previously, it is not uncommon for antisocial adolescents to show immature moral judgment, particularly when the persons hurt are strangers. One participant, Joe, explained that if the victim was a stranger, then the theft was "on him"—somehow his fault. Other group members pointed out to Joe that he was making a blaming others mistake in his thinking, and Joe acquiesced to a unanimous "no, not all right" group decision on Question 4.

Jerry's Problem Situation

Jerry had just moved to a new school and was feeling pretty lonely until one day a guy named Bob came up and introduced himself. "Hi, Jerry. My name is Bob. I heard one of the teachers say you're new here. If you're not doing anything after school today, how about coming over to shoot some baskets?" Pretty soon Jerry and Bob were good friends.

One day when Jerry was shooting baskets by himself, the basketball coach saw him and invited him to try out for the team. Jerry made the team, and every day after school he would practice with the rest of the team. After practice, Jerry and his teammates would always go out together to get something to eat and sit around and talk about stuff. On weekends they would sometimes take trips together.

As Jerry spends more time with the team, he sees less and less of Bob, his old friend. One day, Jerry gets a call from Bob. "Say, I was wondering," says Bob, "if you're not too busy on Thursday, my family is having a little birthday party for me. Maybe you could come over for dinner that night." Jerry tells Bob he'll try to come to the party. But during practice on Thursday, everyone tells Jerry about the great place they're all going to after practice.

What should Jerry say or do?

1. Should Jerry go with the team?

   go with team / go to Bob's party / can't decide *(circle one)*

2. What if Jerry calls Bob from school and says he's sorry, but something has come up and he can't come over after all? Then would it be all right for Jerry to go with the team?

   go with team / go to Bob's party / can't decide *(circle one)*

3. What if Jerry considers that his teammates may be upset if Jerry doesn't come—that they may start to think Jerry's not such a good friend? Then would it be all right for Jerry to go with the team?

   go with team / go to Bob's party / can't decide *(circle one)*

4. What if Jerry thinks that, after all, Bob came along and helped Jerry when Jerry was lonely. Then should Jerry go with the team?

   go with team / go to Bob's party / can't decide *(circle one)*

5. Let's change the situation a bit. Let's say that before Bob asks Jerry to come over, the teammates ask if Jerry will be coming along on Thursday. Jerry says he thinks so. Then Bob asks Jerry. Then what should Jerry do?

   go with team / go to Bob's party / can't decide *(circle one)*

6. Which is more important: to have one close friend or to have a group of regular friends?

   one close friend / group of regular friends / can't decide *(circle one)*

7. Let's change the situation a different way. What if Jerry and Bob are not good friends but instead are just acquaintances? Then should Jerry go with the team?

   go with team / go to Bob's party / can't decide *(circle one)*

LEADER NOTES

Discussion of Jerry's Problem Situation typically promotes a more profound or mature understanding of friendship. Some group members (those who reason at a level no higher than Stage 2) may actually become stimulated to construct Stage 3 moral judgment. For others who already understand and use Stage 3 to some extent, mature reasoning may become more prominent. In either event, at least with respect to the value of friendship or affiliation, this problem situation should facilitate moral judgment development. Also important is the contribution such discussions make to the group itself. Discussion of the value of close friendships seems to promote such friendships in the group and hence contributes to the group's social cohesion.

In our experience, most group members advocate going to Bob's party in response to most questions. The main consideration is that of friendship: Group members point out that Jerry and Bob used to be good friends, and here would be a chance to renew that friendship. An additional consideration is the importance of Jerry's keeping the commitment made to Bob so as to be honest and not let Bob down. After all, in fairness, "Bob was there first when Jerry was lonely, before there was any team for Jerry." Mindful of the friendship, commitment, and/or fairness considerations, group members may suggest that Jerry will feel bad if he goes with the team.

Group members may also make pragmatic points to support going to Bob's party: "Jerry does lots of things with the team, but birthday parties only come once a year" or "Maybe Jerry would like a break from doing things with the team all the time." Pragmatic group members may also suggest that Jerry avoid the problem by attending Bob's party for a while, then catching up with the team. Especially with group leader prompting, pro-Bob group members will counter that leaving early solves nothing: "That's as bad a dump on Bob as not going at all," as one group member once put it.

Group discussion typically reaches the heart of the matter with Question 6; often the choice of "one close friend" is unanimous. Reasons are as follows: "You can tell a close friend anything"; "You need someone you can talk to, who will listen to you"; "You can go to that person with problems"; "Close friends are really friends"; and "A close friend can be trusted not to take advantage of you."

Once a positive peer atmosphere is cultivated through listing and discussion of the reasons for the majority position, attention can turn to the dissenting group members. The few members advocating that Jerry go with the team tend to be unabashed hedonists ("Jerry would have more fun with the team"). They may also try to minimize the harm done to Bob ("Bob won't even notice Jerry didn't come"). These members typically do not care strongly about their positions, however, and will not argue long against majority objections (e.g., that Bob will of course notice). Hence, the choice for going to Bob's party can be made a unanimous group decision on most questions.

The main question on which the majority typically chooses "go with the team" is Question 7, which demotes the relationship between Jerry and Bob from friendship to acquaintance. Hence, Question 7 makes clear the relevance of Question 6 to the original problem situation, in which Jerry and Bob are friends: Jerry should go to Bob's party because a group of regular buddies just isn't the same as a close friend—and here is a chance to restore such a friendship.

To a lesser extent, the majority may also choose "go with the team" for Question 5, which has Jerry making the first commitment (of sorts) to the team rather than to Bob. Those group members for whom the prior commitment to Bob was the important factor will tend to switch to the "team" response on Question 5.

Mark's Problem Situation

Mark has been going steady with a girl named Maria for about 2 months. It used to be a lot of fun to be with her, but lately it's been sort of a drag. There are some other girls Mark would like to go out with now. Mark sees Maria coming down the school hallway.

What should Mark say or do?

1. Should Mark avoid the subject with Maria so Maria's feelings aren't hurt?

    should avoid subject / should bring it up / can't decide (*circle one*)

2. Should Mark make up an excuse, like being too busy to see Maria, as a way of breaking up?

    excuse / no excuse / can't decide (*circle one*)

3. Should Mark simply start going out with other girls so that Maria will get the message?

    yes / no / can't decide (*circle one*)

4. How should Mark respond to Maria's feelings?

    _____

    _____

    _____

5. Let's change the situation a bit. What if Mark and Maria have been living together for several years and have two small children? Then should Mark still break up with Maria?

    should break up / no, shouldn't break up / can't decide (*circle one*)

6. Let's go back to the original situation. This is what happens: Mark does break up with Maria—he lets her know how he feels and starts dating another girl. Maria feels hurt and jealous and thinks about getting even somehow. Should Maria get even?

    yes, should get even / no, shouldn't get even / can't decide (*circle one*)

7. What if the tables were turned, and Maria did that to Mark?

    yes, should get even / no, shouldn't get even / can't decide (*circle one*)

LEADER NOTES

Mark's Problem Situation continues the theme of mature, caring relationships but focuses on the problem of ending a dating relationship
that is going nowhere. The main value of this problem situation for
moral judgment development arrives with discussion of the last question,
which concerns vengeance.

As with most of the problem situations, many group members do
choose positive responses. The majority position tends to be that Mark
should discuss breaking up (Question 1) rather than making up an
excuse (Question 2) or simply starting to date other girls (Question 3).
Accordingly, most of the open-ended suggestions (in response to
Question 4) are positive: "Just tell her you'd like to date other girls"; "Be
considerate and remember she's human, too"; "Explain how you feel,
that you don't want to settle down"; "Listen to what she has to say about
it." Of the responses we have heard, our favorite is "I think we should
see other people. What do you think?" The group member who gave
this response also indicated that he would first try to "work things out"
before breaking up with Maria. As to the reasons for bringing the subject up (Question 1), one group member pointed out that Mark "should
be man enough to tell her"; if he doesn't, another suggested, "Maria
might lose a chance to get another boyfriend" and "would be hurt more
in the long run" than by just being told. Speaking more pragmatically
(against the idea of simply starting to date other girls), another group
member suggested that then those girls could find out how Mark treated
Maria and dump him for being a two-timer.

Of course, not all of the responses are positive. On the open-ended
question, one group member wrote, "Do things to try to make Maria
drop him." Another wrote that he would say, "I'm dumping you, bag!"
These group members may also advocate avoiding Maria or making up
an excuse. After discussion, however, they are often willing to acquiesce to
the majority position and thereby make a positive group decision possible.

An abrupt turnabout occurs on Question 5, in which Mark and
Maria are live-in partners with two small children. Then the majority
favors not breaking up, on the grounds that Mark has a responsibility to
the children (e.g., "The kids should have both a dad and a mom"). If he
left "it would hurt the kids, because they would feel it was their fault."
One group member suggested, "He loved her once. Why should one
argument make him not love her again?" A pragmatic group member
pointed out that he might have to pay child support if he leaves.

The majority position continues to be positive on the vengeance questions, 6 and 7. The majority is against either Maria's getting even if Mark breaks up (Question 6) or Mark's getting even if the tables are turned (Question 7). Suggestions are that "Mark should just tell himself that it's her loss"; that "it's no big deal, there are other fish in the sea"; or that Mark or Maria should "let bygones be bygones." Mark "wouldn't want her to get even with him [so he shouldn't do that to her; Stage 3]," and if one of them retaliated "there would just be more trouble." One group member suggested, somewhat ominously, that Mark shouldn't get even because he "might do something really bad and wind up in here."

Count on several group members advocating retaliation, however—especially by Mark against Maria. Reasons included "Give her a taste of her own medicine" and "He would feel better after he showed her how she hurt him." One group member suggested that Mark should get even because "he'd be mad" and, as further justification, disclosed that he himself had gotten mad and beaten up several girls who had left him for other guys. He remained silent when a peer asked, "Does that make it right?" and asked why he nonetheless thought it was wrong if Maria got even with Mark. Nor would he acquiesce to a group decision against getting even. At least he felt peer group opposition and perhaps for this reason was more accommodating to positive majority positions on subsequent occasions.

It is sometimes helpful to ask the group exactly what is meant by "getting even." Responses range from "showing off [to Maria] with a new girlfriend" to "telling him [the new boyfriend] that she was a good lay for you" to "slashing their tires"—or faces! These responses, once stated for group consideration, will often be branded as immature or destructive by the majority. Nonetheless, many group members will comment that although Mark or Maria—or they—shouldn't get even, they probably would. If the group is still developing, the group leader may need to model relabeling—that is, comment on how much strength and courage it takes not to "give in to childish desires to get even."

The degree of positive content may be surprising and should be encouraged. The group leader should comment on the great potential the group has shown for becoming a positive group. Using relabeling, the leader should emphasize that a strong group is one where members care about another's feelings. Bear in mind, however, that the group members expressing more negative sentiments may be speaking more candidly; their words may be consistent with the actual behavior of the majority. After all, consider how common "payback" or vengeance is in the daily life of the troubled school or correctional facility! Similarly, in social skills exercises, the initial absence of caring about another's feelings is striking. Clearly, the group challenge is to accomplish the translation of responsible words into responsible actions.

George's Problem Situation

One day George's older brother, Jake, tells him a secret: Jake is selling drugs. George and Jake both know that the kind of drug Jake is selling is highly addictive and causes lung and brain damage. It can even kill people. George asks his brother to stop selling. But the family is poor, and Jake says he is only doing it to help out with the family's money problems. Jake asks his younger brother not to tell anyone.

What should George say or do?

1. Should George promise to keep quiet and not tell on his brother?

   should keep quiet / should tell / can't decide *(circle one)*

2. What if Jake tells George that selling drugs is no big deal, that plenty of Jake's friends do it all the time? Then what should George do?

   keep quiet / tell / can't decide *(circle one)*

3. What if George finds out that Jake is selling the drug to 10-year-olds outside a school? Then what should George do?

   keep quiet / tell / can't decide *(circle one)*

4. What if Jake himself won't be harmed by the drug—he tells George he knows how addictive and harmful the stuff is and never touches it? Then what should George do?

   keep quiet / tell / can't decide *(circle one)*

5. What if George finds out that Jake isn't using any of the money at all to "help out the family" but instead is spending it on booze and other things for himself? Then what should George do?

   keep quiet / tell / can't decide *(circle one)*

6. Is it ever right to tell on someone?

   sometimes right / never right/ can't decide *(circle one)*

7. Who's to blame in this situation?

   George (younger brother) / Jake (drug dealer) / other / can't decide *(circle one)*

8. How important is it for judges to send drug dealers to jail?

very important / important / not important *(circle one)*

LEADER NOTES

With George's Problem Situation, the stakes are raised with respect to the issue of dealing with an irresponsible friend. Instead of a tape deck (Jim's Problem Situation), the lives of those who buy drugs from George's brother are at stake.

The majority positions tend to be responsible: George should tell on his brother (Questions 1 through 5), it is sometimes right to tell on someone (Question 6), Jake is to blame in this situation (Question 7), and it is very important for judges to send drug dealers to jail (Question 8).

The reasons for the majority positions tend to be mature. Many of the pro-telling reasons focus on Jake: George would care about Jake; Jake may start taking the drug and die or get messed up himself; Jake could get caught and sent to jail; or Jake could get beaten up or killed in the drug world. Furthermore, Jake is endangering his family because the drug world may get at Jake by killing a member of his family. There is also a concern that Jake is selling a drug that kills, and a particular objection is that he is selling such a drug to kids (Question 3). After reading that Jake actually isn't even helping out the family with his profits (Question 5), some group members may offer the general reason that Jake is self-centered. It is sometimes right to tell on someone (Question 6) when human lives are at stake, as they are with Jake's drug dealing. Jake is the one to blame in this situation (Question 7) because, as the older brother, he should be more responsible and because by selling drugs he has caused the situation (the "Jake" response to Question 7 is often unanimous).

The momentum of responsible reasoning that can be generated through discussion of the earlier questions can be maintained for discussion of the final question (Question 8), concerning the reasons it is "very important" for judges to send drug dealers to jail. Some of the reasoning concerns rehabilitation: "So the dealers will learn a lesson and change"; "So the junkies can get their lives together"; "If they can't find a fix, maybe they'll recover and start using their money to pay their rent." The preponderance of reasoning, however, concerns safety to society: "To make things less violent"; "So people won't die"; "To keep druggies off the streets, protect your family"; "So there won't be so many break-ins"; "To set an example for, send a message to, other drug dealers";

and "To save some kids from being pressured into becoming users and pushers."

George's Problem Situation is controversial, however. After all, many antisocial youths are themselves drug traffickers and identify with Jake. Group members who advocate not telling assert that what Jake does is none of George's business, that George should let Jake learn a lesson, that Jake could be making a lot of money and not be in danger at all, that somebody else will sell the stuff and make money if Jake doesn't, that Jake isn't forcing anybody to buy anything, and that George could get killed if he tells on Jake. Alert majority-position group members can rebut these points: It is George's business if the family is endangered, the "lesson" is too expensive if it's a brother's death, Jake is forcing the drug on 10-year-olds (Question 3) because "they don't know what they're doing," and "Jake is kidding himself if he thinks he's not in any danger—you can't sell drugs and not be in danger." Positive group members may also point out the hypocrisy involved in Jake's not taking the drug himself (Question 4): "He won't hurt himself, but he'll make money off hurting others, dealing death to others."

Some controversy will probably also arise concerning the importance of sending drug dealers to jail (Question 8). Some group members may argue for merely "important" or even "not important" on the grounds that sending drug dealers to jail is "useless" or "hopeless" because you can't send enough of them to make a dent in the problem. Again, alert majority-position group members may brand this assuming the worst. They may argue that this is exactly how the drug world wants you to think and that avoiding this mistake means doing what you can rather than doing nothing.

Leon's Problem Situation

Just after Leon arrived at an institution for boys, he tried to escape. As a result, he was given extra time. It took Leon nearly 4 months to earn the trust of the staff again. He now thinks it is stupid to try to go AWOL. However, Bob, a friend of Leon's, tells Leon he is planning to escape that night. "I've got it all figured out," Bob says. "I'll hit the youth leader on the head with a pipe and take his keys." Bob asks Leon to come along. Leon tries to talk Bob out of it, but Bob won't listen.

What should Leon say or do?

1. Should Leon tell the staff about Bob's plan to go AWOL?

   tell / keep quiet / can't decide (*circle one*)

2. What if Bob is a pretty violent type of guy and Leon thinks that Bob might seriously injure, maybe even kill, the youth leader? Then what should Leon do?

   tell / keep quiet / can't decide (*circle one*)

3. What if the youth leader is mean and everyone hates him? Then what should Leon do?

   tell / keep quiet / can't decide (*circle one*)

4. Is it any of Leon's business what Bob does?

   can be Leon's business / is none of Leon's business / can't decide (*circle one*)

5. Is it ever right to nark on somebody?

   yes, sometimes right / no, never right / can't decide (*circle one*)

6. Let's change the situation a bit. Let's say the youth leader is Leon's uncle. Then what should Leon do?

   tell / keep quiet / can't decide (*circle one*)

7. Let's change the situation a different way. Let's say Bob is Leon's brother. Then what should Leon do?

   tell / keep quiet / can't decide (*circle one*)

8. Which is the most important?

   not telling on your friend / not letting other people get hurt/
   minding your own business (*circle one*)

LEADER NOTES

Again, the group faces the problem of dealing with a troublesome friend. Like George, Leon must deal with someone whose actions may be life threatening. Although Leon's friend is not dealing in deadly drugs, he is planning a crime (going AWOL from the institution) in which someone could get killed.

The majority positions with respect to Leon's Problem Situation tend to be responsible. Leon should tell about Bob's plan (Questions 1 through 3, Questions 6 and 7), it is Leon's business what Bob does (Question 4), it is sometimes right to nark on somebody (as when a life is at stake; Question 5), and what is most important is not letting other people get hurt (Question 8). The majorities are especially strong when the youth leader is Leon's uncle (Question 6) and when Bob is Leon's brother (Question 7).

Although part of the supportive reasoning for the majority position is pragmatic ("Leon would just get caught and have extra time added"), much of the reasoning is mature: "Leon could prevent someone getting hurt," "It's not worth killing somebody to get out of an institution," "Human life is precious," and "The entire youth group could suffer if Bob goes AWOL."

A few group members may argue that what Bob does is none of Leon's business and so Leon shouldn't get involved. After all, Bob would be knocking off somebody everyone hates (Question 3). Alert majority-group members may counter that Bob has made it Leon's business by telling Leon of his plans, and the youth leader doesn't deserve to get killed.

Sam's Problem Situation

Sam and his friend John are shopping in a music store. Sam has driven them to the store. John picks up a CD he really likes and slips it into his backpack. With a little sign for Sam to follow, John then walks out of the store. But Sam doesn't see John. Moments later, the security officer and the store owner come up to Sam. The store owner says to the officer, "That's one of the boys who were stealing CDs!" The security officer checks Sam's backpack but doesn't find a CD. "OK, you're off the hook, but what's the name of the guy who was with you?" the officer asks Sam. "I'm almost broke because of shoplifting," the owner says. "I can't let him get away with it."

What should Sam say or do?

1. Should Sam keep quiet and refuse to tell the security officer John's name?

   keep quiet / tell / can't decide (*circle one*)

2. From the store owner's point of view, what should Sam do?

   keep quiet / tell / can't decide (*circle one*)

3. What if the store owner is a nice guy who sometimes lets kids buy tapes or CDs even if they don't have quite enough money? Then what should Sam do?

   keep quiet / tell / can't decide (*circle one*)

4. What if the store owner is Sam's father? Then what should Sam do?

   keep quiet / tell / can't decide (*circle one*)

5. Is it ever right to tell on someone?

   yes, sometimes / no, never / can't decide (*circle one*)

6. Who's to blame in this situation?

   Sam / John / the store owner / other / can't decide (*circle one*)

7. How important is it not to shoplift?

   very important / important / not important (*circle one*)

8. How important is it for store owners to prosecute shoplifters?

very important / important / not important (*circle one*)

LEADER NOTES

With Sam's Problem Situation, majority positions tend to be responsible: Sam should give the security officer John's name (Questions 1 through 4), it is sometimes right to tell on someone (Question 5), John's to blame in this situation (Question 6), it's very important not to shoplift (Question 7), and it's very important for store owners to prosecute shoplifters (Question 8). The main pragmatic reason in support of telling is that Sam thus protects himself from possible prosecution. Most of the supportive reasons are mature: John was unfair to Sam in getting him into this spot, John's stealing problem will continue until he's stopped and made to think about the consequences, shoplifting makes the prices for everyone go up, the store owner is losing money and will become a popular target if John gets away with it and tells others, the store owner will stop being so nice to kids (Question 3), and John is harming Sam's dad (Question 4). Reasons for the importance of not shoplifting sometimes even reach into Stage 4: "for the sake of order in society" and "because it harms the trust that's needed for society."

Dissenters argue against "ratting on your friend" and suggest that Sam can best stay out of trouble by keeping quiet: "They can't get him— he doesn't have to say anything." These group members may also attribute blame to the store owner (Question 6) on the grounds that the owner should have had customers check things like backpacks before they came in. Alert group members will point out the blaming others error in such an attribution.

Reggie's Problem Situation

"Your father is late again," Reggie's mother tells Reggie one night as he sits down to dinner. Reggie knows why. He passed his father's car on the way home from school. It was parked outside the Midtown Bar and Grill. Reggie's mother and father had argued many times about his father's stopping off at the bar on his way home from work. After their last argument, his father had promised he would never do it again. "I wonder why your father is late," Reggie's mother says. "Do you think I should trust what he said about not drinking any more? Do you think he stopped off at the bar again?" Reggie's mother asks him.

What should Reggie say or do?

1. Should Reggie cover for his father by lying to his mother?

   yes, should cover / no, should tell the truth / can't decide (*circle one*)

2. Was it right for Reggie's mother to put Reggie on the spot by asking him a question about his father?

   yes, right / no, wrong / can't decide (*circle one*)

3. What if Reggie's father drinks a lot when he stops at the bar and then comes home and often beats up on Reggie's mother—sometimes even on Reggie? Then what should Reggie do?

   cover for him / tell the truth / can't decide (*circle one*)

4. Which is most important for Reggie's decision?

   what's best for himself / what's best for his mom / what's best for his dad / what's best for the family (*circle one*)

5. In general, how important is it to tell the truth?

   very important / important / not important (*circle one*)

LEADER NOTES

Unique among the problem situations, Reggie's Problem Situation concerns parental rather than peer pressure. Furthermore, whereas in peer situations the peer has a negative or irresponsible aim, in Reggie's Problem Situation the mother is at least well intentioned in her questions about the father.

This situation is problematic for groups until Question 3 ("What if Reggie's father drinks a lot when he stops at the bar and then comes home and often beats up on Reggie's mother—sometimes even on Reggie?"); then the majority position tends to be that Reggie should tell his mother what he knows. The majority tend also to choose "what's best for the family" as most important for Reggie's decision (Question 4) and "important" for telling the truth (Question 5). Reasons for telling the truth include the following: By covering, Reggie would be helping his dad become an even worse alcoholic; Reggie should help stop his father's deception and harm to the family; Reggie wouldn't want his mother or himself beaten up (Question 3); the truth will come out sooner or later anyway; someone could get killed by the father's drunk driving. Reasons for the importance of telling the truth are typically mature: You wouldn't want someone to lie to you (otherwise your word would mean nothing), and society is based on truth and trust (an especially mature [Stage 4] reason).

Dissenters emphatically suggest that it was wrong for Reggie's mother to put Reggie on the spot (Question 2) and that getting Reggie involved is too heavy a burden to place on a child—Reggie could feel guilty if his disclosure resulted in a divorce. They may suggest that Reggie could help in a limited way by having a private talk with his dad. Pragmatically, however, if Reggie tells his mother (Question 1), his dad may beat him up. In response to one group member's minimizing comment ("She shouldn't hassle him just because he had a beer on the way home"), other group members countered that it's rarely just one beer, that they know from their personal experience how often it happens that dad is drunk and violent (Question 3) by the time he gets home.

Alonzo's Problem Situation

Alonzo is walking along a side street with his friend Rodney. Rodney stops in front of a beautiful new sports car. Rodney looks inside and then says excitedly, "Look! The keys are still in this thing! Let's see what it can do! Come on, let's go!"

What should Alonzo say or do?

1. Should Alonzo try to persuade Rodney not to steal the car?

   should persuade / should let steal / can't decide *(circle one)*

2. What if Rodney says to Alonzo that the keys were left in the car, that anyone that careless deserves to get ripped off? Then should Alonzo try to persuade Rodney not to steal the car?

   should persuade / should let steal / can't decide *(circle one)*

3. What if Rodney says to Alonzo that the car's owner can probably get insurance money to cover most of the loss? Then should Alonzo try to persuade Rodney not to steal the car?

   should persuade / should let steal / can't decide *(circle one)*

4. What if Rodney tells Alonzo that stealing a car is no big deal, that plenty of his friends do it all the time? Then what should Alonzo do?

   should persuade / should let steal / can't decide *(circle one)*

5. What if Alonzo knows that Rodney has a wife and child who will suffer if Rodney gets caught, loses his job, and goes to jail? Then should Alonzo try to persuade Rodney not to steal the car?

   should persuade / should let steal / can't decide *(circle one)*

6. Let's say the car is your car. Alonzo is Rodney's friend, but Alonzo is also your friend. Alonzo knows it's your car. Then should Alonzo try to persuade Rodney not to steal the car?

   should persuade / should let steal / can't decide *(circle one)*

7. In general, how important is it for people not to take things that belong to others?

   very important / important / not important *(circle one)*

8. Let's say that Alonzo does try to persuade Rodney not to take the car, but Rodney goes ahead and takes it anyway. Alonzo knows Rodney's in bad shape from being high—he could have a serious accident and someone could get killed. Then what should Alonzo do?

contact the police / not contact the police / can't decide *(circle one)*

LEADER NOTES

Like Jim in the earlier problem situation, Alonzo must contend with a friend who has a stealing problem. The majority position is that Alonzo should try to persuade Rodney not to steal the car (Questions 1 through 6) and that it is very important not to steal (Question 7). Mature reasons appeal to the danger and harm to innocent people, including the car owner; to the way one would feel if it were one's own car (a consideration often inspired by Question 6); to the guilt one would feel if one did join Rodney; to the fact that prices have to go up to cover crime; and to the loss of order that would result if everyone stole. At least one group member typically spots the blaming others error in laying blame on the victim (Question 2)—for example, "Everyone's careless at one time or another. That doesn't mean you deserve to get your car stolen." There is concern for what will happen to Rodney's family in Question 5. Pragmatic reasons for not stealing or joining Rodney are also prominent, however: "Alonzo could go to jail, so it's not worth the risk"; "There'd be nothing to do in jail"; "Alonzo could get shot or killed"; "The car owner could get even"; "You wouldn't be able to stop Rodney anyway"; "You'd be drunk and wouldn't care what Rodney did"; "This could even be a set-up against Alonzo"; and "Rodney's a fool and deserves whatever happens to him."

One hears both mature and pragmatic reasons, then, in support of the majority positions. For the opposing positions ("Let Rodney steal it"; "It's not important for people not to steal"), however, pragmatic considerations constitute practically the sum total of reasons—for example, "You'd be a big shot"; "You could have lots of fun"; "It's exciting to steal and get away with it"; "You could get money and booze and girls and do whatever you want"; "If you needed to go somewhere, now you could drive" (self-centered). Pragmatic group members acknowledge that you could get caught for stealing, but they suggest that that's why it's important for you to "know what you're doing" and "act confident"—so you won't get caught. Thinking errors are plentiful in the pragmatic reasoning: for example, "Everyone steals anyway"; "You'd teach the car owner a good lesson, not to be so careless"; and "The car owner is a dummy, fool, or jerk [for leaving the keys]" (minimizing/mislabeling). If group members don't catch and correct these thinking errors, the group leader should intervene to do so.

Question 8 suggests that Rodney goes ahead and—in an intoxicated state—steals the car. Should Alonzo contact the police? Many group members who have persistently advocated trying to persuade Rodney not to steal the car will nonetheless choose against contacting the police because it would mean ratting on a friend and getting him in trouble. They will urge getting Rodney home so he can sleep off his high (alert peers will point out that it's too late for that—Rodney has already stolen the car). Group members who advocate calling the police tend to emphasize the dangers of drunk driving and Rodney's irresponsibility to his family, and they argue that a true friend would contact the police.

Alonzo's Problem Situation is an especially good situation for discussing the gap between moral judgment and moral action. Many group members who proffer superbly mature and compelling reasons for trying to persuade Alonzo against stealing the car will disclose at some point in the discussion that they would probably join Rodney: "I know I shouldn't, but I probably would." The group leader should listen actively but also relabel: "That's right, this is a tough situation to keep your head in. It does take a lot of guts to say no and do the right thing." The group leader can also remind the group of the skill Dealing with Group Pressure, or teach that skill if the group has not learned it yet.

Juan's Problem Situation

Juan and Phil are roommates at a juvenile institution. They get along well and have become good friends. Phil has confided that he has been getting pretty depressed lately and has managed to get hold of some razor blades. Juan sees where Phil hides the blades. The youth leader, having learned of the razor blades, searches their room but doesn't find them. So the youth leader asks Juan where the razor blades are hidden.

What should Juan say or do?

1. Should Juan cover for Phil, saying he doesn't know anything about any razor blades?

   cover for Phil / tell the leader / can't decide *(circle one)*

2. What if Phil has told Juan that he plans to cut his wrists with the razor blades that night? Then what should Juan do?

   cover for Phil / tell the leader / can't decide *(circle one)*

3. Would Phil feel that Juan cared about him if Juan told?

   yes, would feel Juan cared / no, would not feel Juan cared / can't decide *(circle one)*

4. What if Juan and Phil actually don't get along well and are not friends? What if Phil has been a real pest? Then what should Juan do?

   cover for Phil / tell the leader / can't decide *(circle one)*

5. What if Juan isn't Phil's roommate but does know about the razor blades and where they are? The youth leader suspects Juan knows something and asks him about the razor blades. Then what should Juan do?

   cover for Phil / tell the leader / can't decide *(circle one)*

6. How important is it for a juvenile institution to have rules against contraband?

   very important / important / not important *(circle one)*

7. How important is it to live even when you don't want to?

   very important / important / not important *(circle one)*

8. Who might be affected (in addition to Phil himself) if Phil were to commit suicide?

   _____

   _____

   _____

LEADER NOTES

How to deal with an irresponsible friend is again the problem. With Juan's Problem Situation, however, the life threatened by the friend's activity is not someone else's (as with George's Problem Situation) but instead the friend's own life.

The majority positions tend to be positive: that Juan should tell the youth leader (Questions 1, 2, 4, and 5), that rules against contraband are very important (Question 6), and that it is very important to live even when you don't want to (Question 7). Pragmatic reasons for telling are that you can get in trouble if you don't tell and that you might get hurt—Phil might cut you with a razor blade. Following are some mature reasons we have heard: Juan should care about Phil; telling might enable Phil to get some help before he hurts himself; any life is precious and worth saving; Phil's family and friends will be hurt if Phil kills himself; you wouldn't want to watch someone kill himself; you'd feel guilty if you knew you could have done something and didn't. Living even when you don't want to is very important because things get better and there's a lot to live for; there's a reason you're here; there are things to do and see; committing suicide is selfish—you're thinking only about yourself (group members may even identify a self-centered thinking error); think how your family would feel; consider that you may change your mind. Family—especially parents—are mentioned prominently in response to Question 8, "Who might be affected (in addition to Phil himself) if Phil were to commit suicide?" The majority of the group members may also rate rules against contraband "very important" because some things are dangerous to both oneself and others.

A few group members may advocate covering for Phil on the grounds that Juan should mind his own business and not get involved. One is especially likely to see "cover" responses in connection with

Question 4 ("What if Phil has been a real pest?"): Then "you couldn't care less what happens to him." These group members may also assert that living even when you don't want to (Question 7) is not important because "it's your life—you can do whatever you want with it." One group member asserted that rules against contraband are not important because "I want to smoke and stuff" (another group member correctly critiqued that reason as being a self-centered thinking error).

Antonio's Problem Situation

Antonio is in school taking a math test. Suddenly, the teacher says, "I'm going to leave the room for a few minutes. You are on your honor not to cheat." After the teacher has gone, Ed, Antonio's friend, whispers to him, "Let me see your answers, Antonio."

What should Antonio say or do?

1. Should Antonio let Ed copy his answers?

   yes, let cheat / no, don't let cheat / can't decide (*circle one*)

2. What if Ed whispers that cheating is no big deal, that he knows plenty of guys who cheat all the time? Then should Antonio let Ed cheat?

   yes, let cheat / no, don't let cheat / can't decide (*circle one*)

3. What if Antonio knows that Ed is flunking because he doesn't study? Then should Antonio let Ed cheat?

   yes, let cheat / no, don't let cheat / can't decide (*circle one*)

4. What if you were the teacher? Would you want Antonio to let Ed cheat?

   yes, let cheat / no, don't let cheat / can't decide (*circle one*)

5. Is it possible to have a really close, trusting friendship with someone who has a cheating or lying problem?

   yes, possible / no, not possible / can't decide (*circle one*)

6. Let's change the situation a little. What if Antonio hardly knows Ed? Then should Antonio let Ed cheat?

   yes, let cheat / no, don't let cheat / can't decide (*circle one*)

7. In general, how important is it not to cheat?

   very important / important / not important (*circle one*)

8. Is it right for teachers to punish cheaters?

   yes, right / no, not right / can't decide (*circle one*)

LEADER NOTES

Antonio's Problem Situation returns to the theme of negative peer pressure, in this case from a friend who wants to cheat on a test.

Majority positions tend to be that Antonio should not let Ed cheat (Questions 1 through 3, Question 6), that the respondent in the position of the teacher would not want Ed to cheat (Question 4; this position may be unanimous from the outset), that a close relationship with someone who cheats is not possible (Question 5), that it's very important not to cheat (Question 7), and that it is right for teachers to punish cheaters (Question 8). Pragmatic reasons are that the teacher might come back unexpectedly and catch both of you and that if Ed isn't caught he might wind up with a grade higher than yours. Mature reasons are that it's unfair for Ed to get the benefit of Antonio's work, that letting Ed cheat will encourage his attitude that he can let other people do his work for him (alert group members will identify such an attitude as a self-centered thinking error), that Ed deserves to flunk and needs to learn a lesson, that Ed is hurting himself in the long run by cheating instead of learning, that Ed is also hurting his parents, and that the teacher has placed trust in Ed and you, and you are on your honor not to cheat. One cannot have a close relationship with a person who cheats (Question 5) because "you never know when they might be planning to cheat you." Teachers need to punish cheaters (Question 8) because otherwise "there would be no order in the classroom."

Again, alert group members will likely identify the thinking errors in the arguments of dissenters: "There's nothing wrong with giving a little help to a friend" (minimizing/mislabeling); "It's the teacher's fault for leaving the room" (blaming others).

The Transfer Coach

Programs to change the behavior of aggressive adolescents often succeed only at a certain time and in a certain place. That is, the program works, but only at or shortly after the time the program is conducted and only in the same place the program is held. Thus, a program may make a youth behave better during and immediately after the weeks the program is going on and in the school, agency, or institution where the program takes place. But a few weeks later, in the schoolyard, on the school bus, or when out on a field trip, home visit, or elsewhere, the youth may be as aggressive as ever. This temporary success followed by a relapse to old, negative ways of behaving is what is called a *failure of transfer*. Transfer failures are much more the rule than the exception with aggressive or delinquent youths.

During Aggression Replacement Training (ART), in addition to instruction in social skills, anger control, and moral reasoning, adolescents receive a great deal of support, enthusiasm, encouragement, and reward for their efforts. After ART, many of them may receive very little support, reward, or other positive responses. So the common failure of transfer does not surprise us.

However, this outcome can be prevented or at least made less likely. Newly learned and thus fragile constructive skills and ways of thinking need not fade away after ART. If attempts by adolescents to use such skills in the real world are met with success—support, enthusiasm, encouragement, reward—the skill use continues, aggression is decreased, and other positive benefits result. Research shows that people like yourself—teachers, facility staff, community workers, parents, friends, peers, employers—are in an ideal position to provide this valuable skill-promoting support and reward. You can be a powerful *transfer coach*, helping to make sure that the curriculum of skills and ways of thinking practiced in ART turn into long-term or even permanent learning.

What is the ART curriculum, and how exactly can you help?

THE ART CURRICULUM

Adolescents in ART go to three types of classes. One class is Moral Reasoning Training, designed to promote higher levels of ethical understanding. A second class is Anger Control Training, which teaches techniques for reducing and managing feelings of anger in provocative situations. The third class is Skillstreaming, in which a series of constructive skills is taught, each one of which is a positive alternative to a destructive or aggressive response an adolescent would usually make in a certain situation.

Anger Control Training

Transfer coaches respond with praise and encouragement when a youth, finding himself or herself in a provoking situation (one in which he or she usually responds with anger), responds instead by using one or more of the anger-reducing techniques learned in Anger Control Training. These techniques include ignoring the provocation or turning away, counting backwards, pausing and taking deep breaths, or imagining a calm, peaceful place. If the transfer coach rewards such behavior, the likelihood of its continuation increases.

Skillstreaming

An equal or greater impact is made by the transfer coach when it comes to the use of the Skillstreaming skills, listed next. When each skill is taught, it is broken down into a few behaviors or steps that actually make up the skill. The behavioral steps *are* the skill. The transfer coach looks for, encourages, and rewards these behaviors when they occur.

Group I: Beginning Social Skills

1. Listening
2. Starting a Conversation
3. Having a Conversation
4. Asking a Question
5. Saying Thank You
6. Introducing Yourself
7. Introducing Other People
8. Giving a Compliment

Group II: Advanced Social Skills

9. Asking for Help
10. Joining In

11. Giving Instructions
12. Following Instructions
13. Apologizing
14. Convincing Others

Group III: Skills for Dealing with Feelings

15. Knowing Your Feelings
16. Expressing Your Feelings
17. Understanding the Feelings of Others
18. Dealing with Someone Else's Anger
19. Expressing Affection
20. Dealing with Fear
21. Rewarding Yourself

Group IV: Skill Alternatives to Aggression

22. Asking Permission
23. Sharing Something
24. Helping Others
25. Negotiating
26. Using Self-Control
27. Standing Up for Your Rights
28. Responding to Teasing
29. Avoiding Trouble with Others
30. Keeping Out of Fights

Group V: Skills for Dealing with Stress

31. Making a Complaint
32. Answering a Complaint
33. Being a Good Sport
34. Dealing with Embarrassment
35. Dealing with Being Left Out
36. Standing Up for a Friend
37. Responding to Persuasion
38. Responding to Failure
39. Dealing with Contradictory Messages
40. Dealing with an Accusation
41. Getting Ready for a Difficult Conversation
42. Dealing with Group Pressure

Group VI: Planning Skills

43. Deciding on Something to Do
44. Deciding What Caused a Problem
45. Setting a Goal
46. Deciding on Your Abilities
47. Gathering Information
48. Arranging Problems by Importance
49. Making a Decision
50. Concentrating on a Task

SPECIFIC COACHING TECHNIQUES

Specific statements, procedures, and techniques that you may find valuable in your attempts to be an effective transfer coach are as follows.

Prompting

Under the pressure of real-life situations both in and out of schools, agencies, or institutions, adolescents may forget all or part of the Skillstreaming skills (or anger-reducing techniques) they were taught, and learned, earlier. If their anxiety isn't too great or their forgetting too complete, all that may be needed for them to perform the skill correctly is some prompting. Prompting is reminding the person *what* to do (the skill), *how* to do it (the steps), *when* to do it (now, or the next time the situation occurs), *where* to do it (and where not to), and/or *why* the skill should be used here and now (describing the positive outcomes expected).

Encouraging

Offering encouragement to adolescents to use a given skill assumes they know it well enough (thus, they do not need prompting) but are reluctant to use it. Encouragement is necessary, therefore, when the problem is lack of motivation rather than lack of knowledge. Encouragement is best given by gently urging the adolescent to use what he or she knows, by showing your enthusiasm for the skill, and by communicating optimism about the likely positive outcome of its use.

Reassuring

For particularly anxious youths, skill transfer attempts are more likely to occur if you are able to reduce the fear of failure. Reassurance is often an effective fear-reduction technique. "You can do it," "I'm here to help you if you need it," and "You've used the other skills well—I think you'll do fine with this one, too" are examples of the kinds of reassuring statements the transfer coach provides.

Rewarding

The most important contribution by far that the transfer coach makes for skill transfer is to provide (or help someone else provide) rewards for using a skill correctly. Rewards take the form of approval, praise, or compliments, or they consist of special privileges, points, tokens, recognition, or other reinforcers built into a school's or a facility's behavior management system. All of these rewards increase the likelihood of continued skill use in new settings and at later times. The most powerful reward offered, however, is the success of the skill itself. If a youth prepares well for a stressful conversation and the conversation then goes very well, that reward (the successful conversation itself) helps skill transfer more than any other reward. The same conclusion—that success increases transfer—applies to all of the Skillstreaming skills and all of the Anger Control Training steps. Thus, whenever possible, create the opportunity to reward a youth's skill use by helping him or her succeed. Respond positively to a complaint if it is reasonable, and try to have others also respond positively. Reciprocate or at least show appreciation for the adolescent's skill use. React with whatever behaviors on your part signal your awareness of effective and appropriate skill use. If you do so and encourage other important people in the adolescent's environment to do so also, fragile skills will become lasting skills, and ART will be successful.

REFERENCES

Adler, A. (1924). *The practice and theory of individual psychology.* New York: Harcourt Brace Jovanovich.

Ahlborn, H.H. (1986). *Dilemma session intervention with adult female offenders: Behavioral and attitudinal correlates.* Unpublished manuscript, Ohio Department of Youth Services, Columbus.

Alberto, P. A., & Troutman, A.C. (1982). *Applied behavior analysis for teachers: Influencing student performance.* Columbus, OH: Charles E. Merrill.

American Psychiatric Association. (1997). *Global assessment of functioning.* Washington, DC: Author.

American School Health Association. (1989). *National adolescent student health survey.* Oakland, CA: Third Party Publishing.

Anderson, R.A. (1978). *Stress power.* New York: Human Sciences Press.

Arbuthnot, J., & Gordon, D.A. (1983). Moral reasoning development in correctional intervention. *Journal of Correctional Education, 34,* 133–138.

Argyle, M. (1981). The experimental study of the basic features of situations. In D. Magnusson (Ed.), *Toward a psychology of situations: An interactional perspective.* Hillsdale, NJ: Erlbaum.

Arkowitz, H. (1977). Measurement and modification of minimal dating behavior. In M. Hersen, R.M. Eisler, & P.M. Miller (Eds.), *Progress in behavior modification* (Vol. 5). New York: Academic.

Arms, R.L., Russell, G.W., & Sandilands, M.L. (1979). Effects of viewing aggressive sports on the hostility of spectators. *Social Psychology Quarterly, 42,* 275–279.

Aronson, E., Blaney, N., Stephan, C., Sikes, J., & Snapp, M. (1978). *The Jigsaw classroom.* Beverly Hills, CA: Sage.

Assagioli, R. (1973). *The act of will.* New York: Viking.

Axelrod, S., & Apsche, J. (Eds.). (1982). *The effects and side effects of punishment on human behavior.* New York: Academic.

Ayllon, T., & Azrin, N.H. (1968). *The token economy: A motivational system for therapy rehabilitation.* New York: Appleton-Century-Crofts.

Azrin, N.H., & Holz, W.C. (1966). Punishment. In W.K. Honig (Ed.), *Operant behavior: Areas of research and application.* New York: Appleton-Century-Crofts.

Backman, C. (1979). Epilogue: A new paradigm. In G. Ginsburg (Ed.), *Emerging strategies in social psychological research.* Chichester, England: Wiley.

Bandura, A. (1969). *Principles of behavior modification.* New York: Holt, Rinehart & Winston.

Bandura, A. (1973). *Aggression: A social learning analysis.* Englewood Cliffs, NJ: Prentice-Hall.

Baron, R.A. (1977). *Human aggression.* New York: Plenum.

Baumrind, D. (1975). Early socialization and adolescent competence. In S.E. Dragastin & G.H. Elder (Eds.), *Adolescence in the life cycle.* Washington, DC: Hemisphere.

Bayh, B. (1975). *Our nation's school—A report card: "A" in school violence and vandalism* (Preliminary report of the Subcommittee to Investigate Juvenile Delinquency). Washington, DC: U.S. Senate.

Benson, H. (1975). *The relaxation response.* New York: Avon.

Berkowitz, L. (1964). The effects of observing violence. *Scientific American, 210,* 35–41.

Block, A. (1977). The battered teacher. *Today's Education, 66,* 58–62.

Brantingham, P. J., & Brantingham, P. L. (1991). *Environmental criminology.* Newbury Park, CA: Sage.

Brown, P., & Fraser, C. (1979). Speech as a marker of situations. In K. Scherer & H. Giles (Eds.), *Social markers in speech.* Cambridge, England: Cambridge University Press.

Bryan, J.H., & Test, M.A. (1967). Models and helping. Naturalistic studies in aiding behavior. *Journal of Personality and Social Psychology, 6,* 400–407.

California Department of Education. (1990). *School crime in California for the 1988–1989 school year.* Sacramento: Author.

Campbell, A. (1986). The streets and violence. In A. Campbell & J.J. Gibbs (Eds.), *Violent transactions.* Oxford, England: Basil Blackwell.

Canale, J.R. (1977). The effect of modeling and length of ownership on sharing behavior of children. *Social Behavior and Personality, 5,* 187–191.

Carr, E.G. (1981). Contingency management. In A.P. Goldstein, E.G. Carr, W. Davidson, & P. Wehr (Eds.), *In response to aggression.* New York: Pergamon.

Cartledge, G., & Johnson, C.T. (1997). School violence and cultural sensitivity. In A.P. Goldstein & J.C. Conoley (Eds.), *School violence intervention: A practical handbook.* New York: Guilford.

Center to Prevent Handgun Violence. (1990). *Caught in the crossfire: A report on gun violence in our nation's schools.* Washington, DC: Author.

Chandler, M., Greenspan, S., & Barenboim, C. (1974). Assessment and training of role-taking and referential communication skills in institutionalized emotionally disturbed children. *Developmental Psychology, 10,* 546–553.

Clarke, R.V. (1992). *Situational crime prevention: Successful case studies.* New York: Harrow & Hestan.

Colby, A., Kohlberg, L., Speicher, B., Hewer, A., Candee, D., Gibbs, J., & Power, C. (1987). *The measurement of moral judgment* (Vol. 2). Cambridge, England: Cambridge University Press.

Colby, A., & Speicher, B. (1973). *Dilemmas for applied use.* Unpublished manuscript, Harvard University, Cambridge, Massachusetts.

Coleman, M., Pfeiffer, S., & Oakland, T. (1991). *Aggression Replacement Training with behavior disordered adolescents.* Unpublished manuscript, University of Texas.

Comstock, G.A., & Paik, H. (1994). The effects of television on antisocial behavior: A meta-analysis. *Communication Research, 21,* 516–546.

Cordilia, A.T. (1986). Robbery arising out of a group drinking context. In A. Campbell & J. J. Gibbs (Eds.), *Violent transactions.* Oxford, England: Basil Blackwell.

Cronbach, L.J., & Snow, R.E. (1977). *Aptitudes and instructional methods.* New York: Irvington.

Csikszentmihalyi, M., & Larson, R. (1984). *Being adolescent.* New York: Basic.

Curran, J.P. (1977). Skills training as an approach to the treatment of heterosexual-social anxiety: A review. *Psychological Bulletin, 84,* 140–157.

Curulla, V. L. (1990). *Aggression Replacement Training in the community for adult learning disabled offenders.* Unpublished manuscript, University of Washington, Seattle.

Deffenbacher, J.L. (1996). Cognitive-behavioral approaches to anger reduction. In K.S. Dobson & K.D. Craig (Eds.), *Advances in cognitive-behavior therapy.* Thousand Oaks, CA: Sage.

DeLange, J.M., Lanham, S.L., & Barton, J.A. (1981). Social skills training for juvenile delinquents: Behavioral skill training and cognitive techniques. In D. Upper & S. Ross (Eds.), *Behavior group therapy, 1981: An annual review.* Champaign, IL: Research Press.

Dil, N. (1972). *Sensitivity of emotionally disturbed and emotionally non-disturbed elementary school children to emotional meanings of facial expressions.* Unpublished doctoral dissertation, Indiana University, Bloomington.

Dodge, K.A. (1980). Social cognition and children's aggressive behavior. *Child Development, 51,* 162–170.

Dodge, K.A. (1990). The structure and function of reactive and proactive aggression. In D. Pepler & K.H. Rubin (Eds.), *The development and treatment of childhood aggression.* Hillsdale, NJ: Erlbaum.

Dodge, K.A., Price, J.M., Bachorowski, J.A., & Newman, J.P. (1990). Hostile attributional biases in severely aggressive adolescents. *Journal of Abnormal Psychology, 99,* 385–392.

Donnerstein, E., Slaby, R.G., & Eron, L.D. (1994). The mass media and youth aggression. In L.D. Eron, J.H. Gentry, & P. Schlegel (Eds.), *Reason to hope: A psychosocial perspective on violence and youth.* Washington, DC: American Psychological Association.

Ellis, H. (1965). *The transfer of learning.* New York: Macmillan.

Emery, J.E. (1975). *Social perception processes in normal and learning disabled children.* Unpublished doctoral dissertation, New York University.

Epps, S., Thompson, B.J., & Lane, M.P. (1985). *Procedures for incorporating generalization programming into interventions for behaviorally disordered students.* Unpublished manuscript, Iowa State University, Ames.

Eron, L.D., & Huesmann, L.R. (1984). *Advances in the study of aggression.* Orlando, FL: Academic.

Evers, W.L., & Schwartz, J.C. (1973). Modifying social withdrawal in preschoolers: The effects of filmed modeling and teacher praise. *Journal of Abnormal Child Psychology, 1,* 248–256.

Feindler, E.L. (1979). *Cognitive and behavioral approaches to anger control training in explosive adolescents.* Unpublished doctoral dissertation, West Virginia University, Morgantown.

Feindler, E.L. (1981). *The art of self-control.* Unpublished manuscript, Adelphi University, Garden City, NY.

Feindler, E.L., & Ecton, R.B. (1986). *Adolescent anger control: Cognitive-behavioral techniques.* New York: Pergamon.

Feindler, E.L., & Fremouw, W. J. (1983). Stress inoculation training for adolescent anger problems. In D. Meichenbaum & M.E. Jaremko (Eds.), *Stress reduction and prevention.* New York: Plenum.

Feindler, E.L., Latini, J., Nape, K., Romano, J., & Doyle, J. (1980, November). *Anger reduction methods for child-care workers at a residential delinquent facility.* Paper presented at the meeting of the Association for the Advancement of Behavior Therapy, New York.

Feindler, E.L., Marriott, S.A., & Iwata, M. (1984). Group anger control training for junior high school delinquents. *Cognitive Therapy and Research, 8,* 299–311.

Feldman, R.A., Caplinger, T.E., & Wodarski, J.S. (1983). *The St. Louis conundrum: The effective treatment of antisocial youths.* Englewood Cliffs, NJ: Prentice-Hall.

Ferster, C.B., & Skinner, B.F. (1957). *Schedules of reinforcement.* New York: Appleton-Century-Crofts.

Feshbach, N.D. (1982). Empathy, empathy training and the regulation of aggression in elementary school children. In R.M. Kaplen, V. J. Konecni, & R.W. Novaco (Eds.), *Aggression in children and youth.* Alphen den Rijn, The Netherlands: Siuthogy/Noordhoff.

Feshbach, N.D., & Feshbach, S. (1969). The relationship between empathy and aggression in two age groups. *Developmental Psychology, 1,* 102–107.

Field, T. (1981). Early peer relations. In P. S. Strain (Ed.), *The utilization of classroom peers as behavior change agents.* New York: Plenum.

Firestone, P. (1976). The effects and side effects of time out on an aggressive nursery school child. *Journal of Behavior Therapy and Experimental Psychiatry, 6,* 79–81.

Flavell, J.H., Miller, P.H., & Miller, S.A. (1993). *Cognitive development* (3rd ed.). Englewood Cliffs, NJ: Prentice-Hall.

Fluegelman, A. (1981). *More new games.* Garden City, NY: Dolphin.

Ford, D.H., & Urban, H.B. (1963). *Systems of psychotherapy.* New York: Wiley.

Foxx, R.M., & Azrin, N.H. (1973). Restitution: A method of eliminating aggressive-disruptive behavior for retarded and brain damaged patients. *Behaviour Research and Therapy, 10,* 15–27.

Freedman, B.J. (1974). *An analysis of social behavioral skill deficits in delinquent and nondelinquent adolescent boys.* Unpublished doctoral dissertation, University of Wisconsin, Madison.

Freud, S. (1950). Why war? In J. Strachey (Ed.), *Collected papers of Sigmund Freud* (Vol. 5). London: Hogarth.

Galassi, J.P., & Galassi, M.D. (1984). Promoting transfer and maintenance of counseling outcomes. In S.D. Brown & R.W. Lent (Eds.), *Handbook of counseling psychology.* New York: Wiley.

Gibbs, J.C. (1995). The cognitive-developmental perspective. In W. M. Kurtines & J.L. Gewirtz (Eds.), *Moral development: An introduction.* Boston: Allyn & Bacon.

Gibbs, J.C. (1997). Surprise—and discovery?—in the near death experience. *Journal of Near-Death Studies, 15,* 259–278.

Gibbs, J.C., Arnold, K.D., Ahlborn, H.H., & Cheesman, E.L. (1984). Facilitation of sociomoral reasoning in delinquents. *Journal of Consulting and Clinical Psychology, 52,* 37–45.

Gibbs, J.C., Barriga, A.Q., & Potter, G.B. (1995). *The How I Think Questionnaire.* Unpublished manuscript, The Ohio State University, Columbus.

Gibbs, J.C., Basinger, K.S., & Fuller, D. (1992). *Moral maturity: Measuring the development of sociomoral reflection.* Hillsdale, NJ: Erlbaum.

Gibbs, J.C., & Potter, G.B. (1992). *A typology of criminogenic cognitive distortions.* Unpublished manuscript, The Ohio State University, Columbus.

Gibbs, J.C., Potter, G.B., & Goldstein, A.P. (1995). *The EQUIP program: Teaching youth to think and act responsibly through a peer-helping approach.* Champaign, IL: Research Press.

Giebink, J.W., Stover, D.S., & Fahl, M.A. (1968). Teaching adaptive responses in frustration to emotionally disturbed boys. *Journal of Consulting and Clinical Psychology, 32,* 336–368.

Gilliam, J. (1997). *Nonreader's hassle log.* Unpublished form for clinical use, Horseshoe Bay, Texas.

Goldstein, A.P. (1973). *Structured Learning Therapy: Toward a psychotherapy for the poor.* New York: Academic.

Goldstein, A.P. (1978). *Prescriptive psychotherapies.* New York: Pergamon.

Goldstein, A.P. (1981). *Psychological skill training: The structured learning technique.* New York: Pergamon.

Goldstein, A.P. (1988). *The Prepare Curriculum: Teaching prosocial competencies.* Champaign, IL: Research Press.

Goldstein, A.P. (1990). *Delinquents on delinquency.* Champaign, IL: Research Press.

Goldstein, A.P. (1994). *The ecology of aggression.* New York: Plenum.

Goldstein, A.P. (1995). *The psychology of vandalism.* New York: Plenum.

Goldstein, A.P., Apter, S.J., & Harootunian, B. (1984). *School violence.* Englewood Cliffs, NJ: Prentice-Hall.

Goldstein, A.P., & Conoley, J.C. (Eds.). (1997). *School violence intervention: A practical handbook.* New York: Guilford.

Goldstein, A.P., & Glick, B. (1987). *Aggression Replacement Training: A comprehensive intervention for aggressive youth.* Champaign, IL: Research Press.

Goldstein, A.P., & Glick, B. (1994). *The prosocial gang: Implementing Aggression Replacement Training.* Thousand Oaks, CA: Sage.

Goldstein, A.P., Glick, B., Carthan, W., & Blancero, D. (1994). *The prosocial gang.* Thousand Oaks, CA: Sage.

Goldstein, A.P., Glick, B., Irwin, M.J., McCartney, C., & Rubama, I. (1989). *Reducing delinquency: Intervention in the community.* New York: Pergamon.

Goldstein, A.P., Harootunian, B., & Conoley, J.C. (1994). *Student aggression: Prevention, control, replacement.* New York: Guilford.

Goldstein, A.P., Heller, K., & Sechrest, L.B. (1966). *Psychotherapy and the psychology of behavior change.* New York: Wiley.

Goldstein, A.P., & Kanfer, F. H. (1979). *Maximizing treatment gains.* New York: Academic.

Goldstein, A.P., & McGinnis, E. (1997). *Skillstreaming the adolescent: New strategies and perspectives for teaching prosocial skills* (rev. ed.). Champaign, IL: Research Press.

Goldstein, A.P., & Michaels, G.Y. (1985). *Empathy: Development, training and consequence.* Hillsdale, NJ: Erlbaum.

Goldstein, A.P., Palumbo, J., Striepling, S., & Voutsinas, A.M. (1995). *Break it up: A teacher's guide to managing student aggression.* Champaign, IL: Research Press.

Goldstein, A.P., & Stein, N. (1976). *Prescriptive psychotherapies.* New York: Pergamon.

Goldstein, J.H. (1986). Sport and aggression. In A. Campbell & J.J. Gibbs (Eds.), *Violent transactions: The limits on personality.* New York: Basil Blackwell.

Goldstein, J.H., & Arms, R.L. (1971). Effects of observing athletic contests on hostility. *Sociometry, 34,* 83–90.

Goranson, R.E. (1970). Media violence and aggressive behavior: A review of experimental research. In L. Berkowitz (Ed.), *Advances in experimental social psychology* (Vol. 5). New York: Academic.

Grant, J.E. (1987). *Problem solving intervention for aggressive adolescent males.* Unpublished doctoral dissertation, Syracuse University.

Greenwood, C.R., Hops, H., Delquadri, J., & Guild, J. (1974). Group contingencies for group consequences in classroom management: A further analysis. *Journal of Applied Behavior Analysis, 7,* 413–425.

Gregg, V.R., Gibbs, J.C., & Basinger, K.S. (1994). Patterns of developmental delay in moral judgment by male and female delinquents. *Merrill-Palmer Quarterly, 40,* 538–553.

Guralnick, M.J. (1981). Peer influences on the development of communicative competence. In P. Strain (Ed.), *The utilization of classroom peers as behavior change agents.* New York: Plenum.

Heller, K., Price, R.H., Reinharz, S., Riger, S., Wandersman, A., & D'Aunno, T.A. (1984). *Psychology and community change.* Homewood, IL: Dorsey.

Herbert, R.L. (1990). Arson and vandalism in schools: What can the educational psychologist do? *Educational Psychology in Practice, 6,* 65–70.

Hersey, P. (1984). *The situational leader.* Escondido, CA: Warner.

Hickey, J.E., & Scharf, P.L. (1980). *Toward a just correction system.* San Francisco: Jossey-Bass.

Higgins, A. (1995). Educating for justice and community: Lawrence Kohlberg's vision of moral education. In W.M. Kurtines & J.L. Gewirtz (Eds.), *Moral education: An introduction.* Boston: Allyn & Bacon.

Hoberman, H.M. (1990). Study group report on the impact of television violence on adolescents. *Journal of Adolescent Health Care, 11,* 45–49.

Homme, L., Csanyi, A.P., Gonzales, M.A., & Rechs, J.R. (1969). *How to use contingency contracting in the classroom.* Champaign, IL: Research Press.

Hornberger, R.H. (1959). The differential reduction of aggressive responses as a function of interpolated activities. *American Psychologist, 124,* 354.

Horney, K. (1939). *New ways in psychoanalyses.* New York: Norton.

Hunt, D.E. (1971). Matching models for teacher training. In B.R. Joyce & M. Weil (Eds.), *Perspectives for reform in teacher education.* Englewood Cliffs, NJ: Prentice-Hall.

Hyman, I.A. (1997). *School discipline and school violence.* Needham Heights, MA: Allyn & Bacon.

Jacobson, E. (1938). *Progressive relaxation.* University of Chicago Press.

Jones, F. H., & Miller, W. H. (1974). The effective use of negative attention for reducing group disruption in special elementary school classrooms. *Psychological Record, 24,* 435–448.

Jones, L. (1993, March). Why are we beating our children? *Ebony,* pp. 17–22.

Jones, Y. (1990). *Aggression Replacement Training in a high school setting.* Unpublished manuscript, Center for Learning and Adjustment Difficulties, Brisbane, Australia.

Kagan, J. (1966). Reflection-impulsivity: The generality and dynamics of conceptual tempo. *Journal of Abnormal Psychology, 71,* 17–24.

Kagan, S. (1985). Learning to cooperate. In R. Slavin, S. Sharan, S. Kagan, R. Hertz-Lazarowitz, C. Webb, & R. Schmuck (Eds.), *Learning to cooperate, cooperating to learn.* New York: Plenum.

Kanfer, F. H., & Karoly, P. (1972). Self-control: A behavioristic excursion into the lion's den. *Behavior Therapy, 3,* 398–416.

Karchmer, C. (1982). Early intervention in arson epidemics: Developing a motive-based intervention strategy. In J.E. Chidester (Ed.), *Fire research and safety.* Washington, DC: National Bureau of Standards.

Karoly, P., & Steffen, J.J. (Eds.). (1980). *Improving the long term effects of psychotherapy.* New York: Gardner.

Kazdin, A.E. (1975). *Behavior modification in applied settings.* Homewood, IL: Dorsey.

Keefer, R., Goldstein, J.H., & Kasiary, D. (1983). In J.H. Goldstein (Ed.), *Sports violence.* New York: Springer-Verlag.

Keeley, S.M., Shemberg, K.M., & Carbonell, J. (1976). Operant clinical intervention: Behavior management or beyond? Where are the data? *Behavior Therapy, 7,* 292–305.

Keller, F. S. (1966). A personal course in psychology. In R. Ulrich, T. Stachnik, & J. Mabry (Eds.), *Control of human behavior.* Glenview, IL: Scott Foresman.

Kelling, G.L., & Coles, C.M. (1996). *Fixing broken windows.* New York: Free Press.

Kennedy, S.M. (1989). *Anger management training with adult prisoners.* Unpublished doctoral dissertation, University of Ottawa, Canada.

Klausmeier, H.J., Rossmiller, R.A., & Sailey, M. (1977). *Individually guided elementary education.* New York: Academic.

Klein, M. (1995). *The American street gang.* New York: Oxford University Press.

Klett, C.J., & Moseley, E.C. (1963, November). *The right drug for the right patient* (Report No. 54). Washington, DC: U.S. Government Printing Office.

Kohlberg, L. (1969). Stage and sequence: The cognitive-developmental approach to socialization. In D.A. Goslin (Ed.), *Handbook of socialization theory and research.* Chicago: Rand McNally.

Kohlberg, L. (Ed.). (1973). *Collected papers on moral development and moral education.* Cambridge, MA: Harvard University, Center for Moral Education.

Kohlberg, L. (1984). *Essays on moral development: The psychology of moral development.* San Francisco: Harper & Row.

Kohn, A. (1986). *No contest.* Boston: Houghton Mifflin.

Krasner, L. (1980). *Environmental design and human behavior.* Elmsford, NY: Pergamon.

Ladd, G.W., & Mize, J. (1983). A cognitive-social learning model of social skill training. *Pyschological Review, 90,* 127–157.

Leeman, L.W., Gibbs, J.C., & Fuller, D. (1993). Evaluation of a multi-component treatment program for juvenile delinquents. *Aggressive Behavior, 19,* 281–292.

Le Unes, A., & Nation, J.R. (1981). *Saturday's heros: A psychological portrait of college football players.* Unpublished manuscript.

Lickona, T. (1983). *Raising good children.* Toronto: Bantam.

Little, V. I., & Kendall, P. C. (1979). Cognitive-behavioral interventions with delinquents: Problem solving, role-taking, and self-control. In P.C. Kendall & S.D. Hollon (Eds.), *Cognitive-behavioral interventions.* Orlando, FL: Academic.

Loeber, R., & Dishion, T. (1983). Early predictors of male delinquency: A review. *Psychological Bulletin, 94,* 68–99.

Loew, C.A. (1967). Acquisition of a hostile attitude and its relationship to aggressive behavior. *Journal of Personality and Social Psychology, 5,* 335–337.

Lorenz, K. (1966). *On aggression.* New York: Harcourt Brace Jovanovich.

Luria, A.R. (1961). *The role of speech in the regulation of normal and abnormal behavior.* New York: Liveright.

Maller, J.B. (1929). *Cooperation and competition: An experimental study in innovation.* New York: Teachers College, Columbia University.

Maltz, D. (1984). *Recidivism.* New York: Academic.

Manaster, G.J. (1977). *Adolescent development and the life tasks.* Boston: Allyn & Bacon.

McGinnis, E., & Goldstein, A.P. (1990). *Skillstreaming in early childhood: Teaching prosocial skills to the preschool and kindergarten child.* Champaign, IL: Research Press.

McGinnis, E., & Goldstein, A.P. (1997). *Skillstreaming the elementary school child: New strategies and perspectives for teaching prosocial skills* (rev. ed.). Champaign, IL: Research Press.

Meichenbaum, D.H. (1977). *Cognitive-behavior modification: An integrative approach.* New York: Plenum.

Meichenbaum, D.H., & Goodman, J. (1969). The developmental control of operant motor responding by verbal operants. *Journal of Experimental Child Psychology, 7,* 553–565.

Meichenbaum, D.H., & Goodman, J. (1971). Training impulsive children to talk to themselves: A means of developing self-control. *Journal of Abnormal Psychology, 77,* 115–126.

Metropolitan Life Insurance Company. (1993). *Violence in America's public schools: Metropolitan Life survey of the American teacher.* New York: Author.

Meyers, D.W. (1982). *Moral dilemmas at Scioto Village.* Unpublished manuscript, Ohio Department of Youth Services, Columbus.

Miller, G., & Prinz, R.J. (1991). Designing interventions for stealing. In G. Stoner, M.R. Shinn, & H.M. Walker (Eds.), *Interventions for achievement and behavior problems.* Silver Spring, MD: National Association of School Psychologists.

Montagu, E.A. (1978). *Learning nonaggression.* New York: Oxford University Press.

Moos, R. (1974). *Evaluating treatment environments: A social ecological approach.* New York: Wiley.

Morrison, R.L., & Bellack, A.S. (1981). The role of social perception in social skills. *Behavior Therapy, 12,* 69–70.

Naranjo, C., & Ornstein, R.E. (1971). *On the psychology of mediation.* New York: Viking.

National Association of School Security Directors. (1975). *Crime in schools: 1974.* Washington, DC: Author.

National Center for Education Statistics. (1991). *Public school principal survey on safe, disciplined, and drug-free schools.* Washington, DC: U.S. Department of Education.

National Education Association. (1956). Teacher opinion on pupil behavior, 1955–1956. *Research Bulletins of the National Education Association, 34*(2).

National School Safety Center. (1993, May). *Weapons prevention practicum.* Practicum presented at the Conference on Disarming Our Schools, Miami.

Newsom, C., Favell, J.E., & Rincover, A. (1982). The side effects of punishment. In S. Axelrod & J. Apsche (Eds.), *The effects and side effects of punishment on human behavior.* New York: Academic.

Nielans, T.H., & Israel, A.C. (1981). Towards maintenance and generalization of behavior change: Teaching children self-regulation and self-instructional skills. *Cognitive Therapy and Research, 5,* 189–195.

Novaco, R.W. (1975). *Anger control: The development and evaluation of an experimental treatment.* Lexington, MA: D.C. Heath.

O'Leary, K.D., Kaufman, K.F., Kass, R.E., & Drabman, R.S. (1970). The effects of loud and soft reprimands on the behavior of disruptive students. *Exceptional Children, 37,* 145–155.

Orlick, T. (1978). *The cooperative sports and games book.* New York: Pantheon.

Osgood, C.E. (1953). *Method and theory in experimental psychology.* New York: Oxford University Press.

Ostrow, A. (1974). The aggressive tendencies of male intercollegiate tennis team players as measured by selected psychological tests. *New Zealand Journal of Health, Physical Education, and Recreation, 6,* 19–21.

Palmer, T. (1973). Matching worker and client in corrections. *Social Work, 18,* 95103.

Patterson, A. (1974). Hostility catharsis: A naturalistic quasi-experiment. *Personality and Social Psychology Bulletin, 1,* 195–197.

Patterson, G.R., Reid, J.B., Jones, R.R., & Conger, R.E. (1975). *A social learning approach to family intervention* (Vol. 1). Eugene, OR: Castalia.

Pfeiffer, J.W., & Jones, J.E. (1974). *A handbook of structured experiences for human relations training* (Vols. 1–5). La Jolla, CA: University Associates.

Phillips, D.P., & Henley, J.E. (1984). When violence is rewarded or punished: The impact of mass media stories on homicide. *Journal of Communication, 34,* 101–116.

Piaget, J. (1965). *Moral judgment of the child* (M. Gabain, Trans.). New York: Free Press. (Original work published 1932)

Plas, J.M. (1986). *Systems psychology in the schools.* Elmsford, NY: Pergamon.

Positive Alternative Learning Program. (1996). *Program manual.* (Available from Ferguson-Florissant School District, 6038 Caroline Avenue, Berkeley, MO 63134)

Power, C., Higgins, A., & Kohlberg, L. (1989). *Lawrence Kohlberg's approach to moral education.* New York: Columbia University Press.

Price, R.H., & Bouffard, D.L. (1974). Behavioral appropriateness and situational constraint as dimensions of social behavior. *Journal of Personality and Social Behavior, 30,* 579–586.

Proctor, R.C., & Eckerd, W.M. (1976). "Toot-toot" or spectator sports: Psychological and therapeutic implications. *American Journal of Sports Medicine, 4,* 78–83.

Rank, O. (1945). *Will therapy.* New York: Knopf.

Richardson, R., & Evans, E. (1992, September). *African American males: An endangered species and the most paddled.* Paper presented at the Seventh Annual Conference of the Louisiana Multicultural Association, Baton Rouge.

Robins, L.N., West, P.A., & Herjanic, B.L. (1975). Arrests and delinquency in two generations: A study of black urban families and their children. *Journal of Child Psychology and Psychiatry, 16,* 125–140.

Rogers, C.R. (1951). *Client-centered therapy: Its current practice, implications, and theory.* Boston: Houghton Mifflin.

Rothenberg, B.B. (1970). Children's social sensitivity and the relationship to interpersonal competence, interpersonal comfort, and intellectual level. *Developmental Psychology, 2,* 335–350.

Russell, G.W. (1981). Spectator moods at an aggressive sports event. *Journal of Sports Psychology, 3,* 217–227.

Russell, W. (1989, February). *The OCR data on corporal punishment: What does it really mean?* Paper presented at the Third National Conference on Abolishing Corporal Punishment in the Schools, Chicago.

Ryan, E.D. (1970). The cathartic effect of vigorous motor activity on aggressive behavior. *Research Quarterly, 41,* 542–551.

Sarason, I.G., Glaser, E.M., & Fargo, G.A. (1972). *Reinforcing productive classroom behavior.* New York: Behavioral Publications.

Selman, R.L. (1980). *The growth of interpersonal understanding.* New York: Academic.

Shannon, L.W. (1988). *Criminal career continuity: Its social context.* New York: Human Sciences.

Sharon, S., & Sharon, Y. (1976). *Small-group teaching.* Englewood Cliffs, NJ: Prentice-Hall.

Siegel, L.M., & Senna, J.J. (1991). *Juvenile delinquency: Theory, practice and law.* St. Paul: West.

Sipes, R.G. (1973). War, sports, and aggression: An empirical test of two rival theories. *American Anthropologist, 75,* 64–86.

Skinner, B.F. (1938). *The behavior of organisms: An experimental analysis.* New York: Appleton-Century-Crofts.

Skinner, B.F. (1953). *Science and human behavior.* New York: Macmillan.

Slavin, R.E. (1980). *Using Student Team Learning* (rev. ed.). Baltimore, MD: Johns Hopkins University, Center for Social Organization of Schools.

Sobsey, D. (1990). Modifying the behavior of behavior modification. In A. Repp & N. Singh (Eds.), *Perspectives on the use of nonaversive and aversive interventions for persons with developmental disabilities.* Sycamore, IL: Sycamore Publishing.

Spivack, G., Platt, J.J., & Shure, M.B. (1976). *The problem-solving approach to adjustment.* San Francisco: Jossey-Bass.

Stokes, T.F., & Baer, D.M. (1977). An implicit technology of generalization. *Journal of Applied Behavior Analysis, 10,* 349–367.

Straus, M.A. (1994). *Beating the devil out of them: Corporal punishment in American families.* New York: Lexington.

Sullivan, H.S. (1953). *Conceptions of modern psychiatry.* New York: Norton.

Sulzer-Azaroff, B., & Mayer, G.R. (1977). *Applying behavior analysis procedures with children and youth.* New York: Holt, Rinehart & Winston.

Taberg Residential Center. (1994). *Operating manual.* (Available from Taberg Residential Center, 1001 Taberg-Florence Road, Taberg, New York 13471)

Tharp, R.G., & Wetzel, R.J. (1969). *Behavior modification in the natural environment.* New York: Academic.

Thayer, L., & Beeler, K.D. (1975). *Activities and exercises for affective education.* Washington, DC: American Educational Research Associates.

Thomas, J.D., Presland, I.E., Grant, M.D., & Glynn, T.L. (1978). Natural rates of teacher approval and disapproval in grade 7 classrooms. *Journal of Applied Behavior Analysis, 11,* 91–94.

Thorndike, E.L., & Woodworth, R.S. (1901). The influence of improvement in one mental function upon the efficiency of other functions. *Psychological Review, 8*, 247–261.

U.S. Department of Justice. (1993). *Bureau of Justice news release.* Washington, DC: Author.

U.S. Office of Juvenile Justice and Delinquency Prevention. (1994). *Juvenile crime, 1988–1992.* Washington, DC: Author.

Van Houten, R. (1982). Punishment: From the animal laboratory to the applied setting. In S. Axelrod & J. Apsche (Eds.), *The effects and side effects of punishment on human behavior.* New York: Academic.

Vestermark, S.D., & Blauvelt, P. D. (1978). *Controlling crime in the school: A complete security handbook for administrators.* West Nyack, NY: Parker.

Walker, H.M. (1979). *The acting-out child: Coping with classroom disruption.* Boston: Allyn & Bacon.

Walker, H.M. (1995). *The acting-out child: Coping with classroom disruption* (rev. ed.). Longmont, CO: Sopris West.

Wann, D.L., & Branscombe, N.R. (1990). Person perception when aggressive or nonaggressive sports are primed. *Aggressive Behavior, 16*, 27–32.

Werner, E.E., & Smith, R.S. (1982). *Vulnerable but invincible.* New York: McGraw-Hill.

White, G.D., Nielson, G., & Johnson, S.M. (1972). Time out duration and the suppression of deviant behavior in children. *Journal of Applied Behavior Analysis, 5*, 111–120.

White, M.A. (1975). Natural rates of teacher approval and disapproval in the classroom. *Journal of Applied Behavior Analysis, 8*, 367–372.

Wilson, J.Q., & Petersilia, J. (1995). *Crime.* San Francisco: Institute for Contemporary Studies Press.

Wolfgang, M.E., Thornberry, T.P., & Figlio, R.M. (1987). *From a boy to man, from delinquency to crime.* University of Chicago Press.

Yochelson, S., & Samenow, S.E. (1976). *The criminal personality: Vol. 1. A profile for change.* New York: Jason Aronson.

Yochelson, S., & Samenow, S.E. (1977). *The criminal personality: Vol. 2. The change process.* New York: Jason Aronson.

Youth violence. (1991, November 25). *The New York Times,* p. 23.

Zillman, D., Bryant, J., & Sapolsky, B.S. (1979). The enjoyment of watching sport contests. In J.H. Goldstein (Ed.), *Sports, games, and play.* Hillsdale, NJ: Erlbaum.

Zimmerman, D. (1983). Moral education. In Center for Research on Aggression (Ed.), *Prevention and control of aggression.* Elmsford, NY: Pergamon.

NAME INDEX

Adler, A., 156
Ahlborn, H.H., 106
Alberto, P.A., 170
Anderson, R.A., 172
Apsche, J., 150
Arbuthnot, J., 35
Argyle, M., 175–176
Arkowitz, H., 172
Arms, R.L., 23–24
Arnold, K.D., 106
Aronson, E., 173
Assagioli, R., 172
Axelrod, S., 150
Ayllon, T., 135, 147
Azrin, N.H., 135, 147, 150, 151

Bachorowski, J.A., 104
Backman, C., 176
Baer, D.M., 156–157
Bandura, A., 3, 5, 33, 48–49, 150
Barenboim, C., 174
Baron, R.A., 3
Barriga, A.Q., 102–103, 104, 105
Barton, J.A., 174
Basinger, K.S., 99, 102, 199
Baumrind, D., 176
Bayh, Birch, 9
Beeler, K.D., 176
Bellack, A.S., 175
Benson, H., 172
Berkowitz, L., 24
Blancero, D., 170, 201
Blaney, N., 173
Block, A., 10
Bouffard, D.L., 29
Branscombe, N.R., 25
Brantingham, P.J., 30
Brantingham, P.L., 30
Brown, P., 176

Bryan, J.H., 178
Bryant, J., 23

Campbell, A., 30
Canale, J.R., 178
Caplinger, T.E., 29
Carbonell, J., 157
Carr, E.G., 136, 141, 142,
    144–145, 148
Carthan, W., 170, 201
Cartledge, G., 45
Chan, Jackie, 83
Chandler, M., 174
Cheesman, E.L., 106
Clarke, R.V., 30
Colby, A., 102
Coleman, M., 203, 204
Coles, C.M., 29
Comstock, G.A., 5
Conger, R.E., 3
Conoley, J.C., 7, 20, 26, 179
Cordilia, A.T., 30
Cronbach, L.J., 27
Csanyi, A.P., 137, 152
Csikszentmihalyi, M., 5
Curran, J.P., 172

D'Aunno, T.A., 26
DeLange, J.M., 174
Delquadri, J., 132
Dil, N., 175
Dishion, T., 29, 178
Dodge, K.A., 27, 104
Donnerstein, E., 5
Doyle, J., 73
Drabman, R.S., 20

Eckerd, W.M., 22–23
Ecton, R.B., 34, 166

Ellis, H., 162
Emery, J.E., 175
Epps, S., 161, 163, 165
Eron, L.D., 3, 5
Evans, E., 19
Evers, W.L., 178

Fahl, M.A., 174
Fargo, G.A., 140, 174
Favell, J.E., 150
Feindler, E.L., 34, 37, 73, 77n, 166
Feldman, R.A., 29
Ferster, C.B., 130
Feshbach, N.D., 177
Feshbach, S., 177
Field, T., 176
Figlio, R.M., 29
Firestone, P., 144
Flavell, J.H., 103
Fluegelman, A., 174
Ford, D.H., 155–156
Foxx, R.M., 151
Fraser, C., 176
Fremouw, W.J., 73
Freud, S., 22
Fuller, D., 170, 199, 206

Galassi, J.P., 170
Galassi, M.D., 170
Gibbs, J.C., 37, 99, 102–103, 104,
    105, 106, 107, 170, 199, 206
Giebink, J.W., 174
Glick, B., 36, 37, 170, 188, 198, 200,
    201, 204, 206
Glynn, T.L., 19–20
Goldstein, A.P., 5, 7, 11, 12, 20, 21,
    22, 26, 27–28, 30, 32, 33, 36, 37,
    49, 56, 99, 102, 107, 153, 155,
    157, 158, 161, 170, 171, 175,
    177, 179, 188, 195, 198, 200,
    201, 204, 206
Goldstein, J.H., 23–24, 25
Gonzales, M.A., 137, 152
Goodman, J., 70, 71, 72
Goranson, R.E., 25
Gordon, D.A., 35
Grant, J.E., 175
Grant, M.D., 19–20
Greenspan, S., 174

Greenwood, C.R., 132
Gregg, V.R., 99, 102
Guild, J., 132
Guralnick, M.J., 176

Harootunian, B., 5, 26
Heller, K., 26, 158, 161
Henley, J.E., 25
Herbert, R.L., 14
Herjanic, B.L., 178
Hersey, P., 192
Hewer, A., 102
Hickey, J.E., 105
Higgins, A., 105
Hoberman, H.M., 5
Holyfield, Evander, 83
Holz, W.C., 150
Homme, L., 137, 152
Hops, H., 132
Hornberger, R.M., 23
Horney, K., 156
Huesmann, L.R., 3
Hunt, D.E., 27
Hyman, I.A., 19

Irwin, M.J., 37, 170, 200
Israel, A.C., 163
Iwata, M., 73

Jacobson, E., 172
Johnson, C.T., 45
Johnson, S.M., 146
Jones, F.H., 20
Jones, J.E., 176
Jones, L., 19
Jones, R.R., 3
Jones, Y., 205

Kagan, J., 70
Kagan, S., 173
Kanfer, F.H., 157, 163
Karchmer, C., 14
Karoly, P., 143, 163, 166
Kasiary, D., 24
Kass, R.E., 20
Kaufman, K.F., 20
Kazdin, A.E., 36, 135, 138, 147, 161
Keefer, R., 24
Keeley, S.M., 157

Keller, F.S., 27
Kelling, G.L., 29
Kendall, P.C., 69–70
Kennedy, S.M., 204
Klausmeier, H.J., 27
Klein, M., 187
Klett, C.J., 36
Kohlberg, L., 35, 99, 100, 102, 105
Kohn, A., 120
Krasner, L., 26
Kutcher, B., 194

Ladd, G.W., 174
Lane, M.P., 161, 163, 165
Lanham, S.L., 174
Larson, R., 5
Latini, J., 73
Leeman, L.W., 170, 206
Le Unes, A., 23
Lickona, T., 103
Little, V.I., 69–70
Loeber, R., 29, 178
Loew, C.A., 23
Lorenz, K., 22
Luria, A.R., 69, 70

Maller, J.B., 173
Maltz, D., 201
Manaster, G.J., 5
Marriott, S.A., 73
Mayer, G.R., 165
McCartney, C., 37, 170, 200
McGinnis, E., 49, 56, 195
Meichenbaum, D., 34, 70, 71, 72, 73
Michaels, G.Y., 177
Miller, G., 13
Miller, P.H., 103
Miller, S.A., 103
Miller, W.H., 20
Mize, J., 174
Montagu, E.A., 3
Moos, R., 26
Morrison, R.L., 175
Moseley, E.C., 36

Nape, K., 73
Naranjo, C., 172
Nation, J.R., 23
Newman, J.P., 104

Newsom, C., 150
Nielans, T.H., 163
Nielson, G., 146
Novaco, R.W., 34, 72, 73, 89

Oakland, T., 203, 204
O'Leary, K.D., 20
Orlick, T., 174
Ornstein, R.E., 172
Osgood, C.E., 162
Ostrow, A., 23

Paik, H., 5
Palmer, T., 27
Palumbo, J., 11, 12, 27–28, 153
Patterson, A., 23
Patterson, G.R., 3
Petersilia, J., 11
Pfeiffer, J.W., 176
Pfeiffer, S., 203, 204
Phillips, D.P., 25
Piaget, J., 99, 102
Plas, J.M., 26
Platt, J.J., 174
Potter, G.B., 37, 99, 102–103,
    104, 105, 107, 206
Power, C., 102, 105
Presland, I.E., 19–20
Price, J.M., 104
Price, R.H., 26, 29
Prinz, R.J., 13
Proctor, R.C., 22–23

Rank, O., 156
Rechs, J.R., 137, 152
Reid, J.B., 3
Reinharz, S., 26
Richardson, R., 19
Riger, S., 26
Rincover, A., 150
Robins, L.N., 178
Rogers, C.R., 156
Romano, J., 73
Rossmiller, R.A., 27
Rothenberg, B.B., 175
Rubama, I., 37, 170, 200
Russell, G.W., 24
Russell, W., 19
Ryan, E.D., 23

Sailey, M., 27
Samenow, S.E., 102
Sandilands, M.L., 24
Sapolsky, B.S., 23
Sarason, E.M., 140, 174
Sarason, I.G., 140, 174
Scharf, P.L., 105
Schwartz, J.C., 178
Sechrest, L.B., 158, 161
Selman, R.L., 174
Senna, J.J., 10
Shannon, L.W., 29
Sharon, S., 173
Sharon, Y., 173
Shemberg, K.M., 157
Shure, M.B., 174
Siegel, L.M., 10
Sikes, J., 173
Sipes, R.G., 24
Skinner, B.F., 130
Slaby, R.G., 5
Slavin, R.E., 173
Smith, R.S., 178
Snapp, M., 173
Snow, R.E., 27
Sobsey, D., 150
Speicher, B., 102
Spivack, G., 174
Steffen, J.J., 143, 166
Stein, N., 27, 37
Stephan, C., 173
Stokes, T.F., 156–157
Stover, D.S., 174
Straus, M.A., 5
Striepling, S., 11, 12, 27–28, 153
Sullivan, H.S., 156
Sulzer-Azaroff, B., 165

Test, M.A., 178
Tharp, R.G., 136
Thayer, L., 176
Thomas, J.D., 19–20
Thompson, B.J., 161, 163, 165
Thornberry, T.P., 29
Thorndike, E.L., 162
Troutman, A.C., 170

Urban, H.B., 155–156

Van Houten, R., 150
Voutsinas, A.M., 11, 12, 27–28, 153

Walker, H.M., 132, 140, 141, 147,
    148, 150, 172
Wandersman, A., 26
Wann, D.L., 25
Werner, E.E., 178
West, P.A., 178
Wetzel, R.J., 136
White, G.D., 146
White, M.A., 19–20
White, S., 207
Wilson, J.Q., 11
Wodarski, J.S., 29
Wolfgang, M.E., 29
Woodworth, R.S., 162

Yochelson, S., 102

Zillmann, D., 23
Zimmerman, D., 35

SUBJECT INDEX

Abilities, deciding on your, 258, 273, 283, 287, 293
Accusation, dealing with, 252, 272, 282, 287, 292
Actions, aggressive, 6
Activities
    deciding on, 255, 273, 282, 287, 293
    as reinforcers, 134
Addiction, aggression as, 8–9
Adolescents, Skillstreaming skills for, 51, 211–262
Aversive stimulus, effect on behavior, 149
Affection, expression of, 231, 268, 278, 285, 290
Aggression, 1, 127
    as addiction, 8–9
    in an athletic context, 30
    antecedents of, 26–27
    consequences of low-level, 11–12
    as instinctive human behavior, 3
    as learned behavior, 12, 31–32
    learning, 3–9
        in the home, 4–5
        from the media, 5
        in school, 5
    in a prison context, 30
    proactive, 27
    problems in changing, 6–8
    reactive, 27
    responses to
        effective, 25–31
        ineffective, 15–25
    in schools, 9–15, 30
    Skillstreaming alternatives to, 234–242
    in society, 9–15
    in thoughts and actions, 6

Aggression effect, 5
Aggression Replacement Training (ART), 1, 31–32, 33, 325. See also Anger Control Training; Moral Reasoning Training; Skillstreaming
    in addressing limitations of antisocial youth, 99
    components of, 33–35
    curriculum for, 37–42, 326–328
    implementation
        cultural compatibility, 45–46
        trainee selection and preparation, 42–43
        trainer selection and preparation, 43–45
    as multichannel approach, 35–37
    procedures for, 42–43
    purposes of, 42
    specific coaching techniques
        encouraging, 328
        prompting, 328
        reassuring, 328–329
        rewarding, 329
Alcohol-related offenses, 9
Alonzo's Problem Situation, 316–318
Alternative schools, 179–186
American School Health Association, 11
Anchoring (cognitive distortion), 6, 105
Anger, 69
    A-B-C model of, 84, 93
    dealing with someone else's, 230, 268, 278, 285, 290
Anger control chain, 94
Anger control enhancement, 197

Anger Control Training, 1, 34, 35, 36,
        37, 69–97, 171–172, 326
    goals of, 83
    implementation concerns, 74–75
        homework, 77
        modeling, 75
        performance feedback, 76–77
        role-playing, 75–76
    origins of, 69–74
    purposes of, 69
    rules and procedures in, 77,
        83–97
Angry aggression, 27
Angry behavior cycle, 94–95
Annsville Youth Center, 196–198
Antisocial behavior, 105, 119
Antonio's Problem Situation, 322–323
Anxiety inhibition, 172
Apathy, 124–125
Apologizing, 225, 267, 277, 285, 289
Arson, 14
ART, embedding in broader curricu-
        lum, 171–178. *See also*
        Aggression Replacement
        Training
Assaults, 9
Assuming the worst (cognitive
        distortion), 6, 103–104
Athletic context, aggression in, 30
Attendance motivation, 119
Attention, 60
Automatic maintenance and
        transfer, 156

Backward counting, in anger
        control, 88
Battered teacher syndrome, 10
Behavior
    aggression as learned, 31–32
    directive, 192
    supportive, 192
Behavioral facilitation, 58
Behavioral rules, communicating,
        132–133
Behavioral therapist, 47
Behavior modification, 48, 130–132
    contingency contracting, 152
    overcorrection, 151–152

Big Brothers, 178
Big Sisters, 178
Bizarre behavior, 128, 152
Blaming others (cognitive distortion),
        6, 104–105
Bombings, 14
Booster sessions, providing, 165–166
Box cutters, 13
Boy Scouts, 178
Bribery, 120
Brownsville Community
        Neighborhood Action
        Center, 186–188, 202
Bullying, 12, 28, 127, 152
Burglaries, 9
Bystander effect, 5

California Department of Education,
        10, 11
Catharsis, as ineffective intervention
        strategy, 22–25
Center to Prevent Handgun Violence, 10
Character Education movement, 48
Child abuse, 4–5
Children
    oppositional, 4
    self-centered, 6
    temperamental, 3
Children's Village, 193–195
Coaching style, 193, 328–329
Coercive parenting, effects of, 3–4
Cognitive deficits, 128
Cognitive distortions, delay as
        persistent and pronounced,
        102–105
Cognitive inadequacies, 127–128
Cognitive restructuring, 105, 106
Cohabitation, as ineffective interven-
        tion strategy, 25
Collaborative Intensive Community
        Treatment Program, 206
Community-based evaluation, 199–201
Complaints
    answering, 244, 271, 280,
        286, 292
    making, 243, 270, 280, 286, 292
Complexity, as effective intervention
        strategy, 25–27

Compliments, giving, 220, 266, 276, 284, 288
Consistency, 138
Constructive treatment strategy, 36
Contingency, 137
    contracting, 152
    management, 130–132
Contingent observation, 144
Contradictory messages, dealing with, 251, 272, 281, 287, 292
Controversial questions, 107
Conversations
    getting ready for difficult, 253, 272, 282, 287, 292
    having, 215, 266, 275, 284, 288
    starting, 214, 265, 275, 284, 288
Convincing others, 226, 267, 277, 285, 289
Cooperation training, 173–174
Corporal punishment, 3, 4–5, 19
Cost setting, 148
Crime
    violent, by juveniles, 14–15
    quality of life, 29
Cues, in anger control, 73, 86, 87
Cultural compatibility, 45–46
Curriculum, embedding ART in broader, 171–178

Dating relationships, ending, 303–306
Decisions, making, 261, 274, 283, 287, 293
Deep breathing, in anger control, 88
Delegating style, 193
Denials, 8
Digression, 125–126, 152
Directing style, 192
Directive behavior, 192
Direct learning, 5
Disruptiveness, 127, 152
Downsizing-of-deviance perspective, 11–12
Drug offenses, 9

Efficacy evaluations, 203–208
Egocentric bias, 102, 103. *See also* Cognitive distortions, Self-centeredness

Erie (Pennsylvania) School District, 188–189
Embarrassment, dealing with, 246, 271, 281, 286, 292
Emotional disturbances, 127–128
Empathy training, 177
Encouraging, 328
EQUIP Program, 107, 206
Excessive restlessness, 126
Exclusion time-out, 143–144
Extended skill transfer, 197
External triggers, 85
Extinction, 141–143, 144
Extinction burst, 143
Extrinsic motivators, 119, 120

Failure, responding to, 250, 272, 281, 287, 292
Failure management, 166
False consensus (cognitive distortion), 6
Fear, dealing with, 232, 268, 278, 285, 290
Feelings
    expressing your, 228, 268, 278, 285, 290
    knowing your, 227, 268, 277, 285, 290
    Skillstreaming skills for, 227–233
    understanding, in others, 229, 268, 278, 285, 290
Fights, keeping out of, 242, 270, 280, 286, 291
Firearms in school violence, 10–11, 13
Frequency of reinforcement, 138
Friends
    dealing with irresponsible, 307–309, 319–321
    dealing with troublesome, 310–311
    standing up for, 248, 271, 281, 286, 292
Friendship
    importance of trust in, 297–299, 316–318
    promotion of, 300–302

Gang Intervention Project, 187, 201–203, 206
Generalization motivation, 119

Generalization of performance, 155–178
    approaches to enhance, 155–158
    maintenance-enhancing proce-
        dures, 164–171
    transfer-enhancing procedures,
        158–164
George's Problem Situation, 307–309
Goals, setting, 257, 273, 283, 287, 293
Group pressure, dealing with, 254,
        272, 282, 287, 292
Group processes, understanding and
        using, 176

Hassle Logs, 77, 78, 79, 80, 84–85, 96
Help, asking for, 221, 267, 276,
        284, 289
Helping others, 236, 269, 279, 286, 291
Home, learning aggression in, 4–5
Homework, in Anger Control
        Training, 77
Horseplay, 28
Hostile aggression, 27
How I Think Questionnaire,
        102–103, 104
Hyperactivity, 125–126
Hyper-schools, 179

Identical elements, 162–163
If-then thinking ahead, in anger
        control, 94
Imagery, in anger control, 88
Immediacy, 137
Impulse reduction, 197
Inactivity, 124–125
Incremental prescription building,
        36–37
Information, gathering, 259, 273, 283,
        287, 293
Inhibitory and disinhibitory effects, 58
Instructions
    following, 224, 267, 277, 285, 288
    giving, 223, 267, 277, 285, 289
Interruption, 126
Intervention-as-inoculation perspec-
        tive, 155–156
Intervention strategies
    effective, 25–31
    ineffective, 15–25

Intimidation, 127
Intrinsic motivators, 119, 120
Introductions
    of others, 219, 266, 276, 284, 288
    of yourself, 218, 266, 276, 284, 288
Isolation time-out, 143

Jerry's Problem Situation, 108–109,
        300–302
Jim's Problem Situation, 297–299
Joining in, 222, 267, 277, 285, 289
Juan's Problem Situation, 319–321
Justice, U.S. Department of, 10, 11
Juvenile delinquency, 4
Juvenile Justice and Delinquency
        Prevention, U.S. Office
        of, 14
Juveniles, violent crime by, 14–15

Learned behavior, aggression as, 12,
        31–32
Learning
    direct, 5
    observational, 58
    vicarious, 5
Left out, dealing with being, 247, 271,
        281, 286, 292
Leon's Problem Situation, 310–311
Listening, 213, 265, 275, 284, 288
Low-level aggression, consequences of,
        11–12

MacCormick Youth Center, 198–199
Maintenance enhancers, development
        of, 157–158
Maintenance-enhancing procedures,
        164–171
Mark's Problem Situation, 303–306
Material reinforcers, 133
Mature morality
    consolidating, 115–117
    cultivating, 113–114
Me-centeredness, 103. See also
        Self-centeredness
Media, learning aggression from, 5
Mediated generalization, 163–164
Mediation-Reinforcer Incomplete
        Blank, 136–137

Metal detectors in schools, 13
Metropolitan Life Insurance
    Company, 10
Minimal participation, 124–125, 152
Minimal skill transfer, 197
Minimizing/mislabeling (cognitive
    distortion), 6, 105
Model characteristics, 59
Modeling, 34, 58–61
    in Anger Control Training, 75
    stages of, 60–61
Modeling display characteristics, 59
Modeling enhancers, 59
Monopolizing, 126
Moral developmental delay,
    remediating, 114–115
Moral Education, 48
Moral reasoning
    delay, 100, 102
    problem situations, 107, 109,
        295–323
    stages of, 100–101
Moral Reasoning Training, 1, 34–35,
    36, 37, 99–117, 171–172
    procedures, 105–117
        phases of sociomoral
            development, 111,
            113–117
        preparations for the social
            decision making meeting,
            109, 111
        problem situations for teach-
            ing mature moral reasoning,
            107, 109, 295–323
        social decision making
            meeting, 106–107
        sociomoral development and
            delay, 99–105
        youth perceptions of, 117
Motivation, increasing trainee,
    119–124
Motivators, 119–120
Multimodal interventions, 35–36
Multisource assessment, 52

National Association of School Security
    Directors, 9
National School Safety Center, 12, 13

Natural environment
    preparing for nonreinforcement
        in, 166
    programming for reinforcement
        in, 166–167, 170
Natural reinforcers, 170–171
Negative behaviors, minimizing, 128–154
Negative reinforcement, 131, 149, 151
Negativism, 127
Negotiating, 237, 269, 279, 286, 291
Nondirective therapist, 47
Nonexclusion time-out, 144
Nonreinforcement, preparing for in
    natural environment, 166

Oasis program, 195–196
Observational learning, 58
Observing choices, 136
Observing effects, 136
Oppositional children, 4
Oregon Social Learning Center, 3
Overcorrection, 151–152
Overlearning, 160–161

Parental pressure, 314–315
Parenting, coercive, 3–4
Partial reinforcement, 138
Participating style, 193
Passive-aggressive isolation, 126–127
Peer pressure, 322–323
Perceptions of Moral Reasoning
    Training, by youth, 117
Performance feedback, 34
    in Anger Control Training, 76–77
    providing, on role-play, 64–65
Permission, asking, 234, 269, 279,
    285, 291
Persuasion, responding to, 249, 271,
    281, 286, 292
Planning, Skillstreaming skills for,
    255–262
Police Athletic League, 178
Positive Alternative Learning (PAL)
    Program, 179–186
Positive reinforcers, 131
    identifying, 133–137
    presenting, 137–140
    removing, 131, 141–151

Praise, pairing with other reinforcement, 139–141
Prepare Curriculum, 171–178
Prescriptiveness, as effective intervention strategy, 27–29
Primary reinforcement, 133
Prison, aggression in, 30
Proactive aggression, 27
Probe questions, 107
Problems
    arranging, by importance, 260, 283, 287, 293
    deciding on cause of, 256, 273, 282, 287, 293
Problem-solving training, 174–175
Project IMPACT (Interventions to Maintain Parents and Children Together), 193
Project WAY (Work Appreciation for Youth), 193
Prompting, 328
Prompts, fading, 165
Prosocial behaviors, 119
Prosocial modeling, 178
Psychodynamic therapist, 47
Psychological skills training, 48
Psychology, contributions to skills training movement, 48–49
Psychotherapy, 48
Psychotherapy research, 156–157
Punishment, 131, 149–150
    corporal, 3, 4–5, 19
    as ineffective intervention strategy, 15, 19–22

Quality-of-life crimes, 29
Questions
    asking, 216, 266, 276, 284, 288
    controversial, 107
    probe, 107

Rape, 9
Reactive aggression, 27
Reassuring, 328–329
Reducers, in anger control, 73, 88
Refusal, 127
Reggie's Problem Situation, 314–315

Reinforcement. *See also* Rewarding
    amount, 138–139
    delaying, 165
    negative, 148–149, 151
    programming for, in natural environment, 166–167, 170
    thinning, 165
Reinforcers, 131
    activity, 134
    material, 133
    negative, 131
    positive, 131
    social, 134
    tangible, 133
    token, 134
Relapse prevention, 166
Relationships, mature, 303–306
Reminders, in anger control, 73, 89–92
Reprimands, 19–20, 22
Reproduction, 61
Resistance
    reducing, 124
    types of trainee, 124–128
Response cost, 147–148
Responsibility Education program, 48
Responsible, being, 312–313
Retention, 60–61
Rewarding, 233, 269, 278, 285, 290, 329. *See also* Reinforcement
Rights, standing up for your, 239, 270, 279, 286, 291
Robberies, 9
Role-player, selection of, 62, 67
Role-playing, 34
Role-plays
    in Anger Control Training, 75–76, 85, 91–92, 93, 95, 96
    conducting, 63–64
    providing performance feedback on, 64–65
    set-up of, 62
Role reversal, 63
Rules violation, 28

Sam's Problem Situation, 312–313
Satiation effect, 139

Schools
  aggression in, 5, 9–15, 30
  bringing weapons to, 12–13
  metal detectors in, 13
  violence and vandalism in, 16–19
  violence prevention and reduction
    interventions in, 30–31
School suspension, 20, 21
Self-centeredness
  in children, 6
  cognitive distortion, 102, 104
Self-control, using, 238, 269, 279,
    286, 291
Self-evaluation, in anger control, 73,
    92, 93
Self-instruction, 164
Self-instructional training
  for the aggressive youngster, 72–74
  for the impulsive youngster, 71–72
Self-punishment, 164
Self-recording, 163
Self-reinforcement, 163–164
Sexual harassment, 12, 28
Shared skill deficiency, 54
Sharing, 235, 269, 279, 285, 291
Shoplifting, 312–313
Situationality, as effective intervention
    strategy, 29–31
Situational perception training, 175–176
Skill acquisition, 197
Skill alternatives, 121–122
Skill generalization, 172, 174, 177
Skillstreaming, 1, 33–34, 35, 36, 37,
    47–67, 171–172, 326–328
  for adolescents, 51, 211–262
  curriculum, 50
    skill negotiation, 53
    skill selection, 50, 52
  goal of, 119, 121
  grouping chart for, 54, 288–293
  history and development, 47–50
  implementation concerns, 53
    frequency of sessions, 54
    length of program, 55
    room arrangement and
      materials, 55–56
    trainee selection, 53–54
    trainer collaboration, 54

training procedures, 56
  assigning skill homework,
    65–67
  conducting role-plays, 63–64
  defining the skill, 56–57
  establishing trainee skill need,
    61–62
  modeling the skill, 58–61
  providing performance
    feedback, 64–65
  selecting role-player, 62, 67
  setting up role-plays, 62
Skillstreaming checklists, 52, 53
  parent, 275–283
  student, 284–287
  teacher/staff, 265–274
Sleeping, 125
Social decision making meeting,
    106–107
  preparations for, 109, 111
Social learning theory, contributions to
    skills training movement,
    48–49
Social reinforcers, 134
Social skills, Skillstreaming skills as,
    211–226
Society, aggression in, 9–15
Sociomoral development, phases of,
    111, 113–117
Sociomoral developmental delay, 106
Spontaneous recovery, 143
Sport, being a good, 245, 271, 280,
    286, 292
Stealing, 297–299, 316–318
Stimulus variability, 161–162
Stress management, 172
  Skillstreaming skills for, 243–254
Structured Learning, 49. *See also*
    Skillstreaming
Students, as crime victims, 10
Superficiality, 100
Supportive behavior, 192
Supportive models, recruiting, 177–178
Suspension, from school, 20, 21

Taberg Residential Center, 189–193
Tangible motivators, 119, 120
Tangible reinforcers, 133

Tasks, concentrating on, 262, 274, 283, 287, 293
Teachable moments, capturing, 152–154
Teachers, assault on, 10
Teasing, responding to, 240, 270, 280, 286, 291
Television violence, 5
Temperamental children, 3
Temper tantrums, 3
Thank you, saying, 217, 266, 276, 284, 288
Thinking ahead, in anger control, 93–94
Thinking errors. *See* Cognitive distortions
Thoughts, aggressive, 6
Time-out, 143–146, 151
Time-out burst, 146
Token economy, 134
Token reinforcers, 134
Trainees
    characteristics of, 60
    establishing skill need, 61–62
    increasing motivation in, 119–124
    reducing resistance in, 124–128
    selection and preparation of, 42–43, 53–54
Trainers
    collaboration among, 54
    selection and preparation, 43–45
Training, transfer, 34, 158–159
Transfer coach, 167, 186, 325–329
Transference neurosis, 156
Transfer enhancers, development of, 157–158

Transfer failures, 325
Transfer training, 34, 158–159
Triggers, in anger control, 73, 84–86
Trouble, avoiding, with others, 241, 270, 280, 286, 291
Trust, in friendship, 297–299, 316–318

U.S. Department of Justice, 10, 11
U.S. Office of Juvenile Justice and Delinquency Prevention, 14

Values Clarification, 48
Vandalism, 13–14
    deterrence, 16–19
Variety of reinforcement, 139
Verbal mediation, 70
Vicarious learning, 5
Victim effect, 5
Violence
    deterrence, 16–19
    in media, 5
Violent crime by juveniles, 14–15

Weapons, 12–13

Youth perceptions of Moral Reasoning Training, 117
Youth D.A.R.E.S. of Coney Island, 187, 202
Youth Violence, 11

Zero tolerance policies, 28

Arnold P. Goldstein joined the clinical psychology section of Syracuse University's Psychology Department in 1963 and both taught there and directed its Psychotherapy Center until 1980. In 1981, he founded the Center for Research on Aggression, which he currently directs. He joined Syracuse University's Division of Special Education in 1985 and in 1990 helped organize and codirect the New York State Task Force on Juvenile Gangs. Dr. Goldstein has a career-long interest, as both researcher and practitioner, in difficult-to-reach clients. Since 1980, his main research and psychoeducational focus has been youth violence. Dr. Goldstein's many books include, among others, *The Prepare Curriculum: Teaching Prosocial Competencies; Delinquents on Delinquency; The Gang Intervention Handbook; Break It Up: A Teacher's Guide to Managing Student Aggression;* and the recently revised edition of *Skillstreaming the Adolescent: New Strategies and Perspectives for Teaching Prosocial Skills.*

Barry Glick received his Ph.D. from Syracuse University in 1972. Trained as a counseling psychologist, Dr. Glick has devoted his professional career to the development of policies, programs, and services for adolescents. His specialization is in juvenile delinquency as well as the emotionally disturbed adolescent. Dr. Glick has worked in both private child care agencies and state government. He has held positions as a child care worker, a psychologist, an administrator, and a manager. Previously holding the post of Associate Deputy Director for Local Services, New York State Division for Youth, he is currently a national consultant to juvenile and adult correctional agencies, senior editor of *Managing Delinquency: Programs That Work,* and first author of *No Time to Play: Youthful Offenders in Adult Systems.*

John C. Gibbs, Ph.D., is professor of developmental psychology at The Ohio State University. He is a member of the State of Ohio Governor's Council on Juvenile Justice and a faculty associate of The Ohio State University Criminal Justice Research Center. His work has concerned developmental theory, assessment of social cognition and moral judgment development, and interventions with conduct-disordered adolescents. He is first author of *Moral Maturity: Measuring the Development of Sociomoral Reflections* and *The EQUIP Program: Teaching Youth to Think and Act Responsibly through a Peer-Helping Approach*, as well as coauthor (with Lawrence Kohlberg) of the second volume of *The Measurement of Moral Judgment*.